IMAGES
of America

MANHATTAN, BELGRADE, AMSTERDAM, AND CHURCHILL

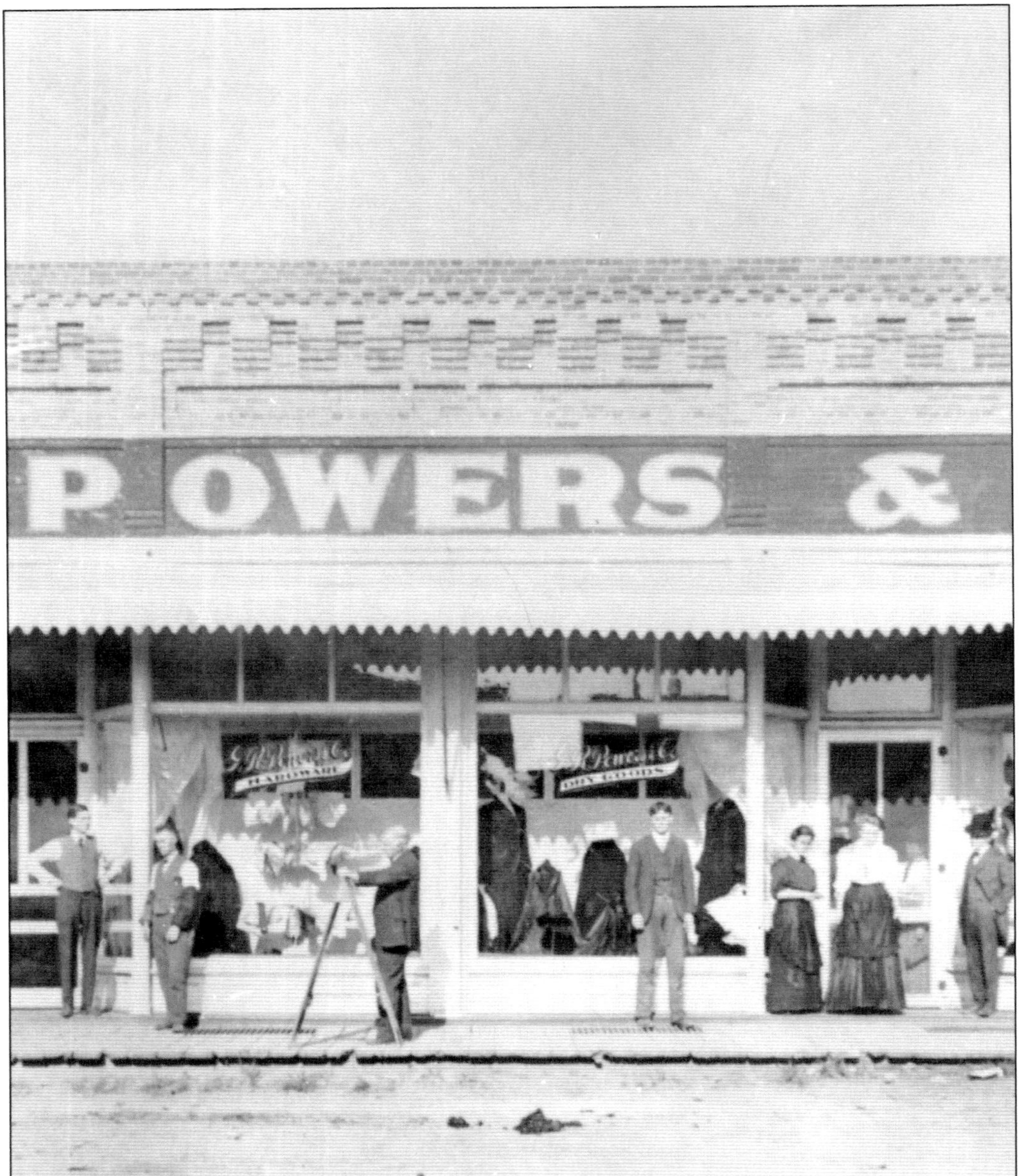

In this early Belgrade scene, well-dressed residents gather in front of Powers hardware store. (Courtesy of the Pioneer Museum and Gallatin Historical Society.)

On the Cover: Pictured in the early 20th century is the Danley & Nason Machine Shop Garage & Auto Livery in Manhattan. Arch Martin is standing on the far left, and Mr. Nason is third from the left. (Courtesy of the Pioneer Museum and Gallatin Historical Society.)

IMAGES
of America

MANHATTAN, BELGRADE, AMSTERDAM, AND CHURCHILL

Bruce Gourley and the
Pioneer Museum of Bozeman

ARCADIA
PUBLISHING

ISBN 978-0-7385-7609-1

Published by Arcadia Publishing
Charleston, South Carolina

Printed in the United States of America

Library of Congress Control Number: 2011926877

For all general information, please contact Arcadia Publishing:
Telephone 843-853-2070
Fax 843-853-0044
E-mail sales@arcadiapublishing.com
For customer service and orders:
Toll-Free 1-888-313-2665

Visit us on the Internet at www.arcadiapublishing.com

This book is dedicated to the living descendants of the early families of the Gallatin Valley.

CONTENTS

Acknowledgments

Thanks to the staff of the Pioneer Museum and Gallatin Historical Society in Bozeman, Montana, for their invaluable assistance in the selection and acquisition of photographs, as well as editorial assistance in answering many questions. Because of the diligent and tireless work of the museum and society, the history of Gallatin County has been well preserved and is easily accessible to any who wish to learn the stories of the region. Images used in this collection are from the archives of the Pioneer Museum and Gallatin Historical Society.

Thanks to Paul Newby, longtime pilot and son of aviation pioneer Al Newby, for his first-hand information about the history of Gallatin Field Airport and airplanes in the Gallatin Valley.

INTRODUCTION

Open space and fertile soil west of Bozeman had beckoned since Montana's Gallatin Valley was formally settled by white inhabitants in the 1860s. Until the 1880s, however, the area remained only lightly populated.

The expanding Northern Pacific Railroad soon provided occasion for a few enterprising businessmen to stake claims to the west of Bozeman. During the 1880s, realtor Thomas B. Quaw envisioned great things alongside the westward rails 10 miles from Bozeman. Growing farm enterprises in the area led Quaw to develop the townsite of what became Belgrade, which he named after the Serbian town. Leaving behind his Bozeman real estate business, Quaw became general manager of the Belgrade Grain and Produce Company in 1886.

In the coming months, the town grew rapidly, convincing Quaw that it would soon be larger than Bozeman. While reality would never match his enthusiasm, the little town with big dreams became an important agricultural and business community in the central Gallatin Valley.

Even as Quaw was establishing Belgrade, wealthy British families were settling farther west, purchasing large acreages and establishing ranching operations. Their sojourn in the valley proved brief, however, and was followed by the arrival of several enterprising New York businessmen who found the soil suitable for the growing of malting barley in 1890. The Manhattan Malting Company acquired large acreages in order to grow the grain needed for the production of beer, and it formally established the town of Manhattan (formerly Moreland, which was formerly Hamilton) in 1891, constructing a malting house and grain elevators. Seeking agricultural workers, the company sent word to the Netherlands, and in a few short years, Hollanders settled the area en masse.

Some early Dutch immigrants purchased land south of Manhattan, establishing the Holland Settlement. Other families followed suit, and the settlement soon became known as the adjacent communities of Churchill (named after a church constructed upon a hill) and Amsterdam. The growing of grains provided earthly sustenance for the early Dutch settlers, while a common faith united the families spiritually. As the decades passed by, the farmers diversified their crops, but the Dutch composition of the communities remained much the same.

Today, Belgrade is one of the fastest-growing small towns in Montana, while Manhattan, Churchill, and Amsterdam remain small, close-knit, quiet communities surrounded by fields and pastures.

One

Belgrade

Little Town with a Big Vision

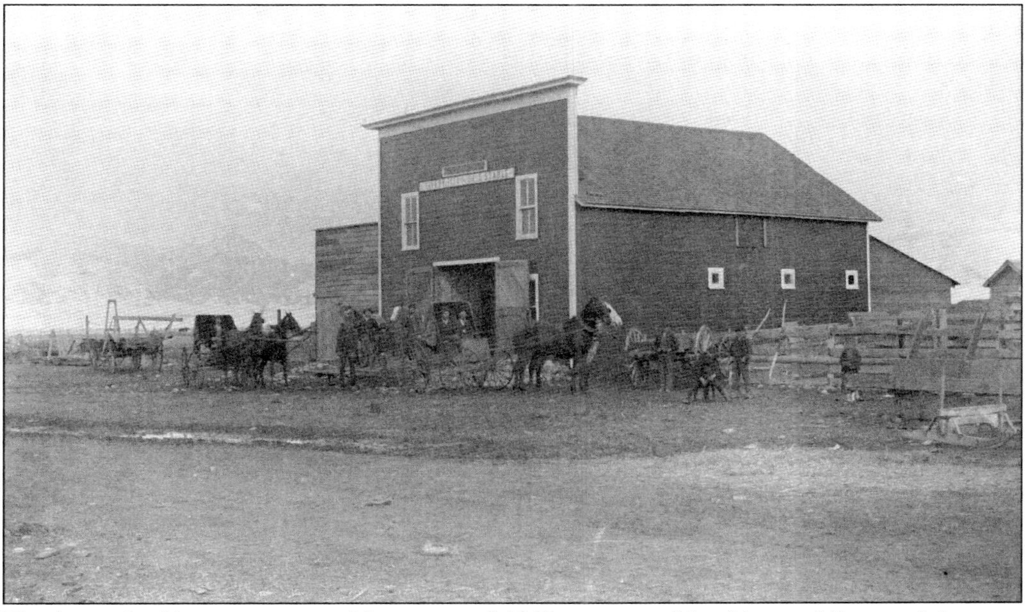

The livery feed business pictured here around 1888 was owned by Alva and Preston Johnston, who were among the earliest businessmen to open shop in Belgrade. The Johnston brothers, though, were best known for Corbett, the "Belgrade Bull," whom they acquired in the early 1890s. Corbett's ability to throw off would-be riders became so legendary that the bull was featured in the *Saturday Evening Post* in 1910.

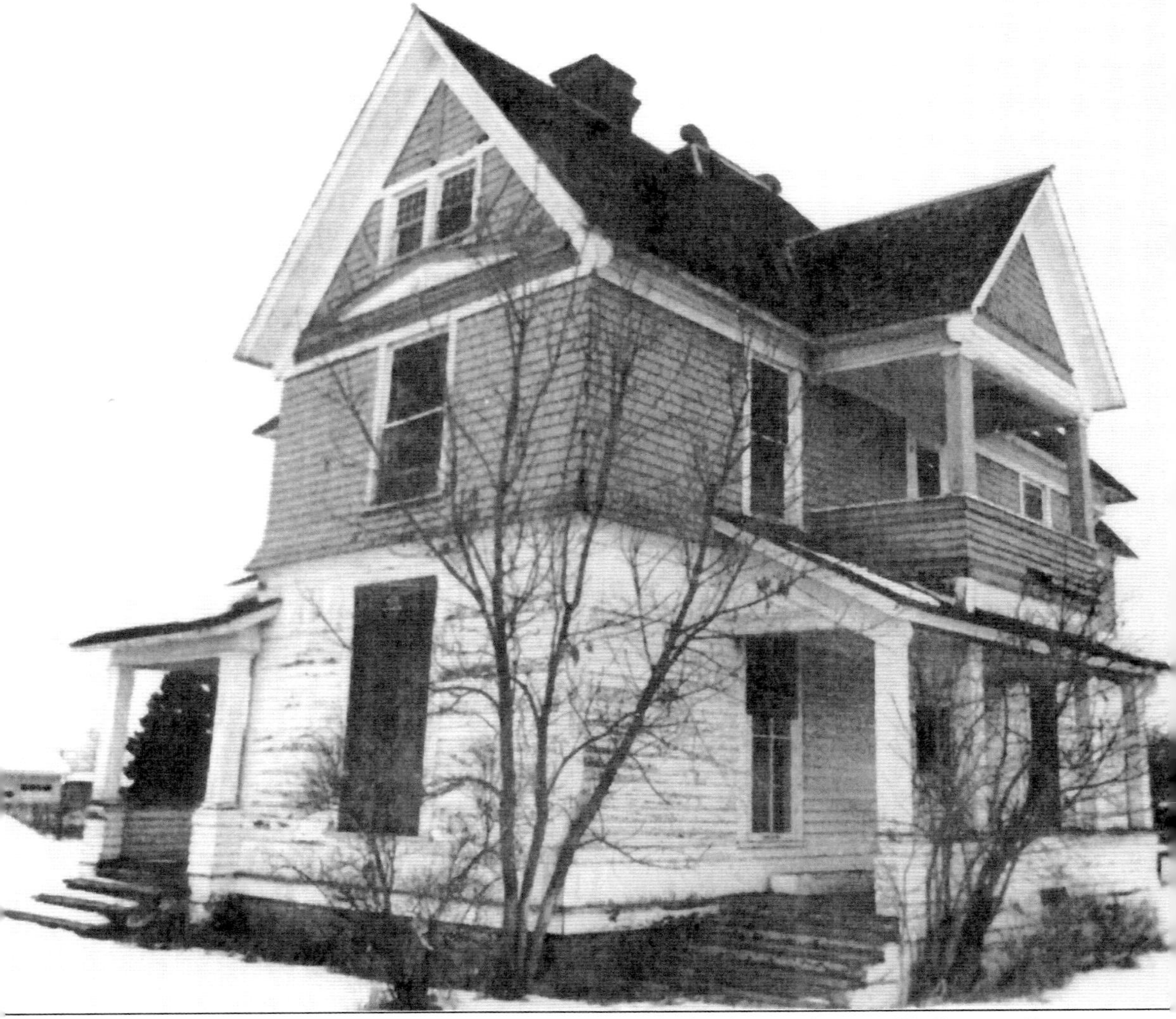

Thomas Buchanan Quaw, founder of Belgrade, built this house about 1885. Quaw, a Bozeman businessman, closed his Bozeman real estate office soon after the house was constructed. Moving to the future townsite that he had picked out about 10 miles west of Bozeman and along the Northern Pacific rail line, Quaw became manager of the Belgrade Grain and Produce Company. Having settled in on December 31, 1886, he hosted a winter ball attended by some 200 couples that was designed to showcase the new townsite. Within a year, Belgrade boasted a telegraph office and a post office with Quaw working as postmaster.

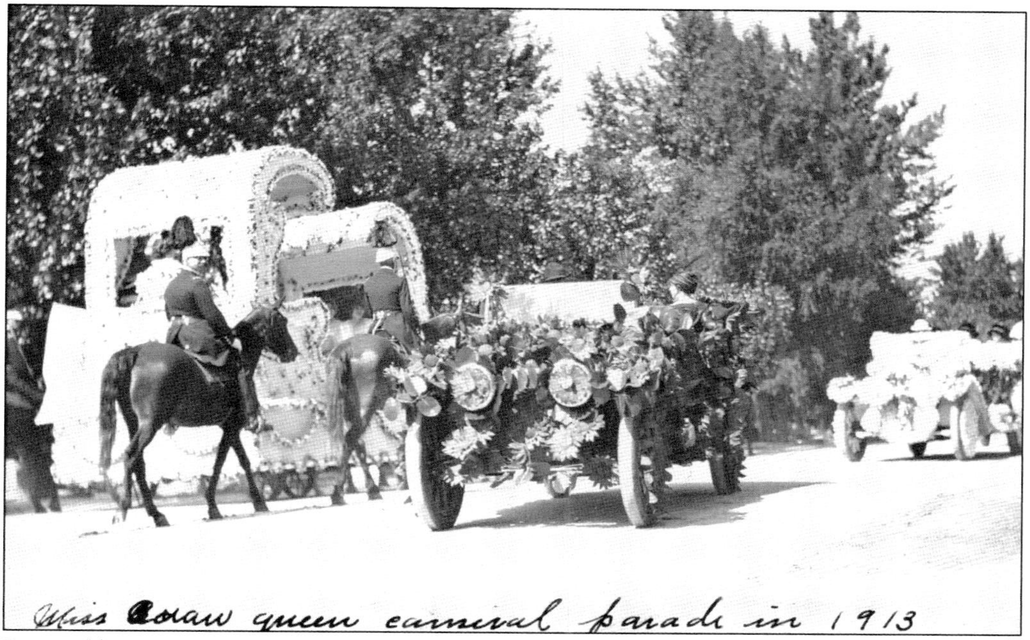

Pictured here is Margaret Georgina, the daughter of Belgrade founder Thomas Buchanan Quaw, as queen of a 1913 parade. Flower-adorned automobiles accompany horses along the parade route. Margaret's brother Thomas Belgrade Quaw was named after the town of Belgrade.

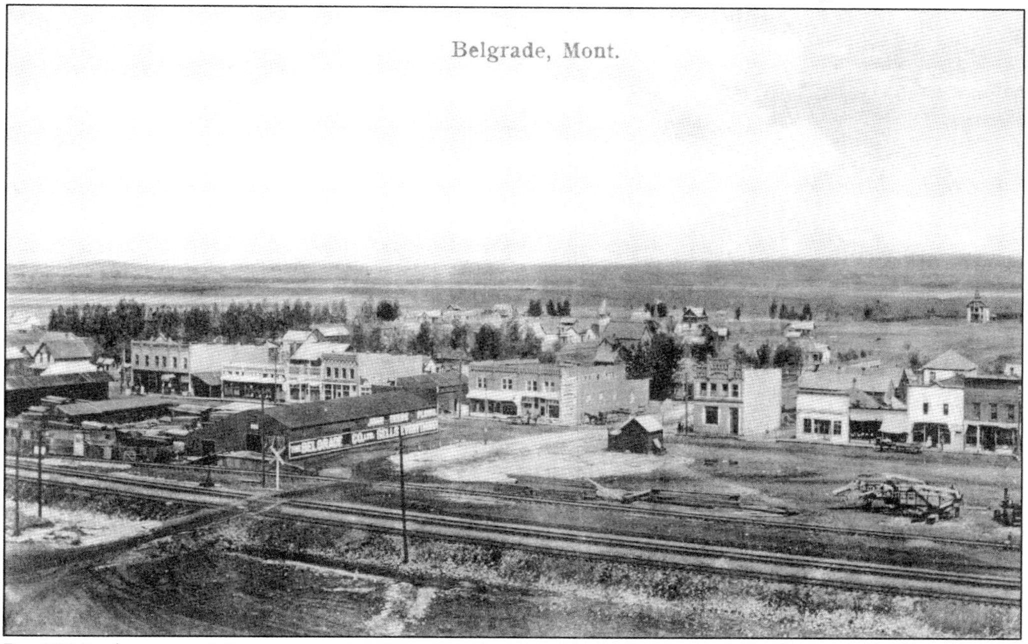

By 1904, the year this panoramic photograph was taken from atop the flour mill, the town of Belgrade had established itself as an agribusiness center in central Gallatin Valley. One block north of the railroad, horses and wagons are interspersed. Nearer the tracks, warehouses are positioned for easy access to distant markets. Parked in the open space to the right are farm implements. The small, dark building in the forefront became John Kyle's shoe cobbler shop.

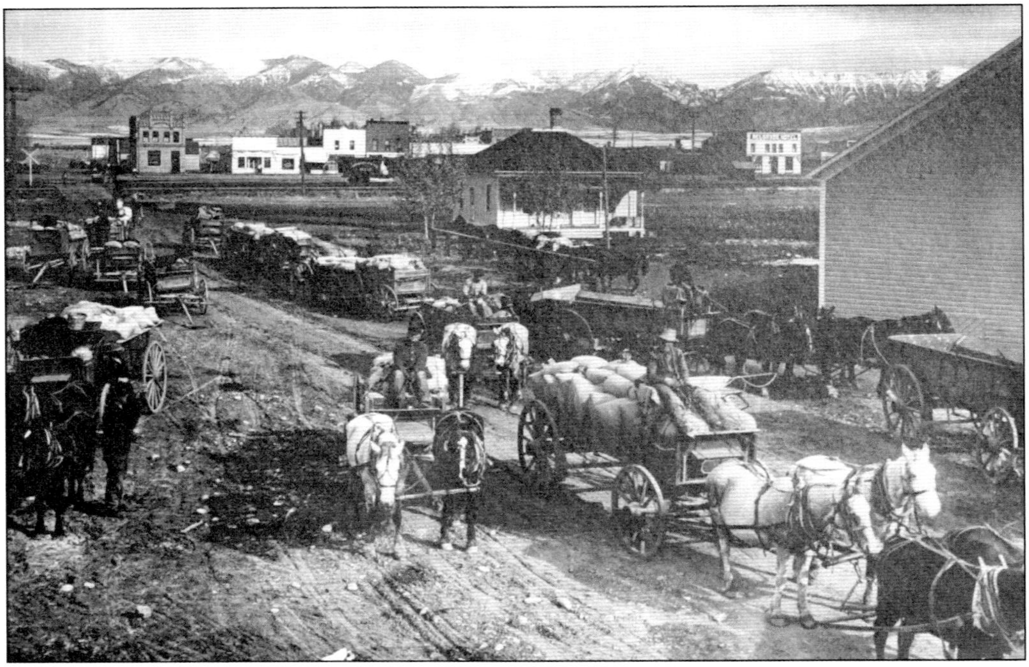

In this c. 1905 photograph, grain harvested from the central Gallatin Valley is hauled by horse and wagon down Broadway Street for processing at the Gallatin Valley Milling Company (formerly the Gallatin Milling Company), owned by Oliver W. Fisher and sons. Fisher, an Ohio native, had served in the Union army before seeking his fortune out West.

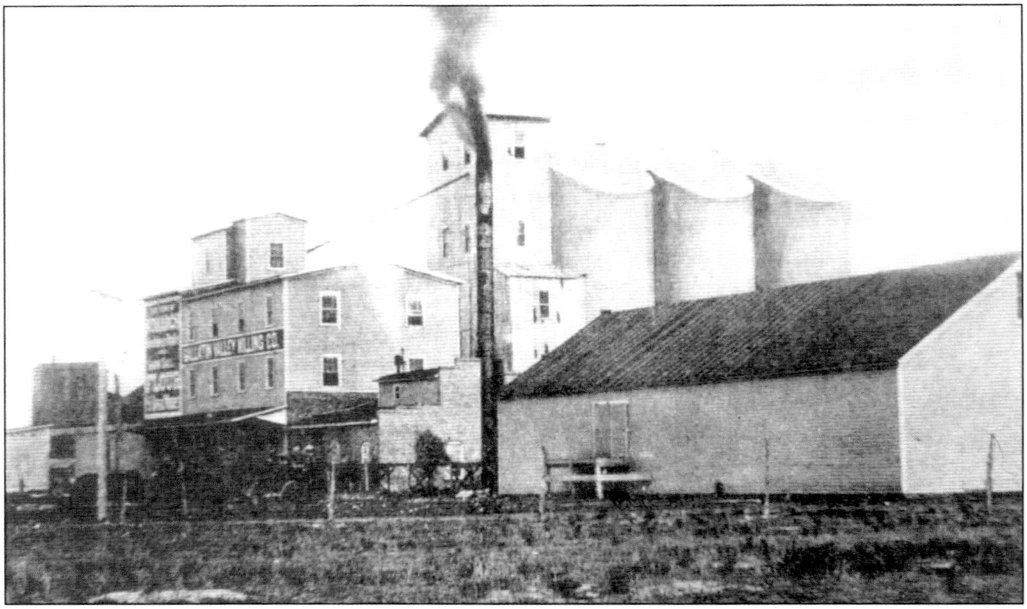

The Gallatin Valley Milling Company, also known as the Fisher Mill, is in operation in this 1905 photograph. Capable of processing 300 barrels of grain daily, the mill produced flour for transport by rail. The Fisher family owned numerous businesses nationwide, and in the summer months, Oliver lived in nearby Bozeman.

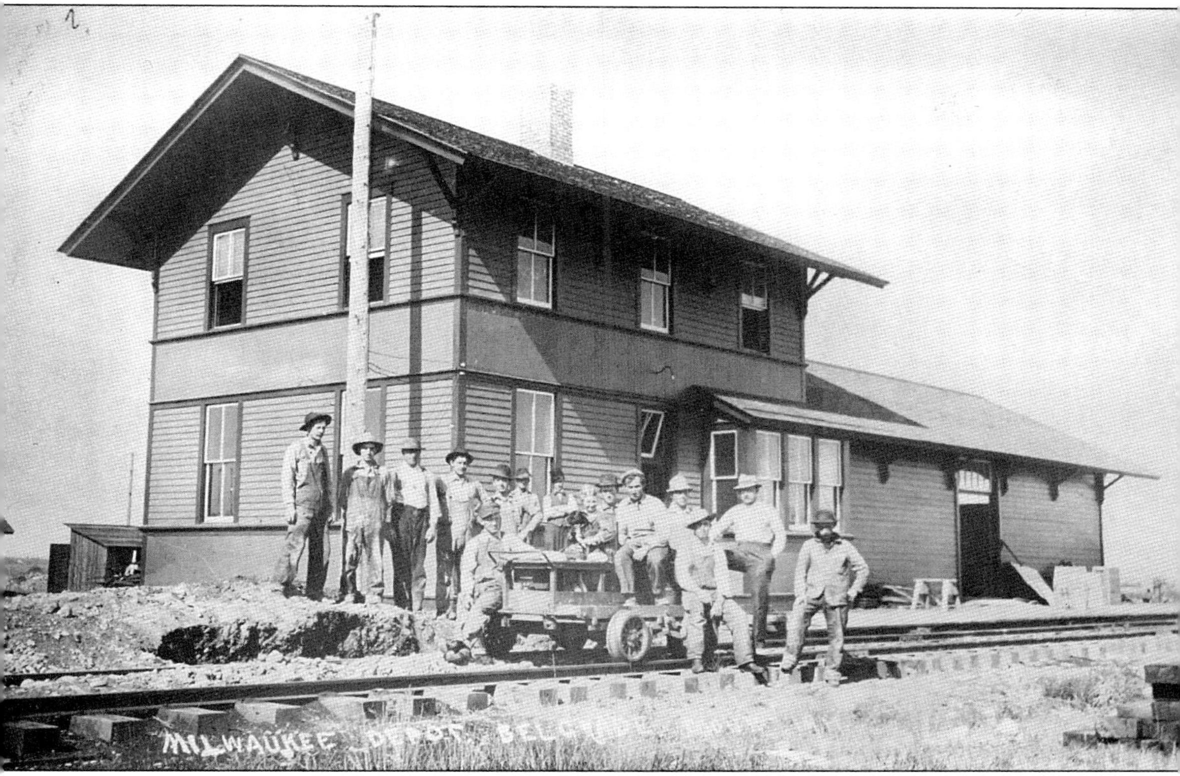

Railroads were essential to the expansion of the Western United States, opening western farmland, natural resources, and new business opportunities to individuals, families, and the nation at large. The Northern Pacific Railway and the Milwaukee Road transported commodities and passengers to and from Belgrade in the early 1900s. Easterners and European immigrants arrived by train, while Gallatin Valley grains and other commodities were shipped to eastern markets. The Milwaukee Road depot, pictured here, served both passengers and freight. For newly arriving settlers, the depot represented the beginning of a new life in Montana's Gallatin Valley. Businessmen also passed through the depot, seeking new opportunities. In addition, the Belgrade depot served tourists en route to Yellowstone and Glacier National Parks.

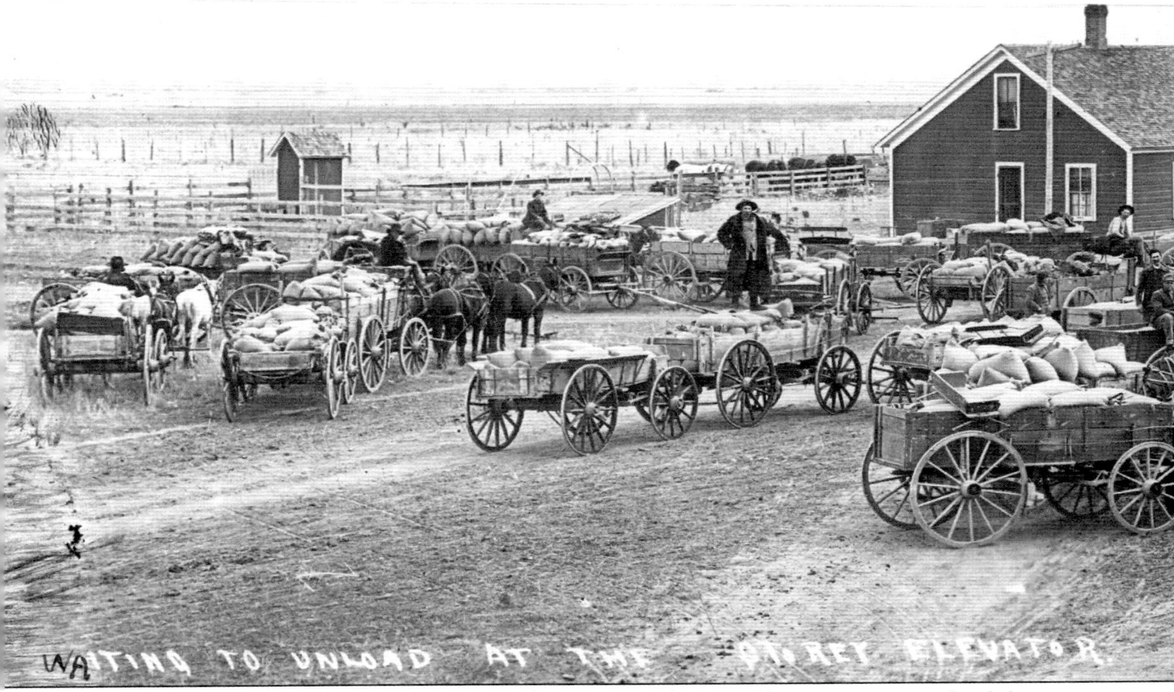

In this 1909 photograph, taken early in the morning, dozens of farmers wait to unload their wagons of grain at Nelson Story's Belgrade grain elevator. A pioneer rancher and entrepreneur who traveled to Montana during the gold rush of the 1860s, Story (1838–1926) became one of the wealthiest citizens of the Gallatin Valley. His business interests included banking, real estate, and milling. The men pictured above represented a second wave of Gallatin Valley settlers—hardworking farmers who found an opportunity in the spacious valley to own land and support their families

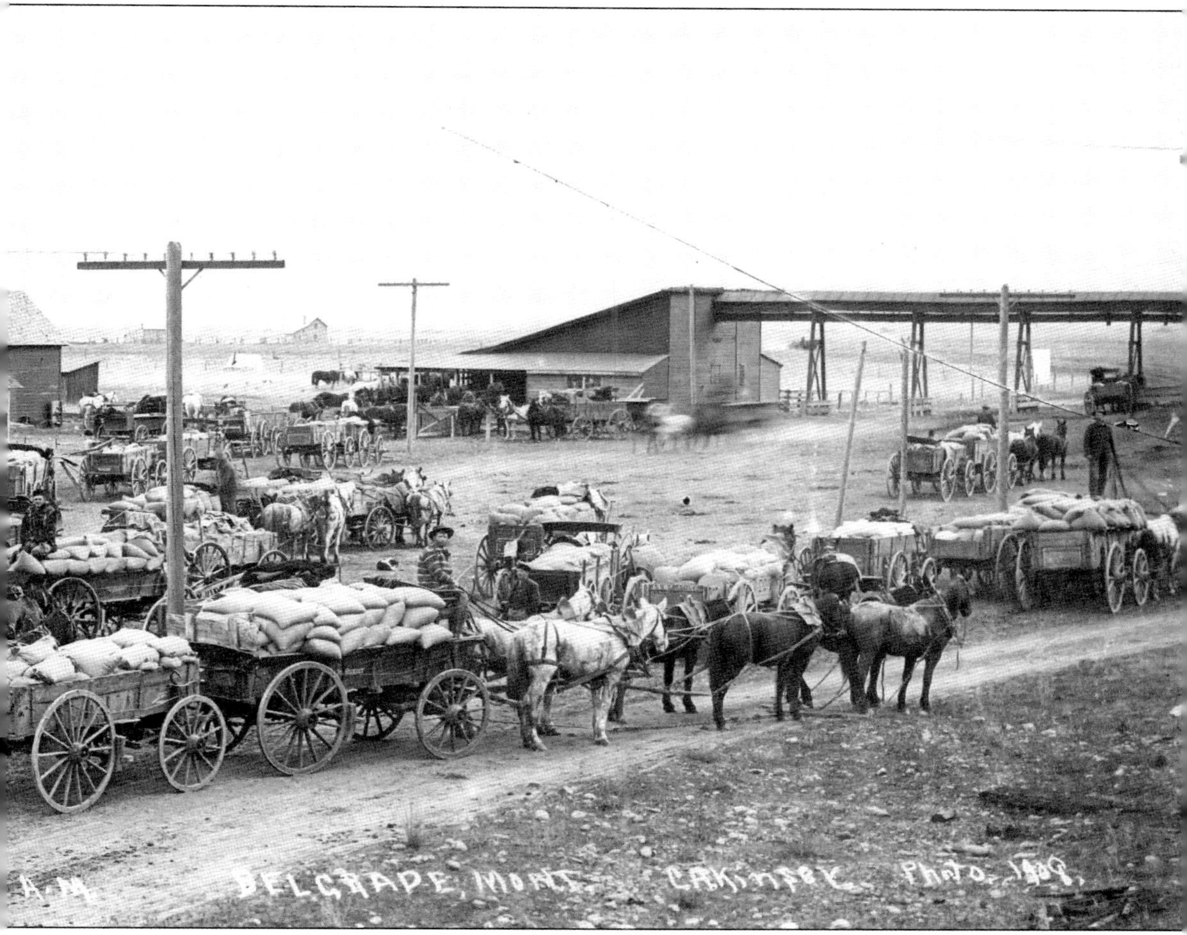

at a time when eastern cities were increasingly overcrowded and besmirched by pollution. Solemn faces greeted the photographer of this image. The farmer's life, dependent upon the weather and swings in market prices, was never secure. Income earned by the sale of one's grain (each sack weighed about 100 pounds) might or might not provide enough cash for the coming year. Yet, for many early settlers living outside of town, the opportunity to work in the clean air and wide-open spaces of Montana was invaluable.

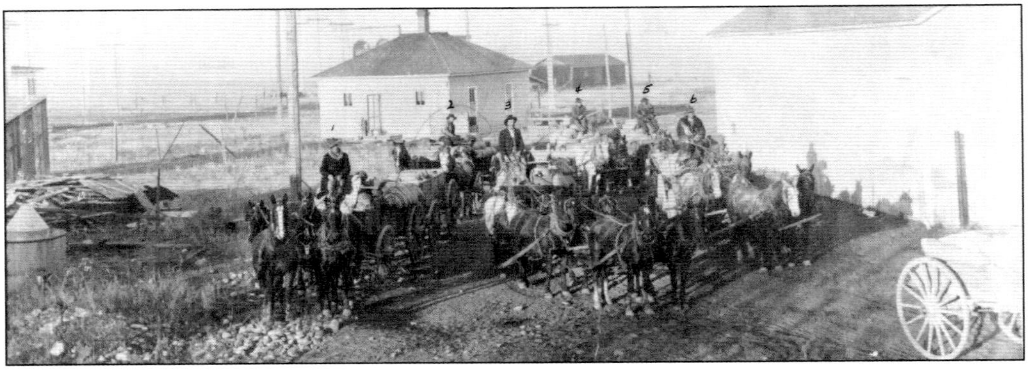

The farmers hauling grain into Belgrade in the image above were participants in an annual ritual. So fertile were the fields that the Gallatin Valley became one of the prime grain suppliers for US markets. In the early 20th century, many Americans ate bread and drank beer made from grains raised in the Belgrade area. Though farming was hard work, play was also a part of the rhythm of life for farmers and ranchers. A highlight of each year was the Belgrade rodeo, as seen in the 1907 image below, which was an opportunity for men to compete against one another in riding and roping contests. Evoking the fading ruggedness of the American frontier, rodeos thrilled participants and spectators alike, while capturing the imagination of distant city dwellers.

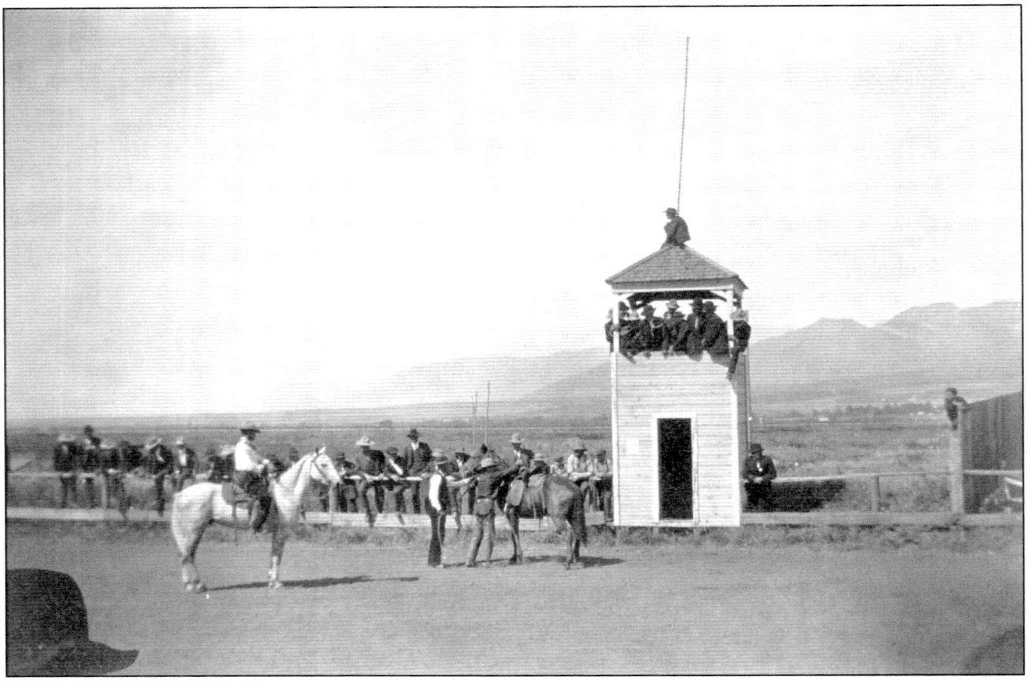

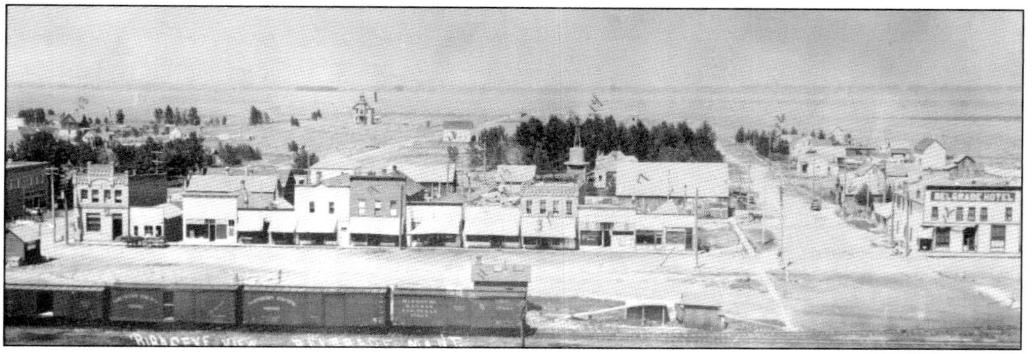

Pictured above is a panoramic view of the town of Belgrade around 1909. Horses and wagons traversed the dirt streets, as automobiles in the Gallatin Valley remained rare. To the bottom right is the Belgrade Hotel, and in the background, set apart from the rest of the buildings, is the Quaw schoolhouse, named for the town's founding family. The town's water tower is visible to the right. It held water piped from Springhill, about seven miles away to the east.

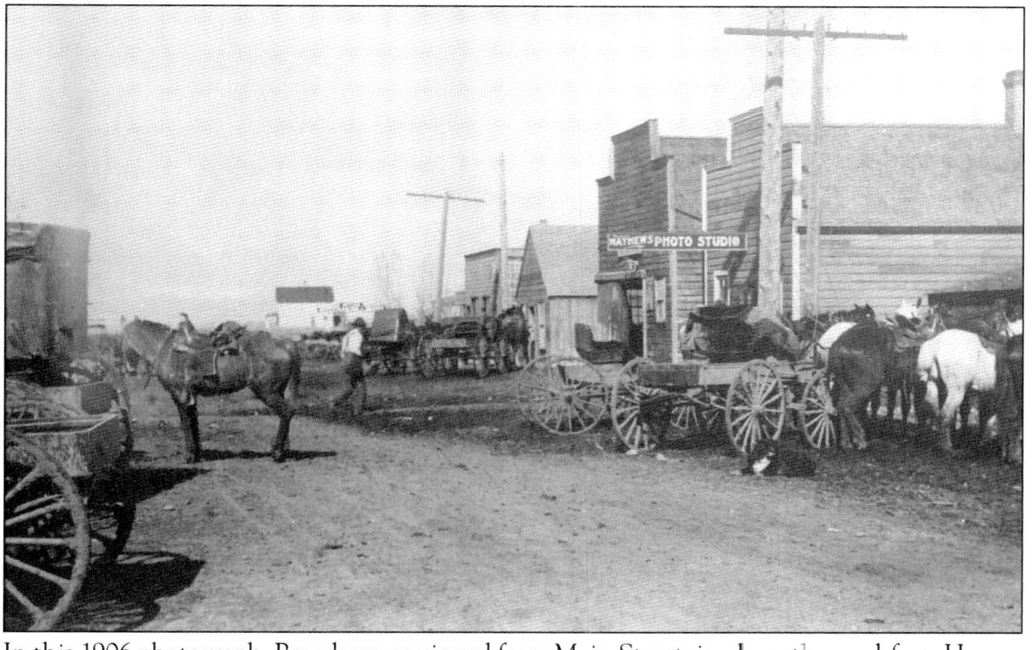

In this 1906 photograph, Broadway, as viewed from Main Street, is a busy thoroughfare. Horses, buggies, and wagons line both sides of the packed-down dirt street, with Matthews Photo Studio visible to the right. By this time, photography had come to be viewed as an art form, and portrait studios were not uncommon in America's small towns.

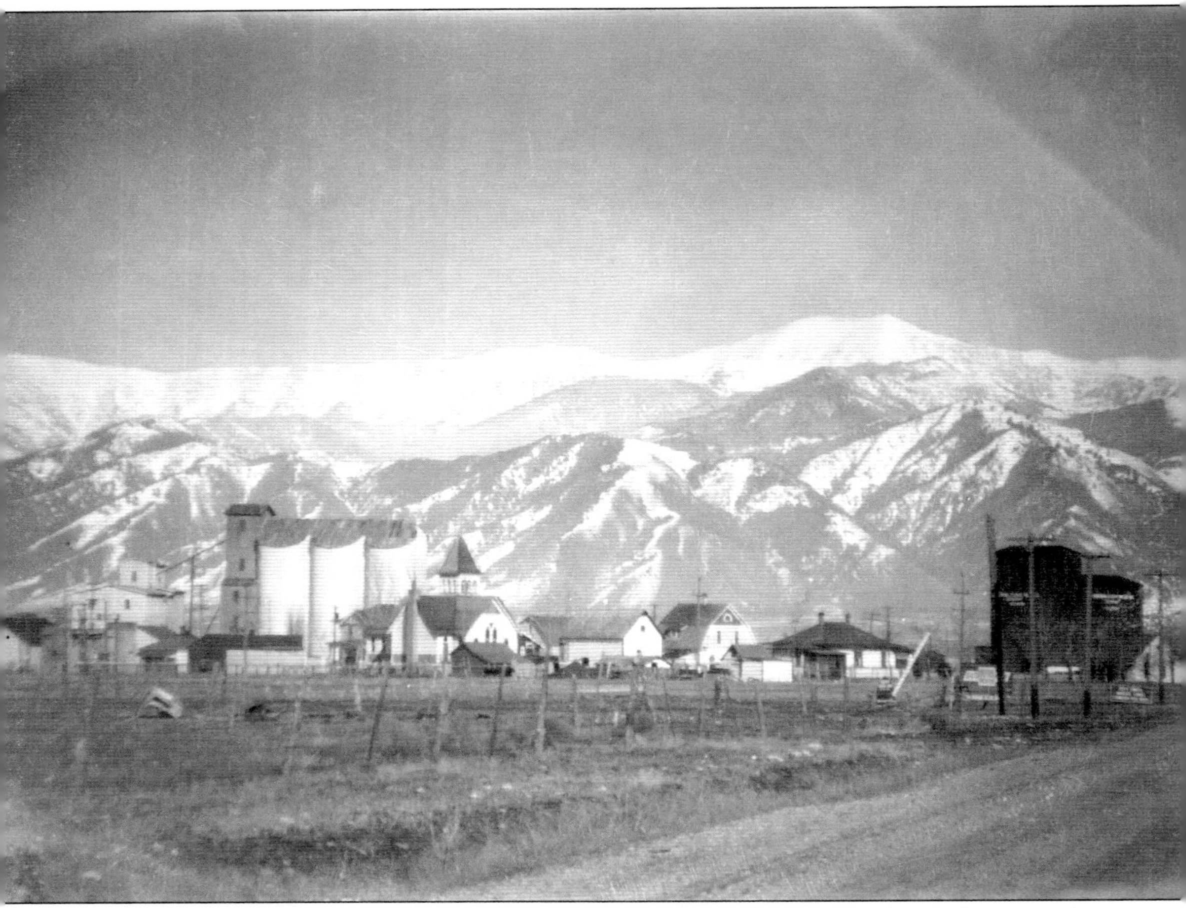

Snow covers the top of the Bridger Mountains in this undated image of Belgrade facing northeast. In the Gallatin Valley, the grittiness of early-20th-century, small-town Montana life, as experienced by many ordinary citizens, unfolded against the backdrop of the beauty and majesty of the Rocky Mountains. The mountains provided game for residents, and some found in the surrounding peaks a sense of spirituality. Organized religion took hold slowly but steadily in Belgrade, offering a sense of community for many persons of faith. The Presbyterian church in the foreground was completed in 1911, and in 1931, the town's Presbyterians and Baptists joined together and created a federated church in the building. Telephone lines and poles visible in this photograph ensured a direct connection to the larger world beyond the mountains ringing the valley. Towering above the other buildings, the grain storage bins and mill, set near the rail tracks, were the lifeblood of the community's economy.

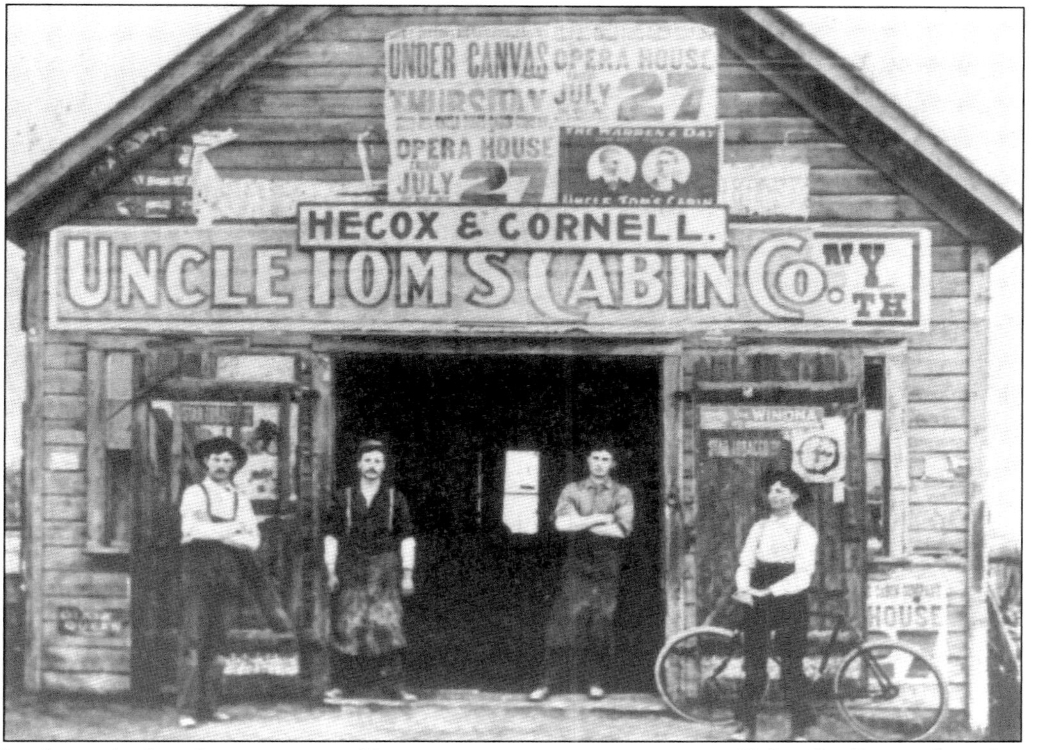

In the early decades, a variety of business enterprises sprung up in Belgrade. Pictured in this undated photograph is the handiwork of early enterprising businessmen Hecox and Cornell. Jesse Nelson, Ed Cornell, Hamp Hecox, and an unidentified bicyclist stand from left to right in front of the Hecox and Cornell Blacksmith Shop, housed in a small wooden building plastered with a variety of signs advertising products and events.

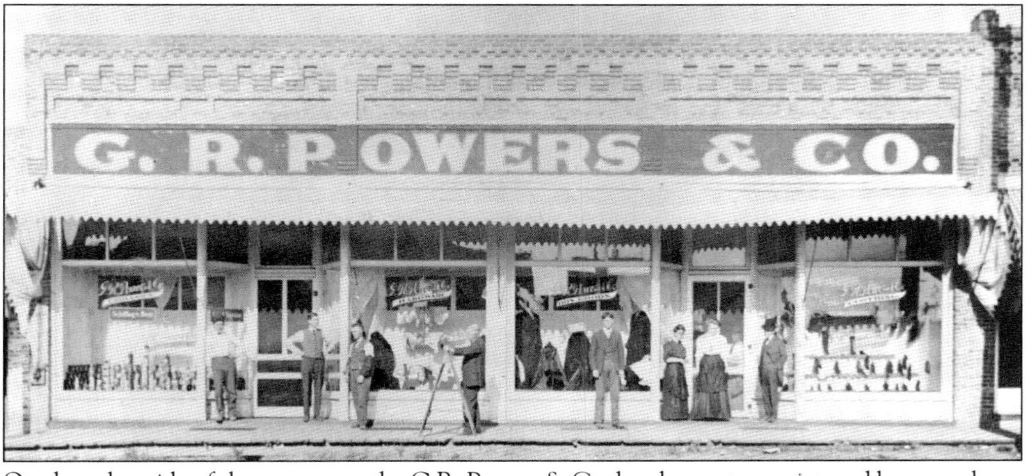

On the other side of the spectrum, the G.R. Powers & Co. hardware store, pictured here, evokes a sense of tidiness and professionalism. The Powers family owned businesses throughout Montana. The well-dressed men and women lounging in front of the store provide little hint of the agricultural nature of Belgrade. Hardware stores of this era served as general stores, selling clothes, food, and other goods.

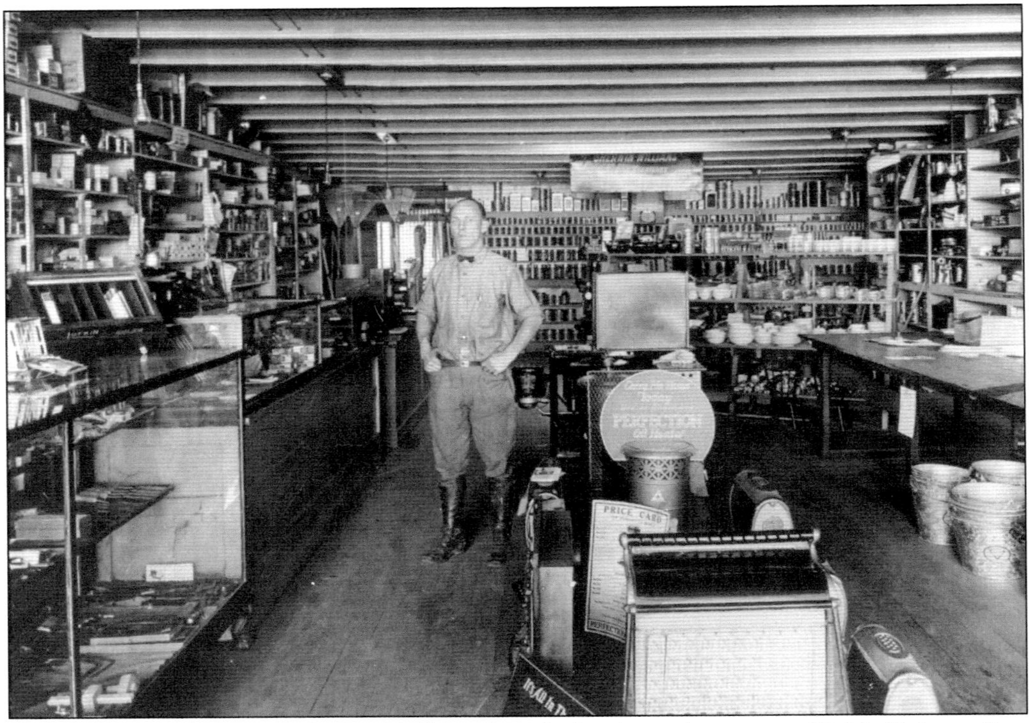

Inside the Belgrade Mercantile, Jim Isbell stands in the hardware department. To Isbell's immediate right is a display advertising oil heaters, an improvement over the more common coal- or wood-burning heaters. Shelves and displays are filled with merchandise. Cans line the rear wall while dishes and kitchen items are visible to the rear right.

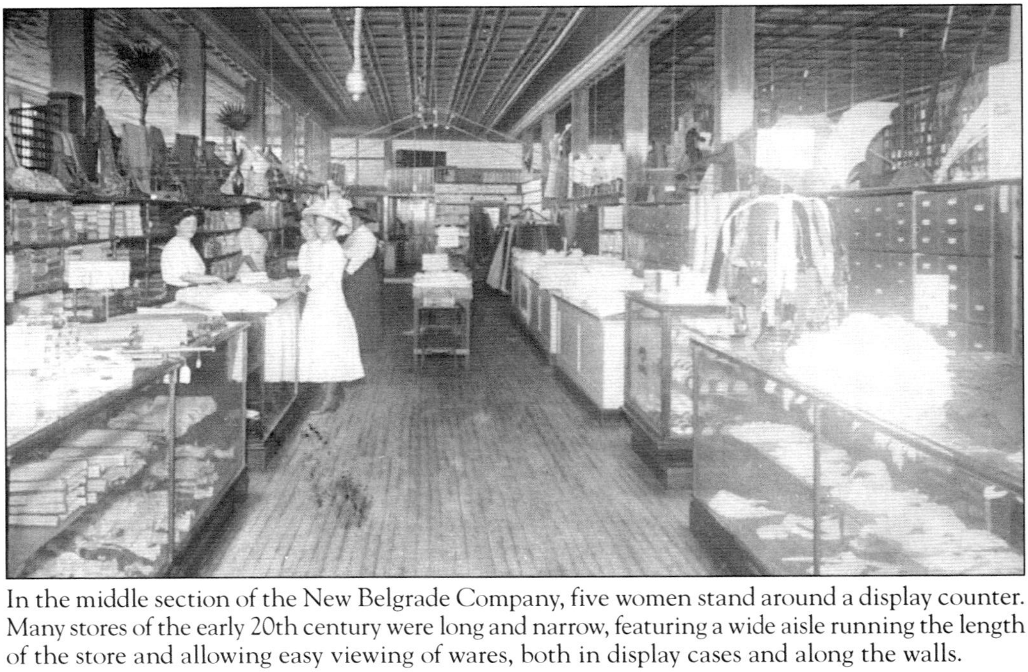

In the middle section of the New Belgrade Company, five women stand around a display counter. Many stores of the early 20th century were long and narrow, featuring a wide aisle running the length of the store and allowing easy viewing of wares, both in display cases and along the walls.

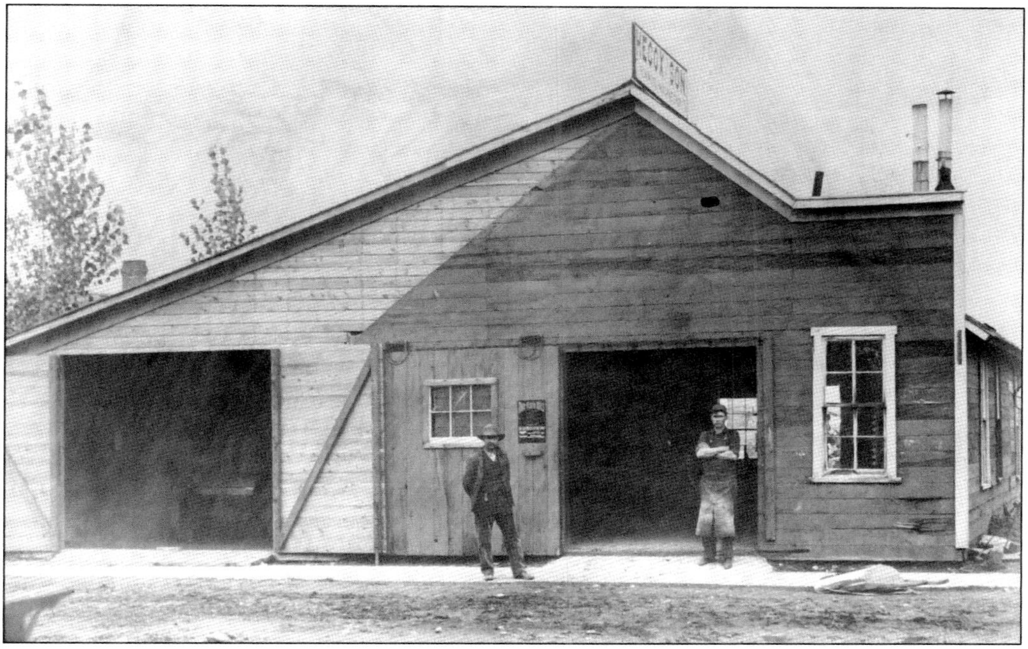

With the introduction and growth of automobiles, the place of the horse in Montana life gradually changed. The Hecox & Son Blacksmith & Auto Shop, pictured here around 1909, serviced both horses and automobiles. C.H. Hecox, left, and H.S. Hecox stand in front of their business alongside a barely visible automobile inside a stall to the left.

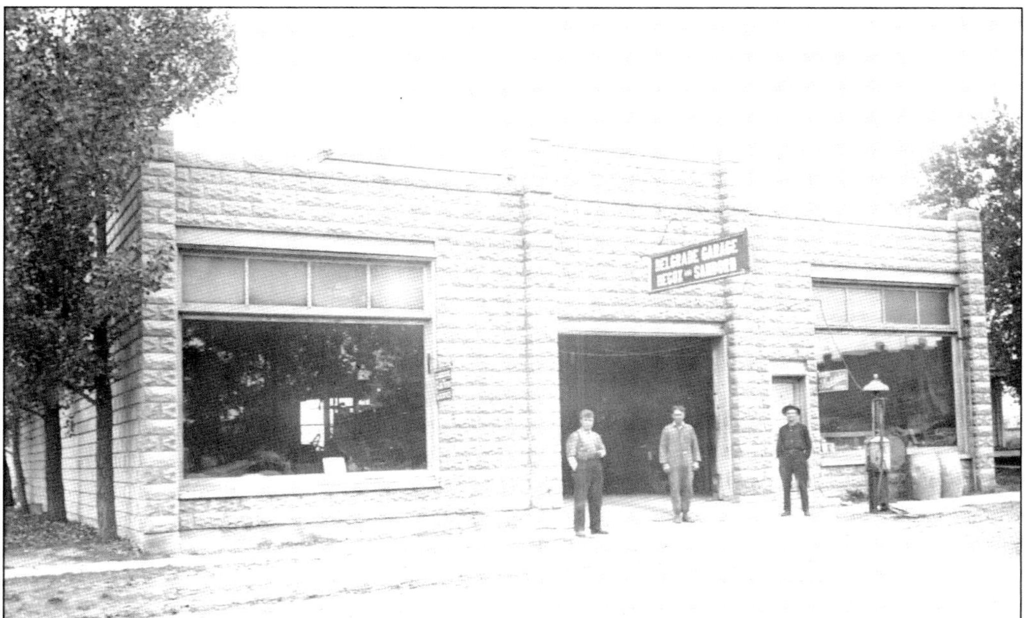

By the second decade of the 20th century, automobiles routinely roamed Belgrade's city streets. Standing in front of the Hecox and Sanborn Garage in 1919 are, from left to right Dudley Hecox, Elmer Templeton, and H.G. Hecox. An early gasoline pump is visible to the right of the three men.

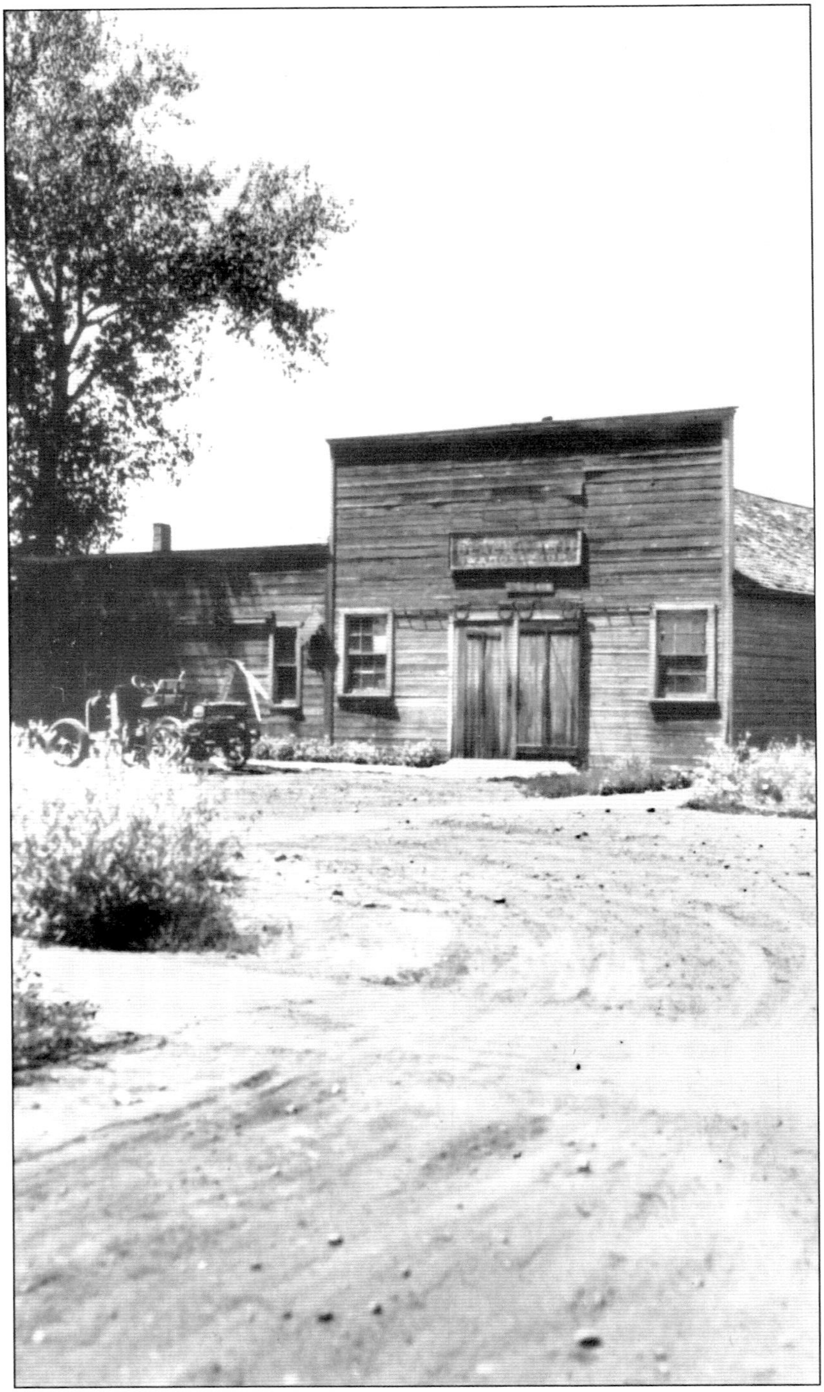

In 1930s Belgrade, Skinner's Blacksmith Shop on Weaver Street offers a snapshot of the changed world of transportation. While horseshoes hang above the doorway beneath the faded shop sign, an automobile is parked in front of the building. However, blacksmithing endured in Montana, as horses remained necessary in ranching operations.

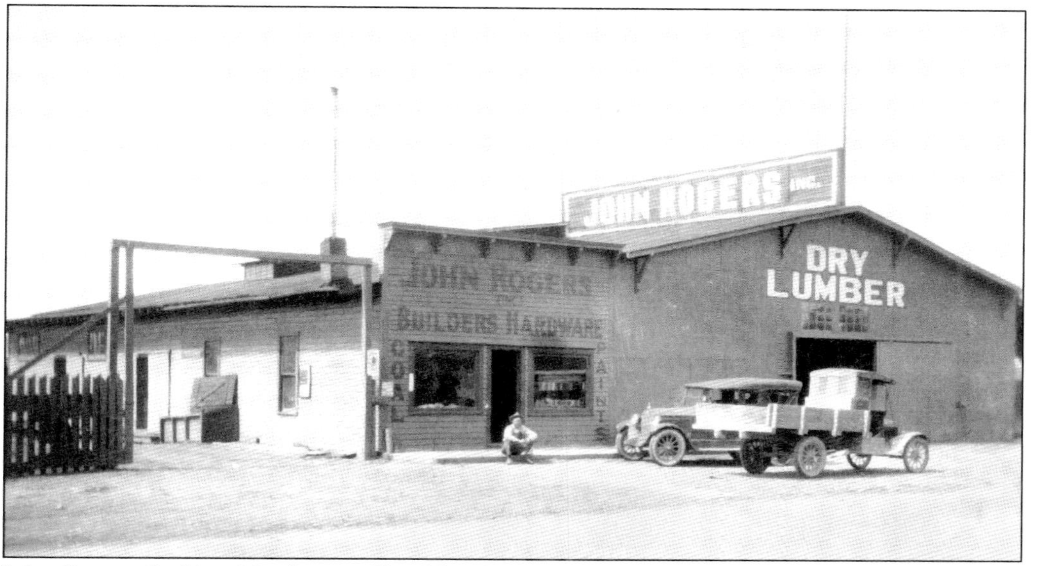

John Rogers Builders Hardware offered lumber, hardware, paints, coal, and more to Belgrade area residents. The progress of the town could be seen in rough-hewn structures giving way to common folks' homes built of planed lumber and painted inside and out. While brick remained a popular building material in some commercial buildings, wood was more practical and less costly for the constructing of houses.

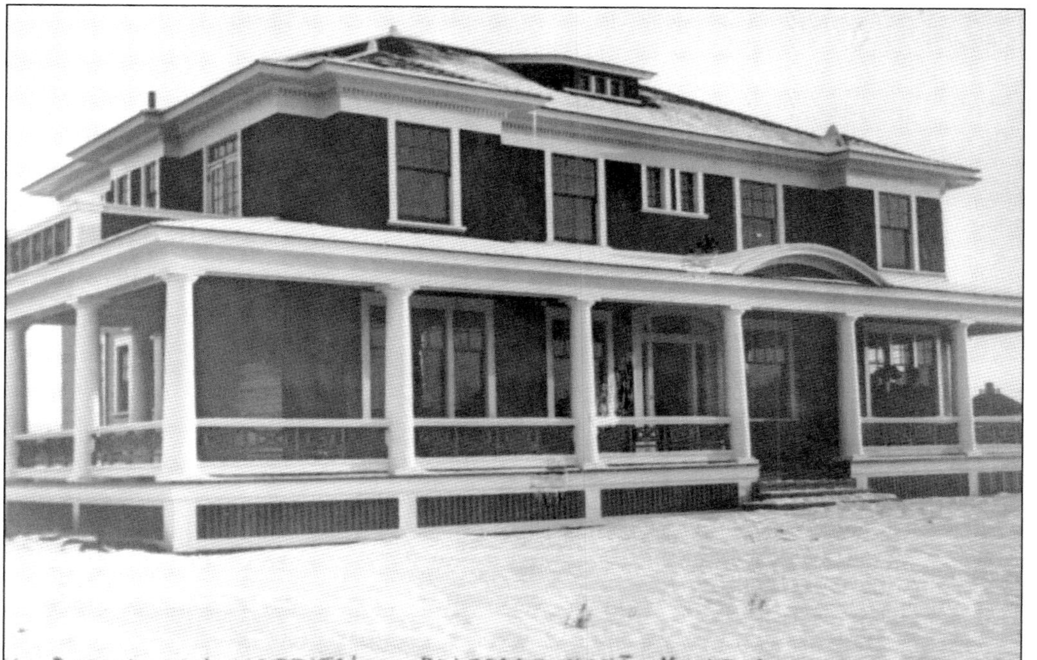

Pictured above in 1910, the Johnston Hospital in Belgrade, which was indicative of many small town hospitals of the era, resembles a large house complete with a wraparound porch supported by large columns. Commonly called sanitariums, many late-19th- and early-20th-century hospitals were designed with spacious room dimensions and an aura of restfulness.

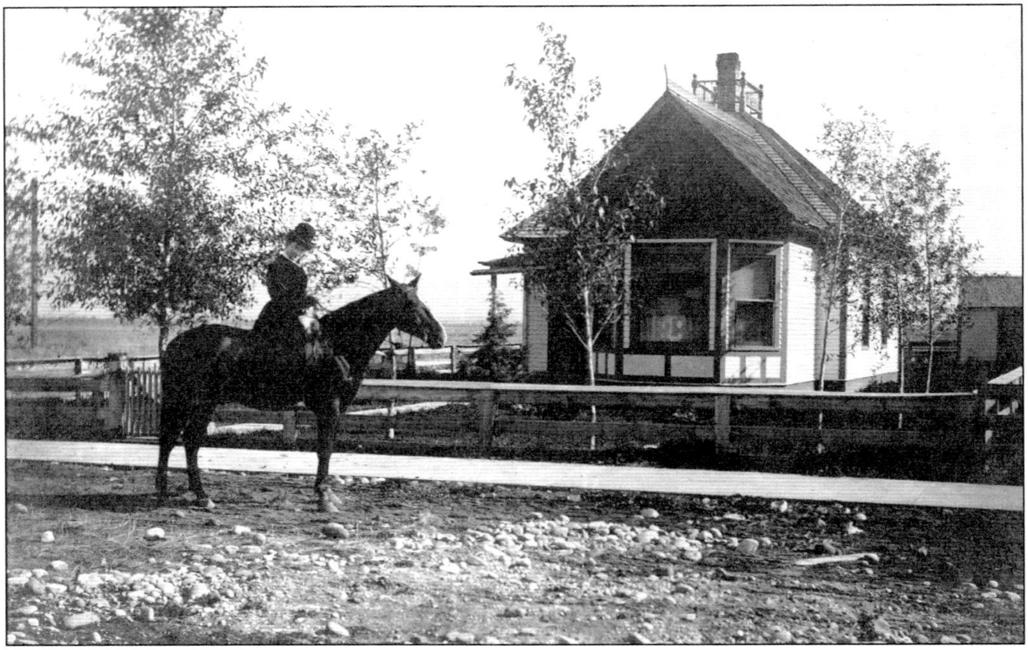

Montana in the late 19th and early 20th centuries was a rugged place, remote from large cities to the east, west, and south. A woman's life in the early Gallatin Valley was often lonely and arduous. Women of means, however, such as Alice Tate, pictured here in 1908, were able to enjoy a variety of activities, including recreational horseback riding.

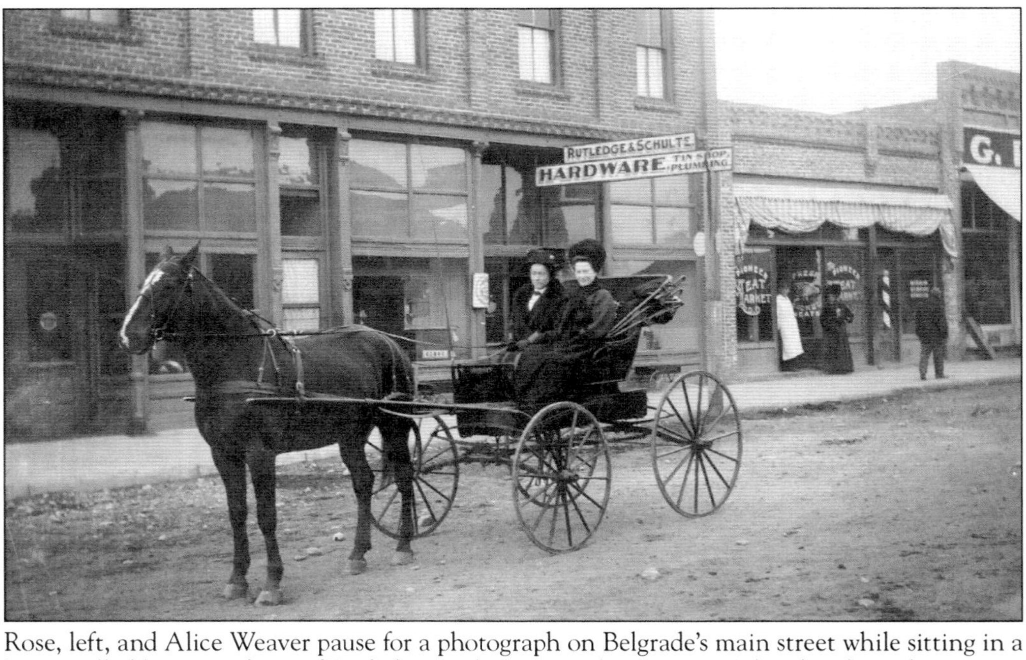

Rose, left, and Alice Weaver pause for a photograph on Belgrade's main street while sitting in a horse-pulled buggy in front of Rutledge & Shulte's Hardware store. A butcher from the Pioneer Meat Market watches from his shop's doorway alongside an unidentified woman holding a parcel. Belgrade's downtown stores provided opportunity for women to socialize, as well as shop.

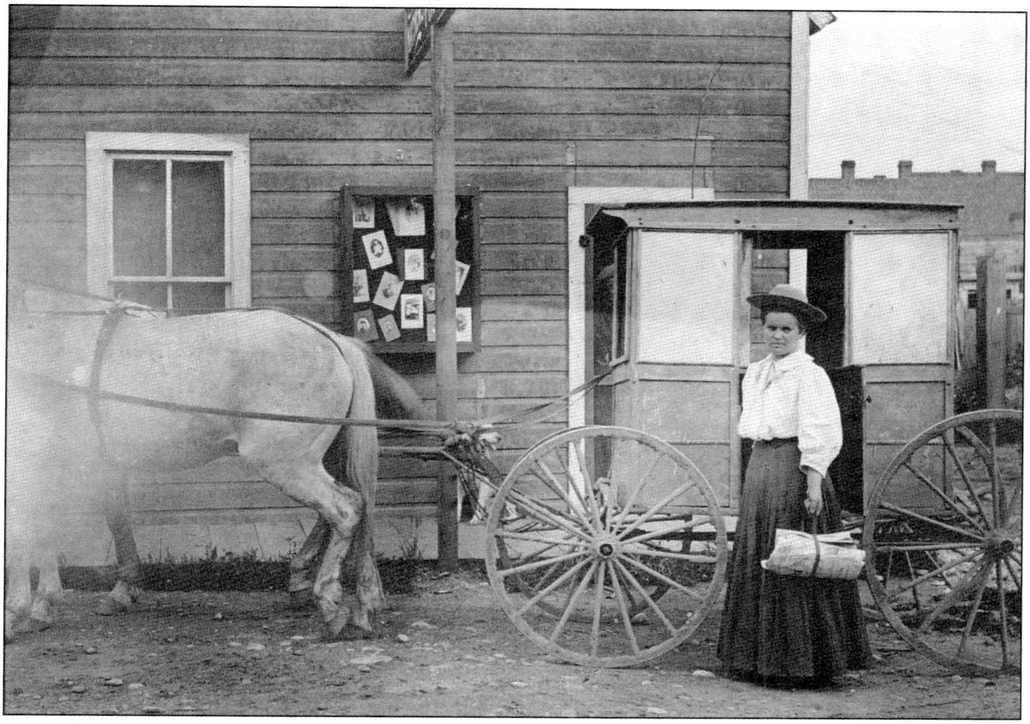

Not all women in early Belgrade worked in the home or fields. Mail carrier Carrie Weaver delivered mail in the Dry Creek area. Due to bad road conditions and rough terrain, the horse and buggy remained essential to Montana rural mail delivery in the early decades of the 20th century. This 1906 image was captured in front of Matthews Photo Studio. Pictures of area residents are tacked to the front of the building.

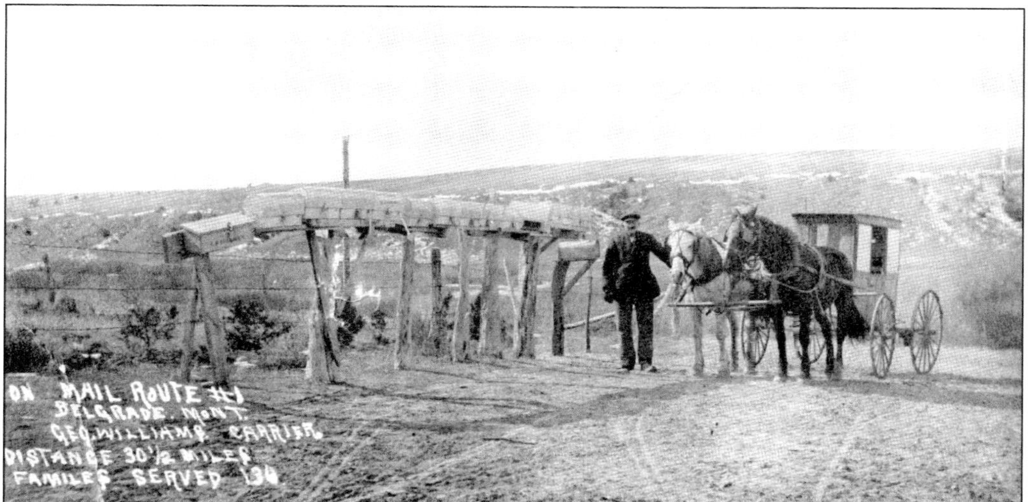

More commonly the domain of men, early postal mail delivery often meant a full day of riding. Mail carrier George Williams delivered mail on Belgrade's route No. 1. The route covered a distance of 30.5 miles and served 130 families. In this photograph, mailboxes in front of Williams are mounted upon homemade poles.

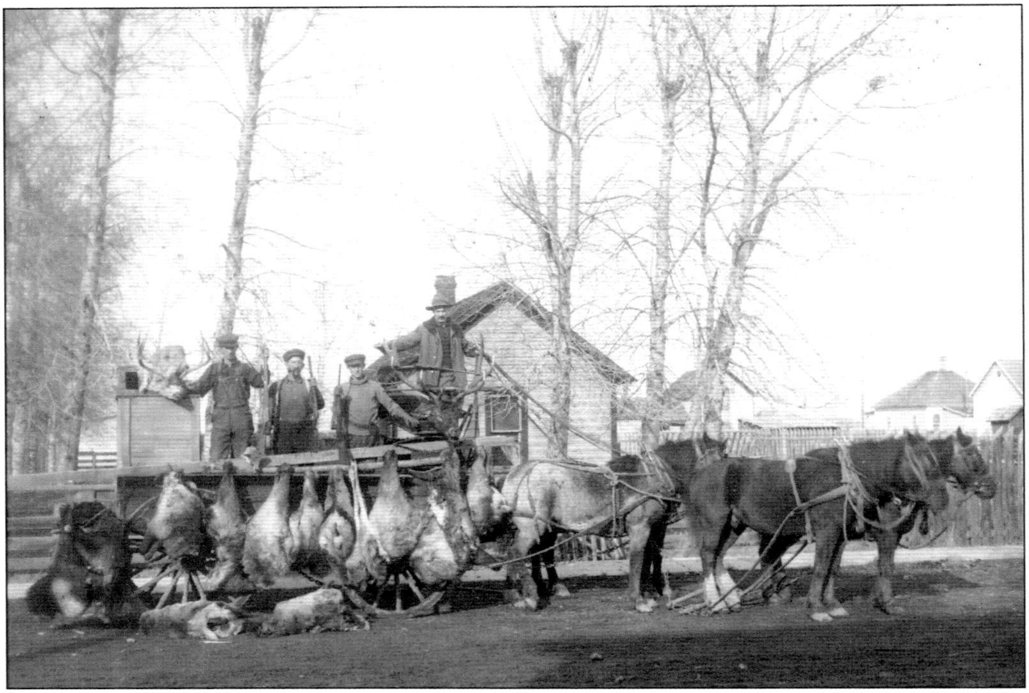

A group of Belgrade hunters pose with their game after a successful outing. Rifles are on display, and deer and elk quarters hang from the side of a wagon. A large elk bull rack is also held aloft for all to see, with a Winchester 30-06 rifle resting across its rack. Wild game provided meat for many family tables in early Belgrade.

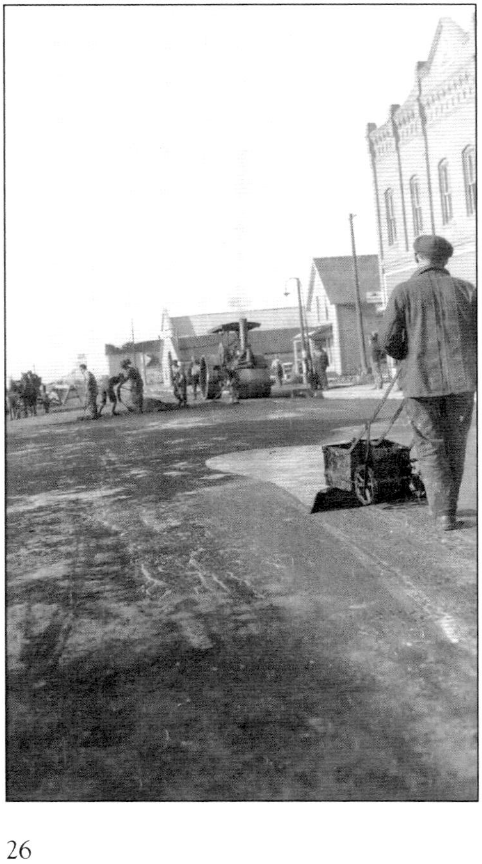

In the 1920s, Belgrade's main street underwent a transformation from dirt to asphalt. In this photograph, a small group of onlookers watch as Main Street is paved. Workers, machinery, and horses share the street as the sticky mixture is spread upon the leveled ground. Main Street would remain the only paved street in town for about three decades.

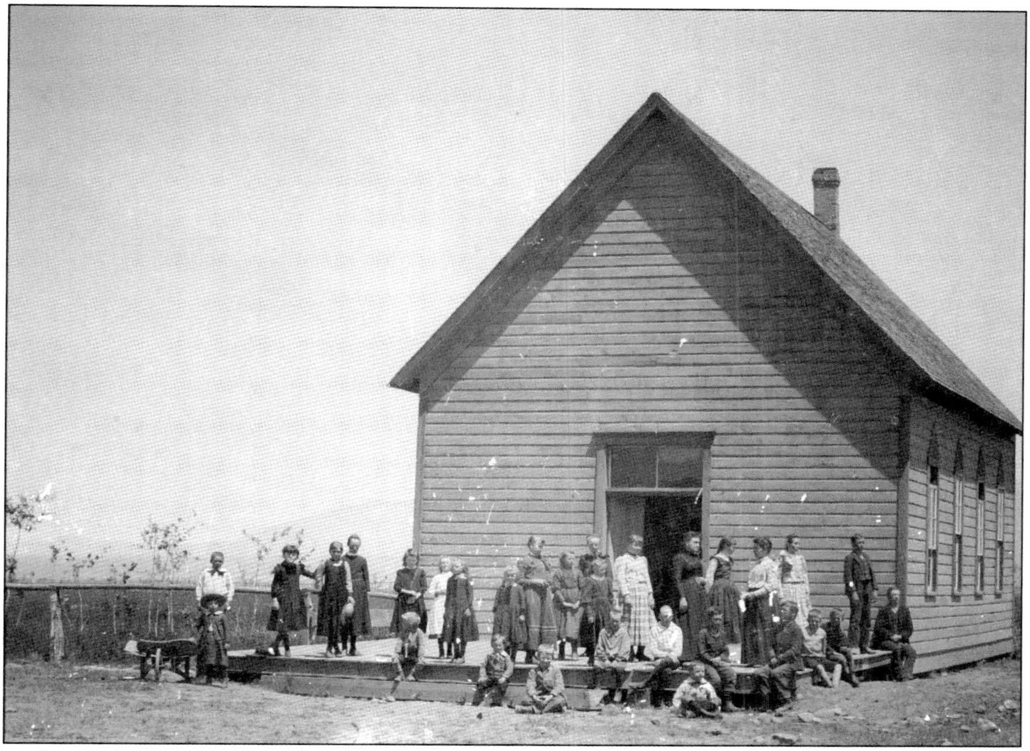

In this 1890s photograph, Belgrade's first schoolhouse is pictured. Children of various ages alongside their teacher stand and sit on the open porch of the simple one-story building that had no windows in front. The town soon outgrew the schoolhouse, which was later used as a church building.

Pictured are Belgrade schoolchildren and adults during the 1895–1896 school year. Among those pictured in this image are Jack Murphy, Nelson Stuart, Charles Stuart, Whitfield Spain, Virginia Spain, Bill Murphy, Frank Monroe, Orvis W. Smith (teacher), Inez Ogle, Vern Holloway, W. Wylie, Mary Hoffman, Kay Murphy, Jane Kennedy, Rose Kennedy, Ann Kennedy, Ed Knadler, and Art Knadler. For more information on the people pictured, visit Bozeman's Pioneer Museum.

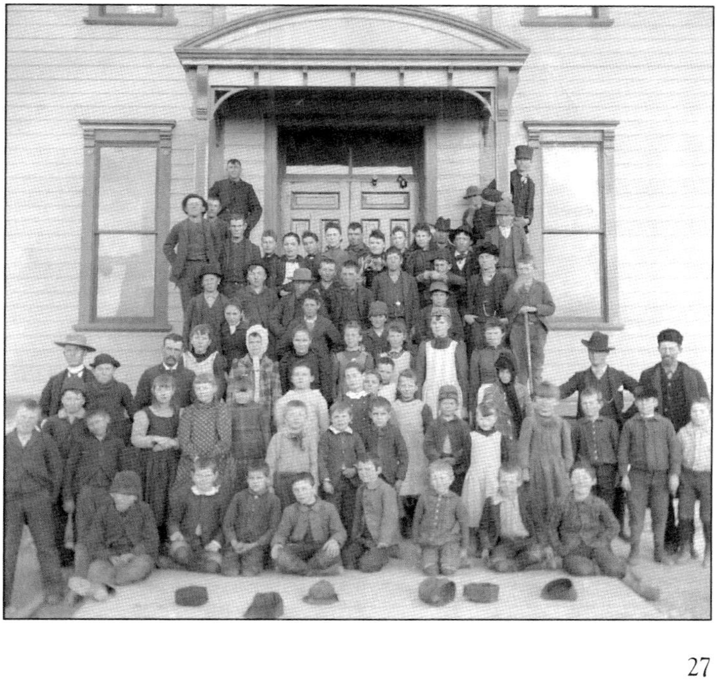

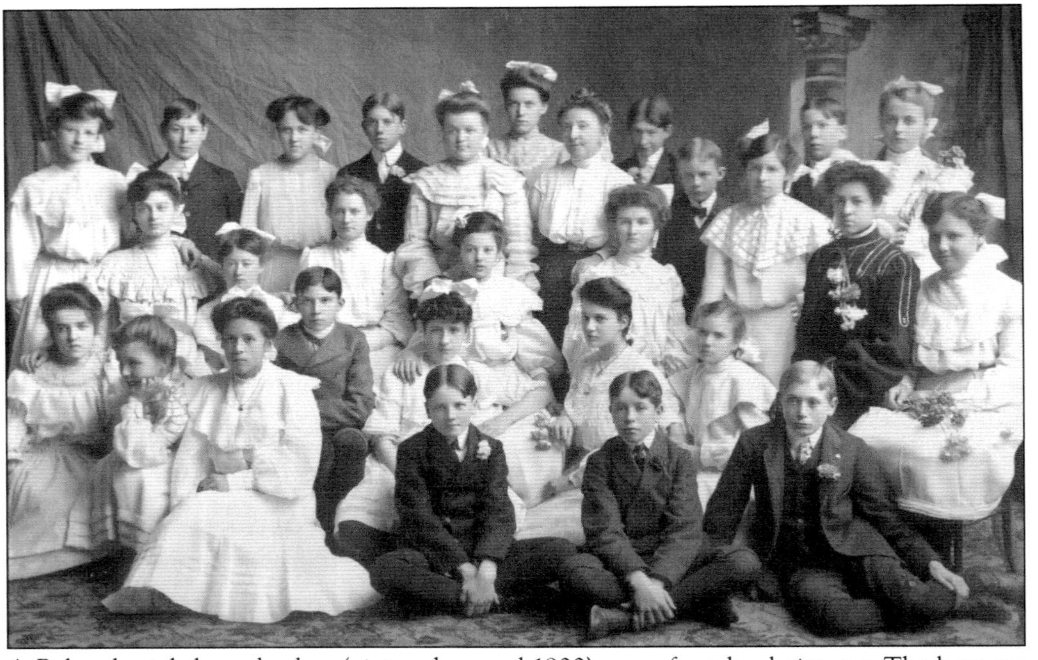

A Belgrade eighth-grade class (pictured around 1900) poses for school pictures. The boys are wearing dark suits, whereas most of the girls wear white dresses. Many children did not attend school beyond eighth grade.

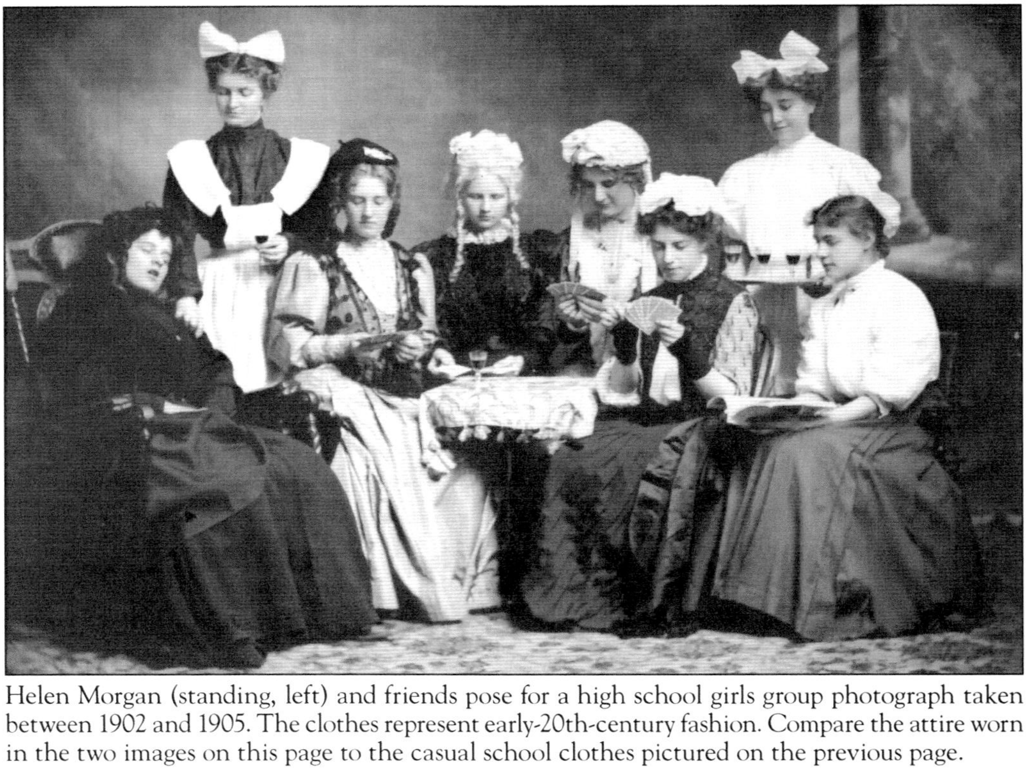

Helen Morgan (standing, left) and friends pose for a high school girls group photograph taken between 1902 and 1905. The clothes represent early-20th-century fashion. Compare the attire worn in the two images on this page to the casual school clothes pictured on the previous page.

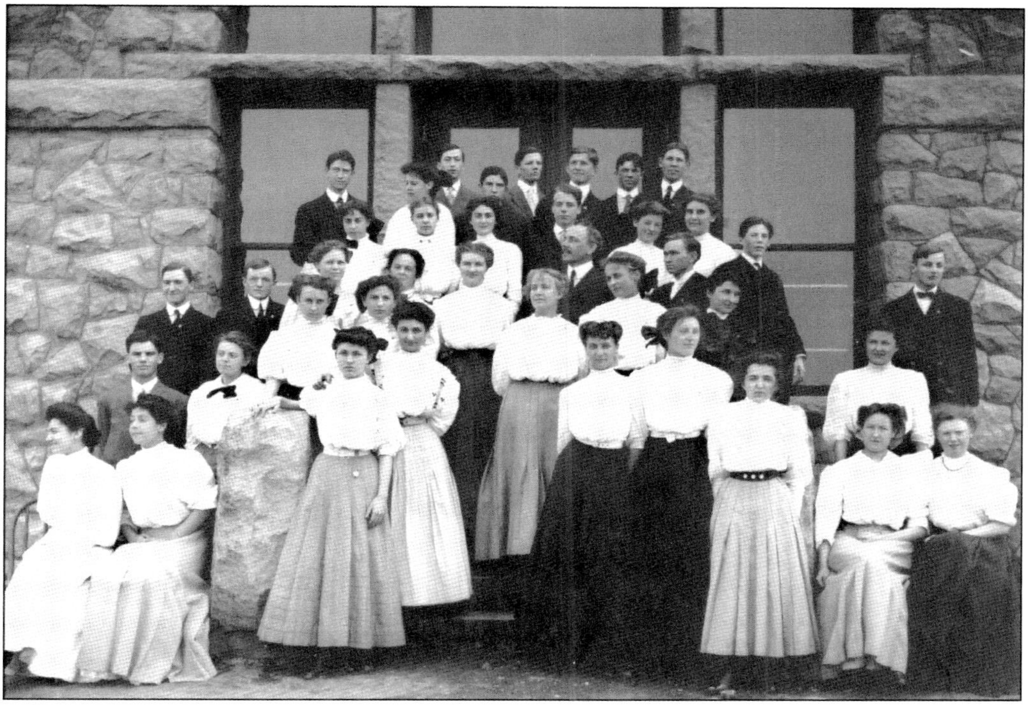

A high school graduating class around 1905 poses for a photograph. Young women noticeably outnumber the young men; however, most graduating women of this era did not pursue further education or a career outside of the home, while many men with high school diplomas continued their education and/or transition into a professional career.

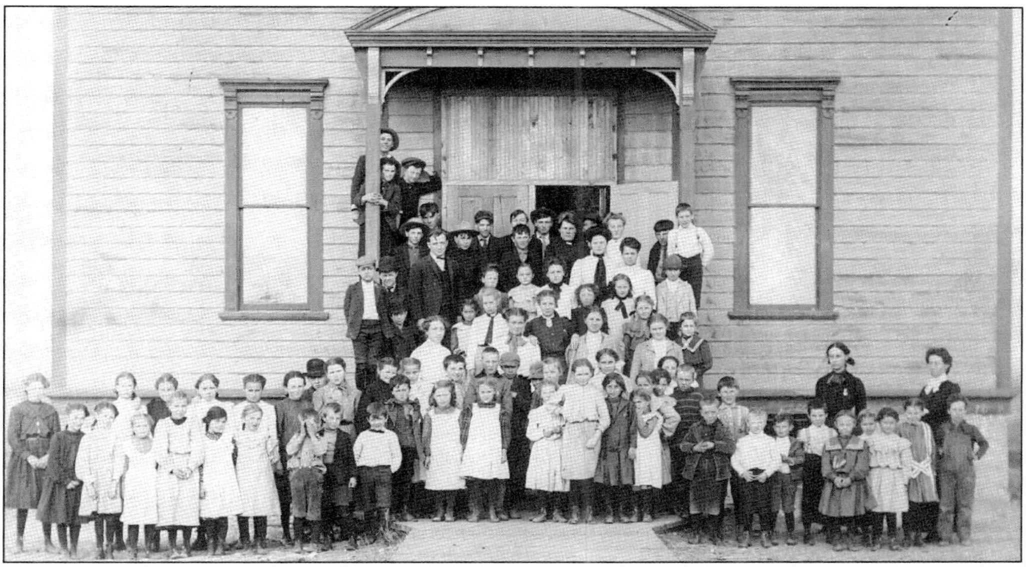

Photographed in the spring of 1906, young public school students are gathered in front of the Belgrade schoolhouse. Teachers pictured somewhere in this image are Bess Humbly, Anna Murphy, and William Fitzstephens. Characteristic of rural schools of the era, many children are dressed in plain clothes. For some, this may be the first time they have ever had their picture taken.

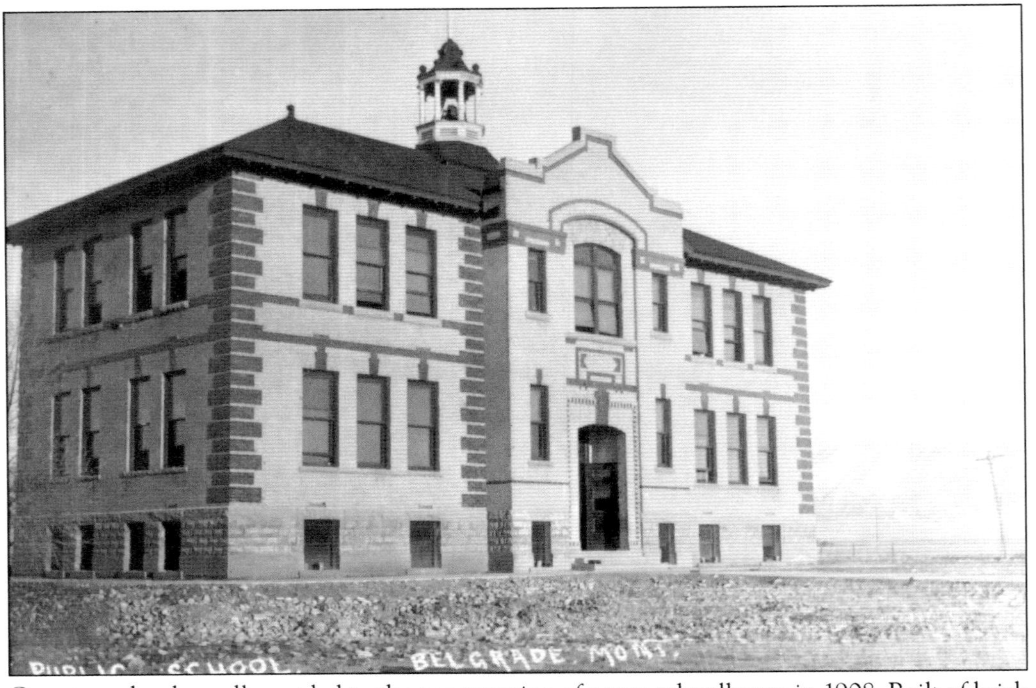

Growing school enrollment led to the construction of a new schoolhouse in 1908. Built of brick and stone, the new facility was a much larger and sturdier structure. Situated away from the downtown area, the Bridger Mountains are visible in the background. Nearby telephone poles indicate the growing importance of communications in rural Gallatin Valley.

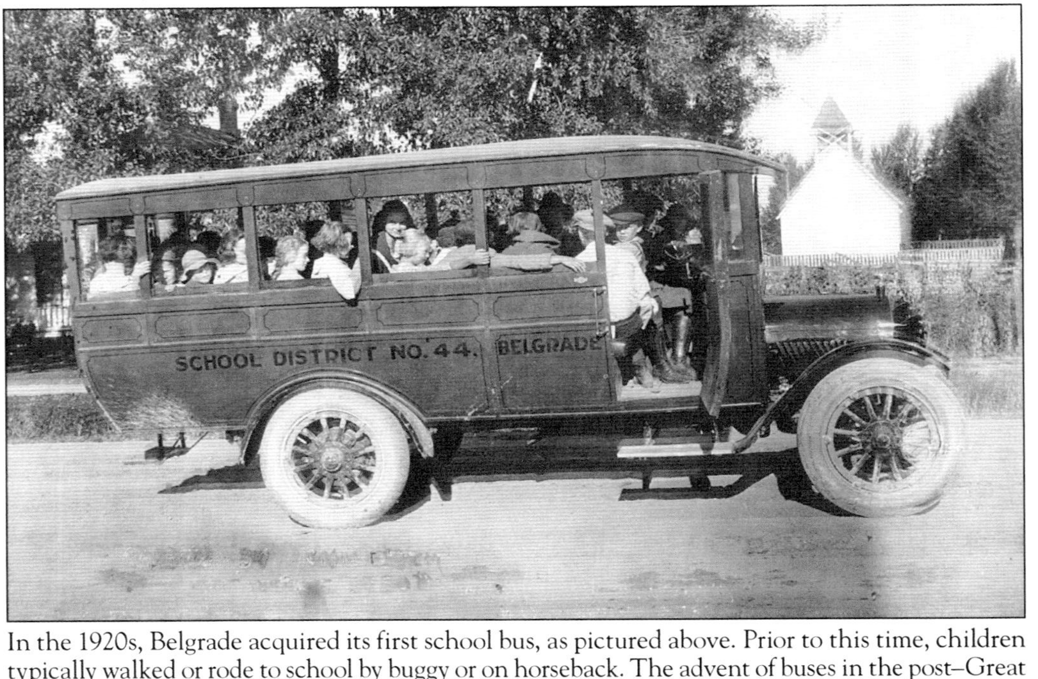

In the 1920s, Belgrade acquired its first school bus, as pictured above. Prior to this time, children typically walked or rode to school by buggy or on horseback. The advent of buses in the post–Great War era made school more accessible to children. Few families owned automobiles at this time.

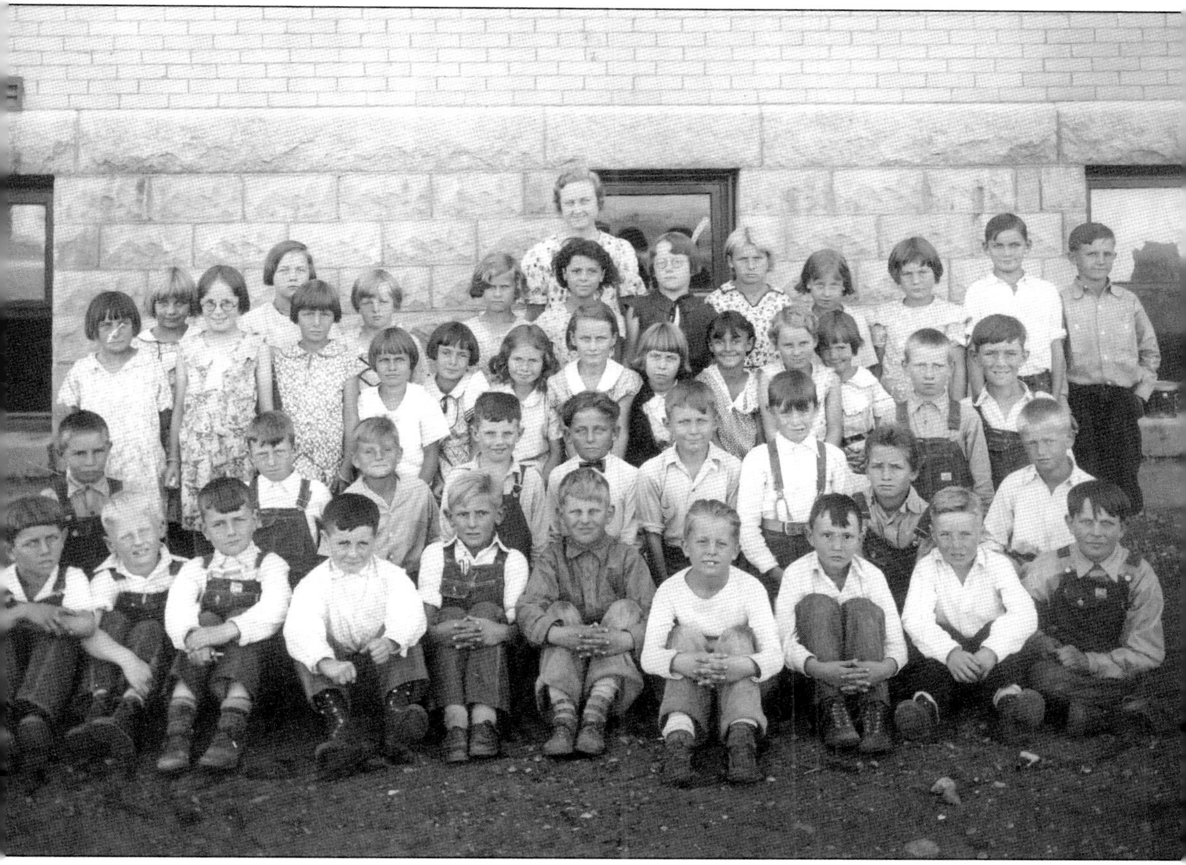

The Great Depression of the 1930s left many American families destitute, but in the Gallatin Valley, hard times had long been a fact of life. A drought in the summer of 1919 led to years of reduced crop prices, followed by a second period of drought beginning in 1929. Farms, banks, and businesses failed. However, the Depression impacted Gallatin County to a lesser degree than in many other parts of the nation, and during the 1930s, the valley grew with the arrival of newcomers seeking a fresh start. By the time of this early 1930s photograph, the public school had been renamed Quaw School after Thomas Quaw, Belgrade's optimistic founder. Among those pictured here, from left to right, are (first row) Ted Arts, Stuart Stone, Bob DiefenderPher, Art Poor, Clark Taylor, Rayford Weaver, Mark Hampton, Don Gowin, and Lyle Burnett; (second row) Francis Kelly, Don Hecox, unidentified, George Richmond, unidentified, Don Heck, unidentified, Ivan Grant, and Jack Sandho; (third row) two unidentified, Naomi Kelly, Patty Pitman, Billie Lou McGuire, Benetta Lawrence, June Chesley, unidentified, Evelyn Hoffman, unidentified, Norm Van Dyken, and Ben Arts; (fourth row) two unidentified, Hazel Maher, seven unidentified, Stan Walker, and Miss Weidman (teacher).

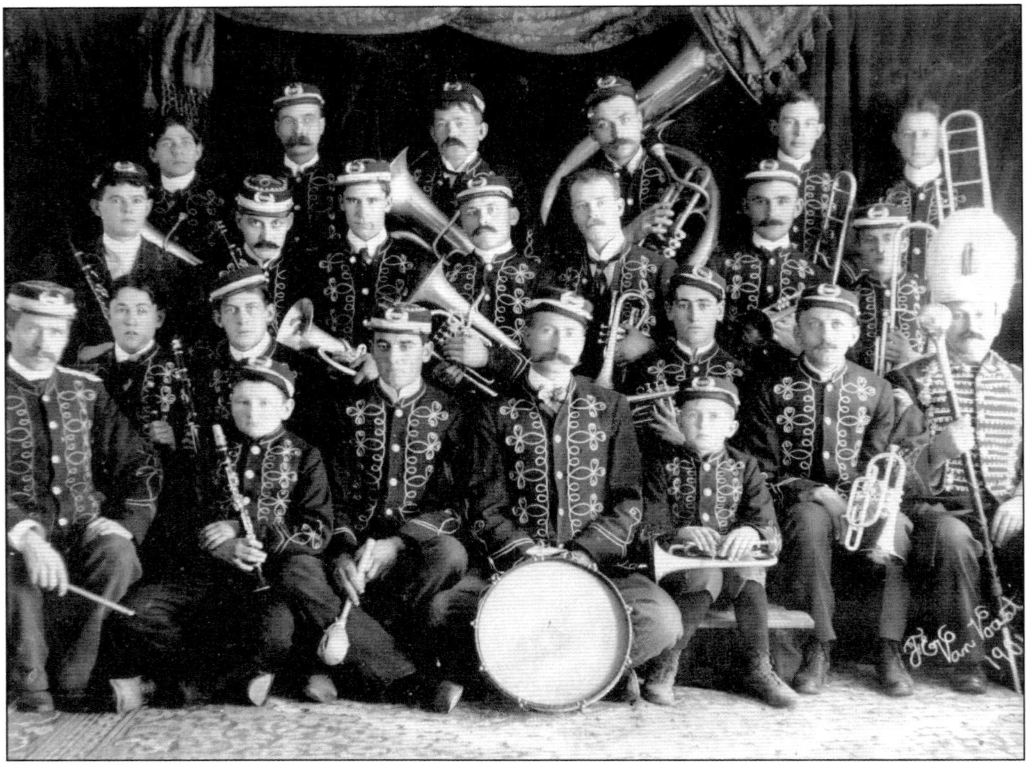

Belgrade's marching band provided an avenue for recreation and musical training in the early 20th century for the town's boys and men. This 1901 photograph of the band's smartly dressed members portrays the group in the attire used for city parades and other events. Town bands were a point of pride for many communities in Montana.

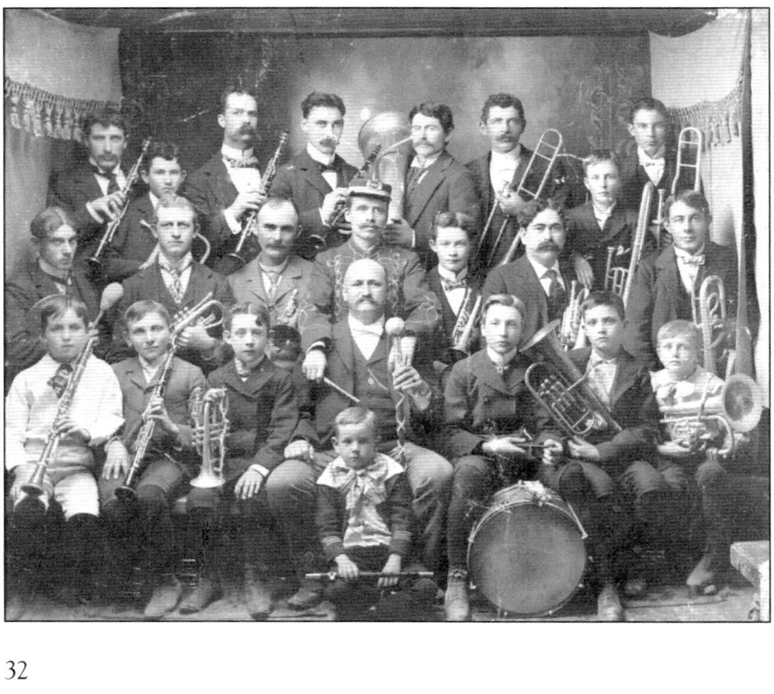

In this undated photograph, the members of Belgrade's marching band are dressed in formal attire in a studio. Comprised of males of all ages, the youngest members of the band are seated in the front row. Musical instruments were a luxury for many families in the early 20th century.

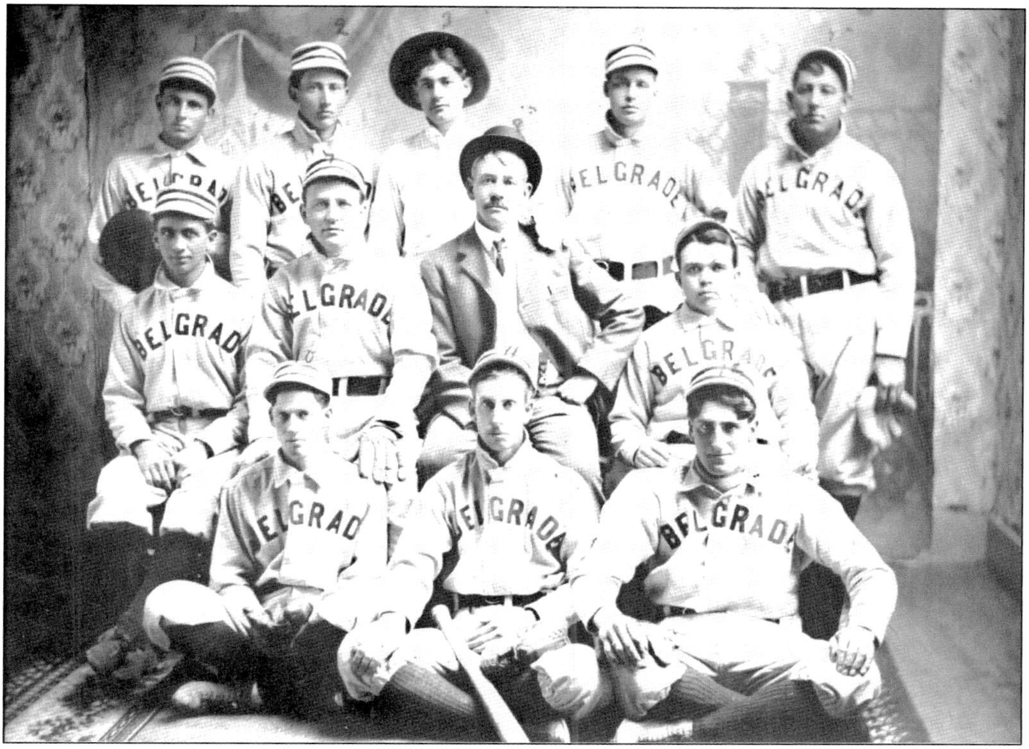

Like many rural towns in early-20th-century America, Belgrade boasted a baseball team. The baseball team offered recreational and leisure time opportunity for young men, and the club played other teams in and around the Gallatin Valley. Pictured in this c. 1908 photograph (order unknown) are Hampton Hecox, Winfred Ferguson, Everett Hamilton, Fred Montgomery, Charles Wilson, George Moody, William Fitzstephens, August Bertelson (manager), Fred Hidman, and Freddy Waterman.

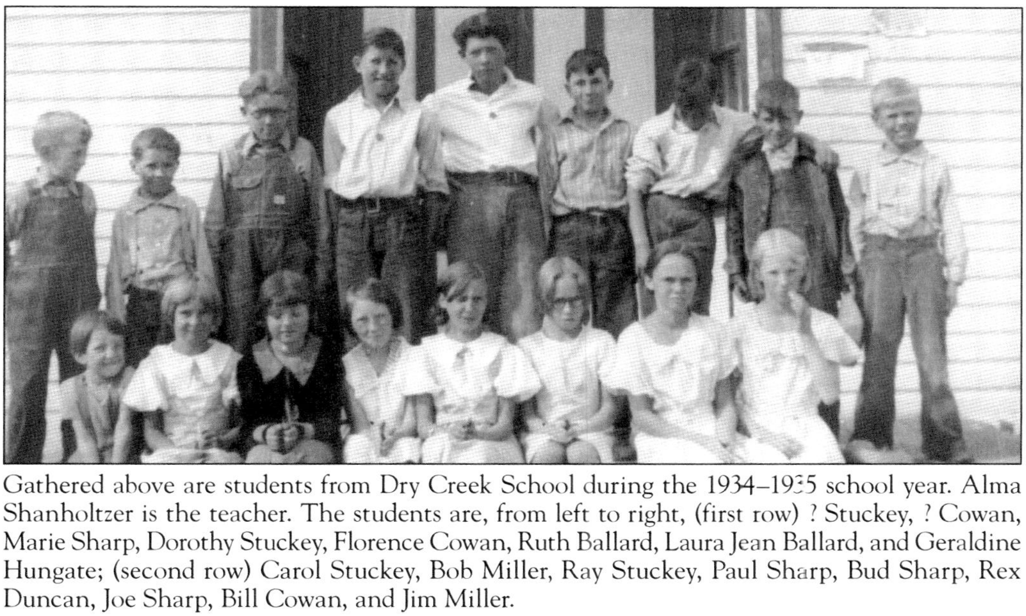

Gathered above are students from Dry Creek School during the 1934–1935 school year. Alma Shanholtzer is the teacher. The students are, from left to right, (first row) ? Stuckey, ? Cowan, Marie Sharp, Dorothy Stuckey, Florence Cowan, Ruth Ballard, Laura Jean Ballard, and Geraldine Hungate; (second row) Carol Stuckey, Bob Miller, Ray Stuckey, Paul Sharp, Bud Sharp, Rex Duncan, Joe Sharp, Bill Cowan, and Jim Miller.

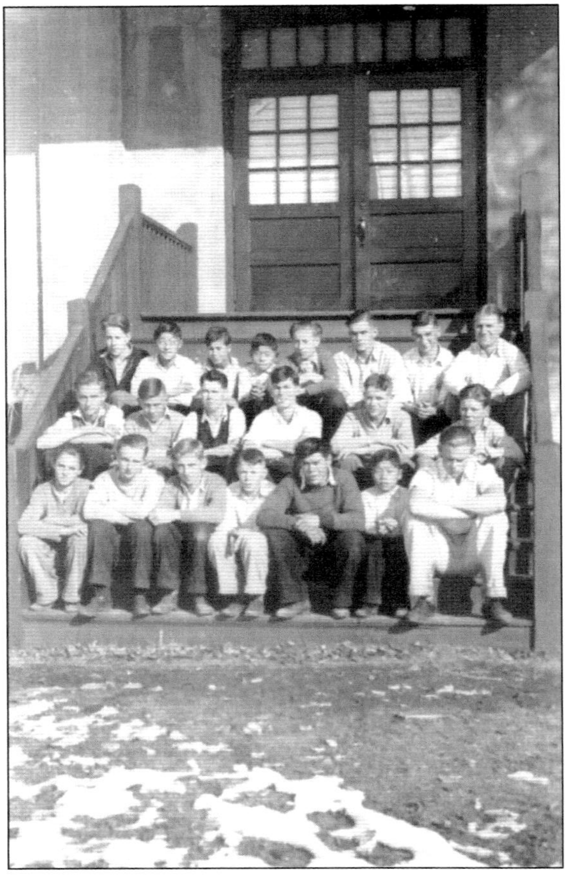

Pictured at left are the 1935 charter members of Belgrade's Future Farmers of America (FFA). They are, from left to right, (first row) Robert Miller, George Lee, Ralph Pike, Jamie Lee, Arnold Doig, Kenneth Pitman, and Earl Coscik; (second row) Ernest Hoffman, Louise Huffine, Wilbur Spring Jr., Floyd Duncan, Ben Truax, and Chad Brown; (third row) Norman Mize, Melvin Hamilson, Edwin Walker, Robert Cline, Bill Ford, Chuck Pike, Louie Lee, and Jack Toohey. Below, from its beginning as a railroad town, Belgrade's early agricultural economy depended upon the rails. Pictured in this 1919 image is the shallow grade line, or "lowline," at Powers, one mile north of Belgrade. The train is sitting on tracks beside the water tower, with the caboose facing the camera, and the conductor standing just outside the door. The powerful Challenger 4-6-4 steam engine and coal car weighed about one million pounds.

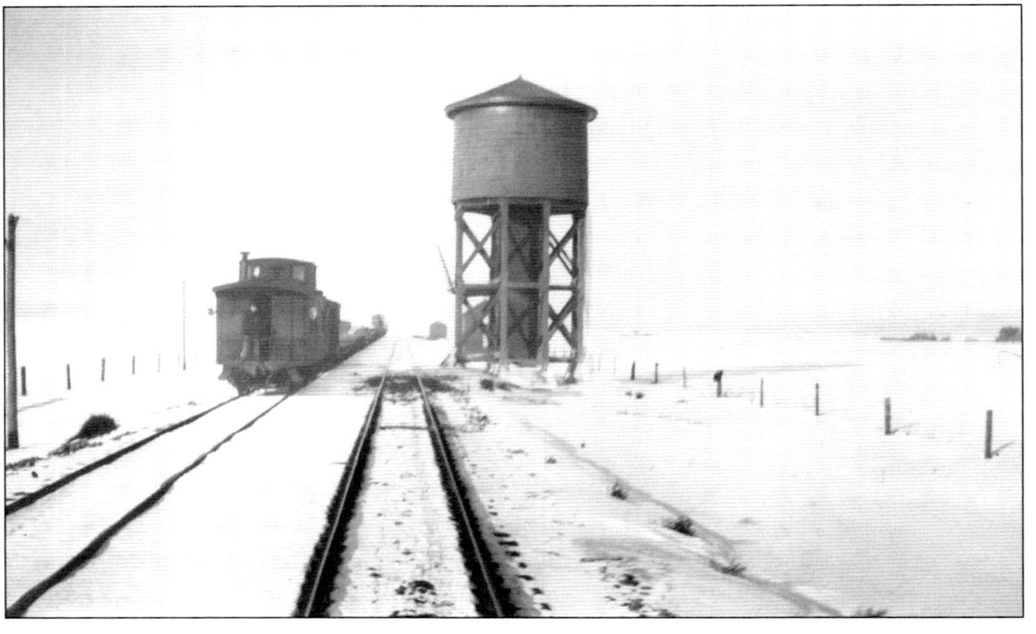

Train mishaps were all too common in the early 20th century. In addition to the ever-present threat of collisions and derailments, steam engines were susceptible to boiler explosions. This April 1905 image (right) chronicles the boiler explosion of engine No. 41, a consolidation engine, now mangled. An unidentified man examines the engine's wheels. Railroad disaster struck Belgrade again on November 4, 1909. Pictured below is a derailed and listing consolidation locomotive. A flatbed car with a crane in the background is positioned to attempt to lift the locomotive back onto the tracks. Montana's railroad workers included men of various nationalities, as evidenced by the men lined up near the wrecked train.

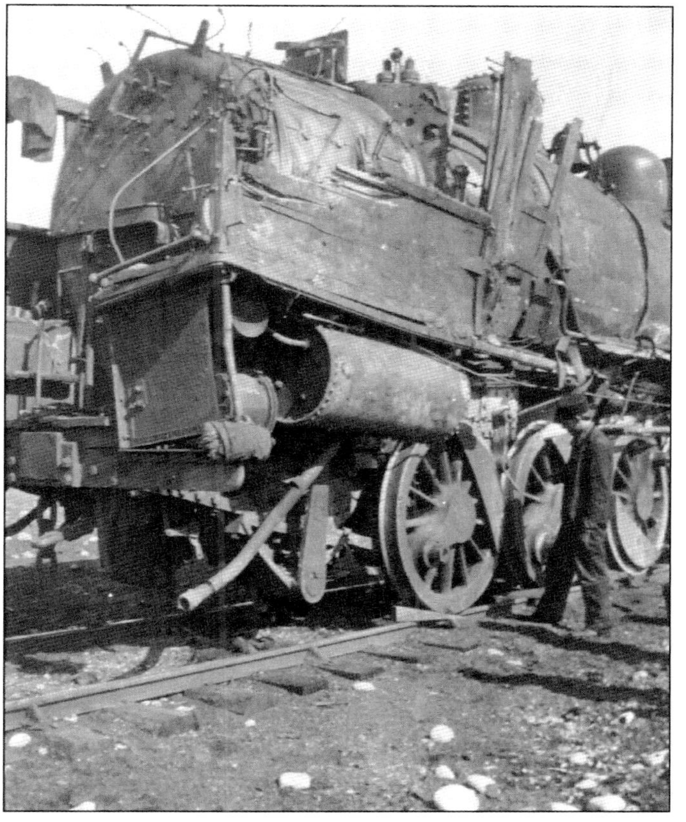

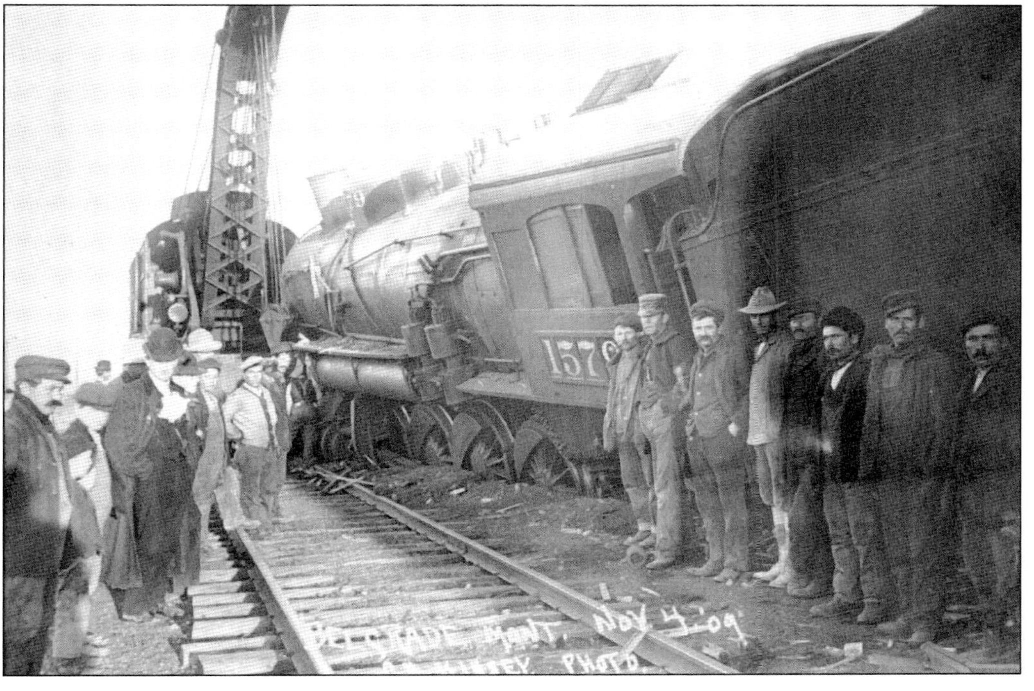

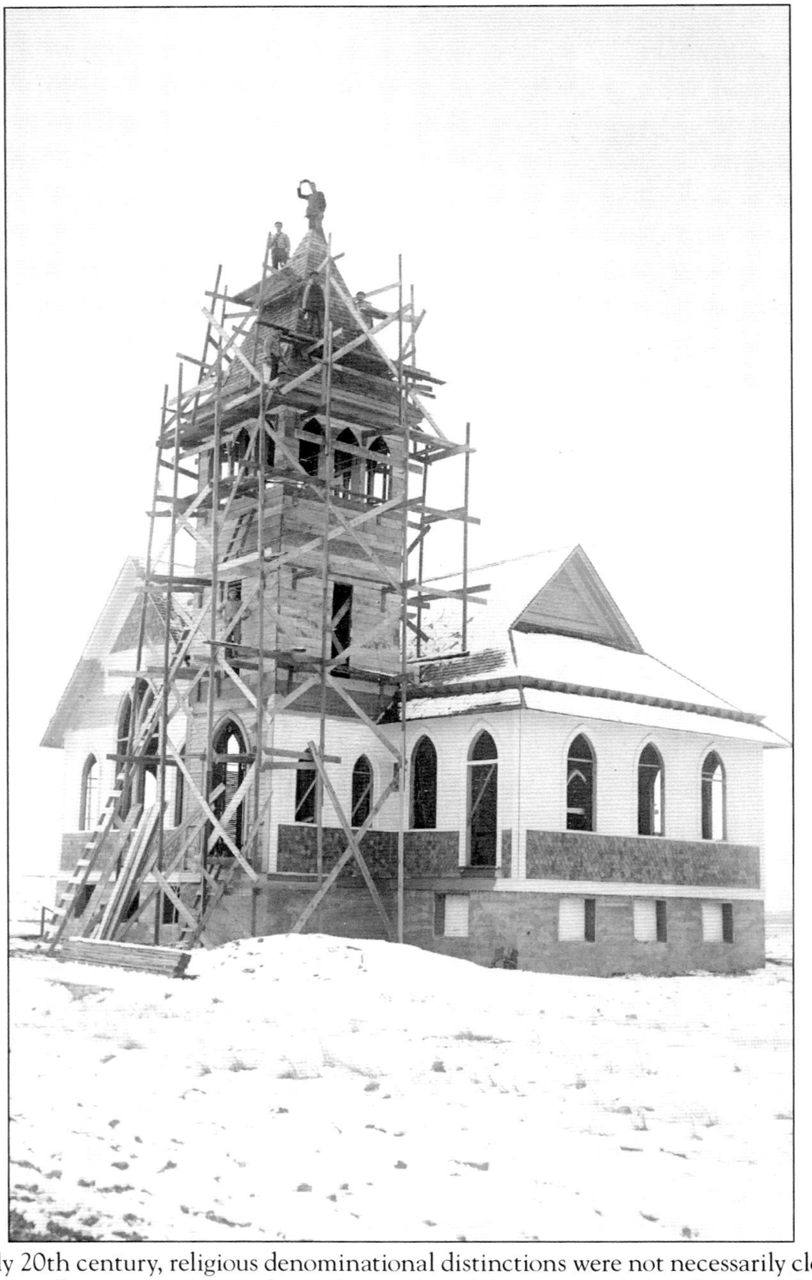

In the early 20th century, religious denominational distinctions were not necessarily clear-cut in Montana's small communities. In the early decades of the century, Belgrade boasted a number of congregations, including Methodist, Presbyterian, and Baptist churches. The church building pictured here is under construction in 1911. While originally housing a Presbyterian congregation, the town's Presbyterians and Baptists joined together in 1931 to create a federated church. From that point forward, the two denominations met together in this church structure on Sundays under the leadership of either a Presbyterian or Baptist pastor. With the departure of a given pastor, the next pastorate was rotated to a clergyman of the other denomination. Such dual-denominational arrangements were not uncommon in Montana.

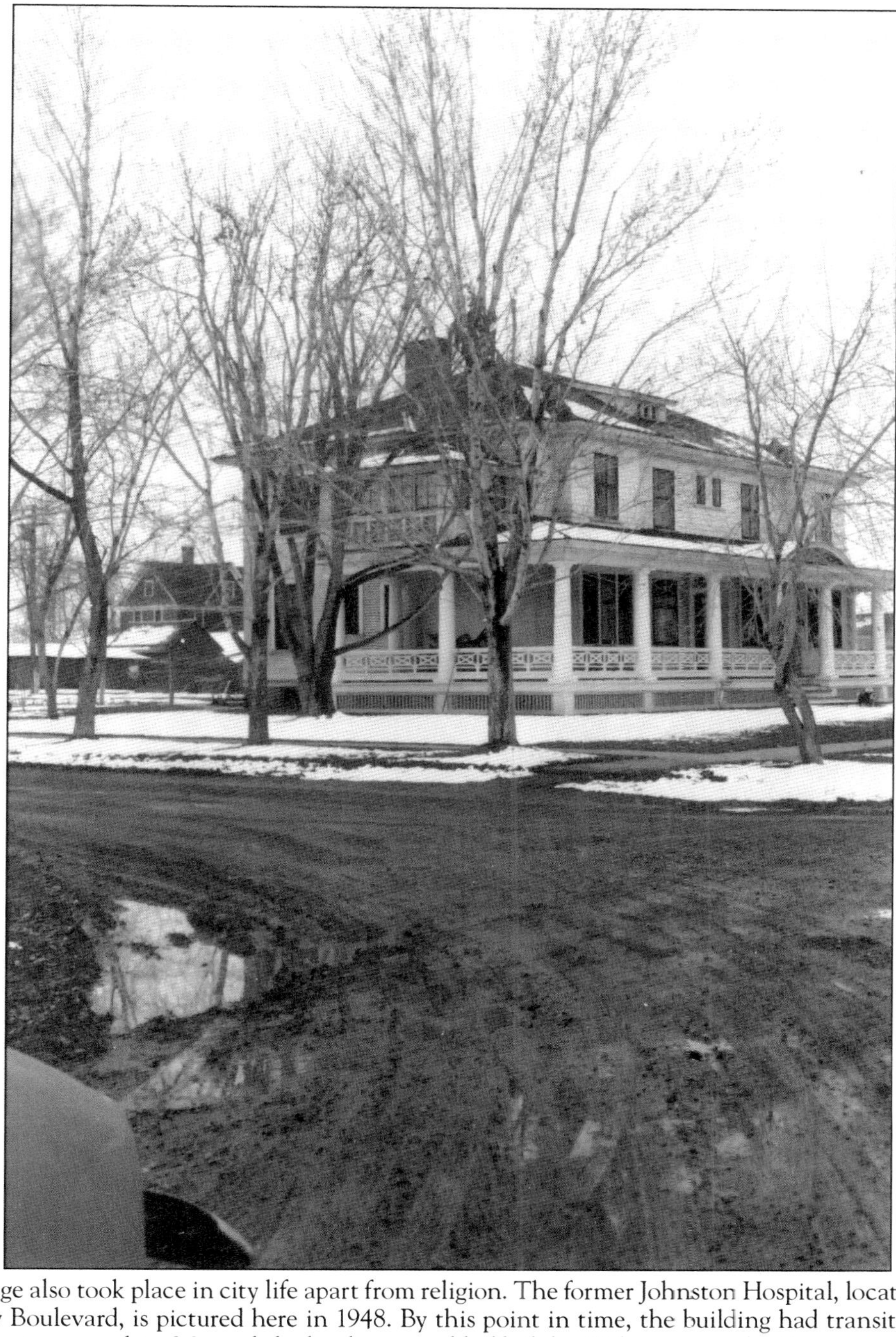

Change also took place in city life apart from religion. The former Johnston Hospital, located on Quaw Boulevard, is pictured here in 1948. By this point in time, the building had transitioned to private ownership. Meanwhile, by the second half of the 20th century, the Quaw name was permanently etched in the city's collective memory. Buildings and street signs alike testified to the legacy of the man who envisioned and brought about the city of Belgrade. By the mid-century, it was evident that Belgrade would remain a small town in the shadow of Bozeman, but residents were pleased with what their town had become: an agricultural hub for the valley with an established business center, community services, and good schools.

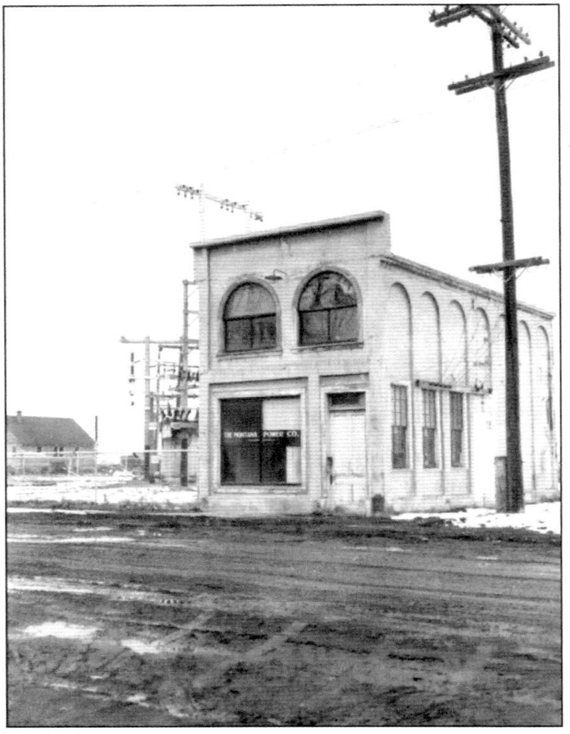

A number of hydroelectric plants were constructed in Montana in the early 20th century, and a need for a centralized power structure soon emerged. In 1912, the Montana Power Company was formed by John Ryan, then-president of Anaconda Copper Mining Company. Belgrade's Montana Power Company substation is pictured at left in 1948.

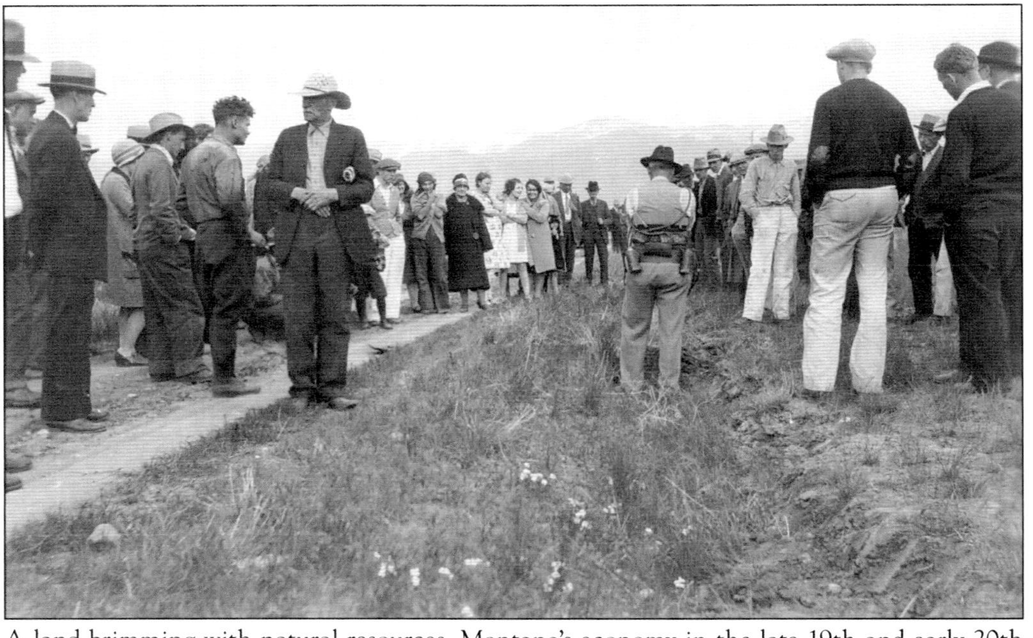

A land brimming with natural resources, Montana's economy in the late 19th and early 20th centuries benefited from logging and extractive industries. Among the riches underground was oil, and in this undated photograph, onlookers gather as tests for oil are conducted in Belgrade. While eastern Montana proved fertile ground for oil, efforts to uncover the black gold in Belgrade and the Gallatin Valley did not pan out.

The Montana Flour Mills Co. elevator is pictured in this 1950s image. At the mid-century mark, wheat continued to drive the economy of Belgrade. The growing and selling of wheat involved the purchase of tractors, trucks, buildings, fertilizers, chemicals, and other farm and building supplies, all of which generated money within the town's economy.

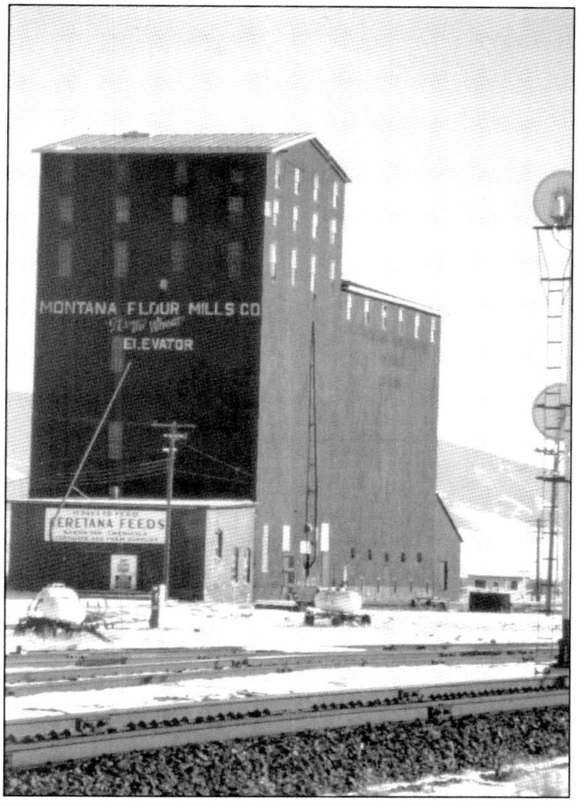

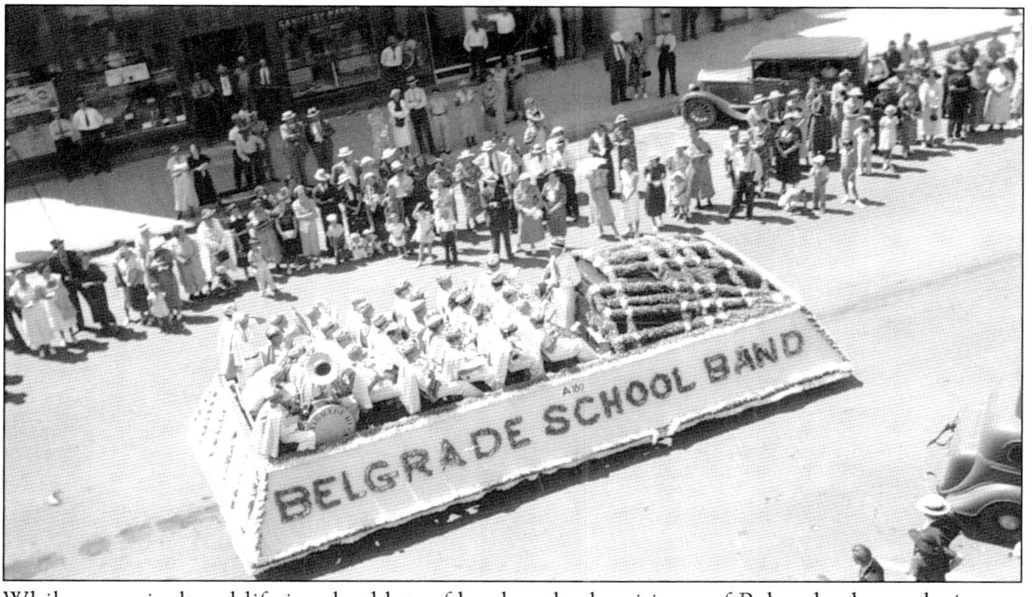

While an agricultural life involved lots of hard work, the citizens of Belgrade also took time to play and celebrate. On July 2, 1937, the First All-Montana Day Parade was held in Bozeman. Surrounding communities were invited to participate. Pictured here is the Belgrade School Band performing as families line Bozeman's Main Street.

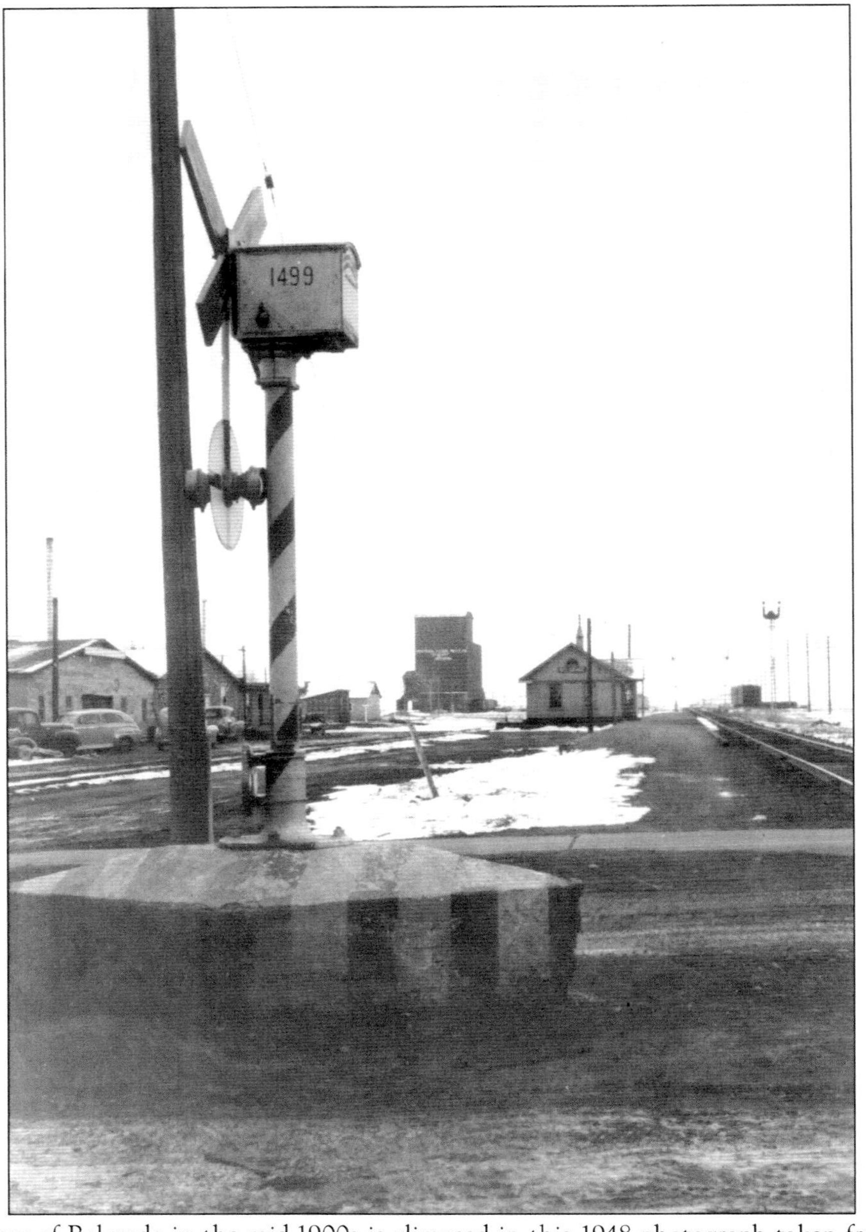

The story of Belgrade in the mid-1900s is glimpsed in this 1948 photograph taken from the Broadway crossing. At the forefront and to the right, the town's railroad infrastructure is pictured: crossing signals, rails, and the Northern Pacific depot. The extension of the Northern Pacific in the 1880s brought about the birth of the town and later fueled its early growth. The rails, traversed by steam engines as well as powerful and much safer diesel locomotives by the mid-century, remained central to Belgrade's success, connecting area agricultural production to markets far away. In the center background is the Montana Flour Mills elevator, representing the predominance of wheat in nearby fields. Pictured to the left are automobiles parked alongside a row of buildings. While horses retained a role in ranch and farm life, by the mid-century, the automobile had long replaced the horse as the primary means of transportation in Belgrade and the Gallatin Valley.

Two

GALLATIN FIELD

THE VALLEY OPENS TO THE WORLD

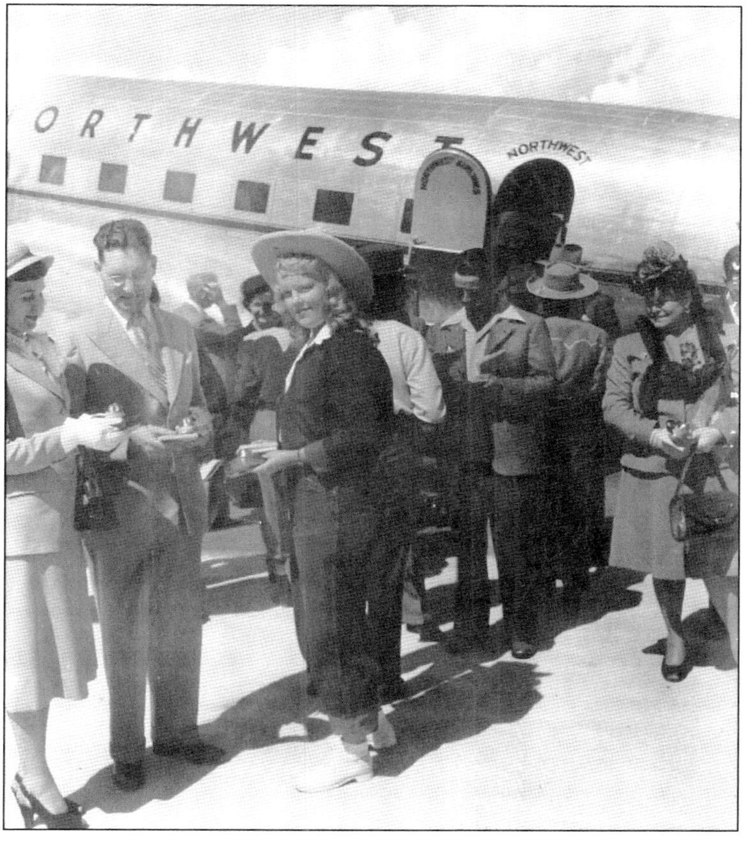

In 1947, Montana's Gallatin County was opened to the world through the arrival of commercial aviation. Pictured here is the first commercial flight into Belgrade's Gallatin Field. Northwest Airlines provided the initial flight services. Standing in the forefront center is Northwest Airlines hostess Margaret Gould (also known as Peggy Malson). Notice the formal attire of passengers. Such dress was standard in the early days of commercial aviation.

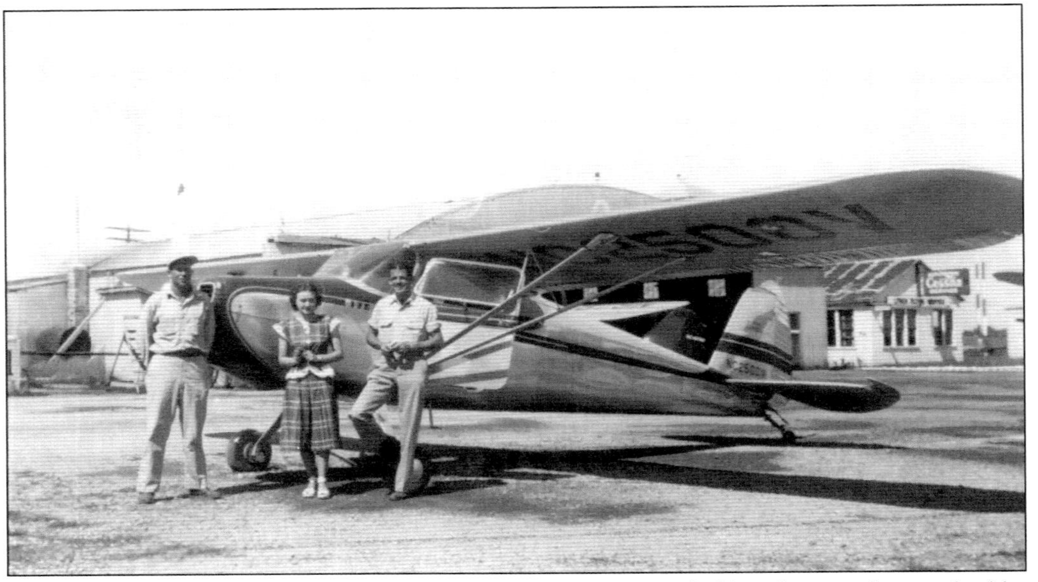

On April 21, 1928, a Gallatin County community meeting was held to discuss where to build a Belgrade airport. Later that year, Seifert Airport was built near Belgrade and named in honor of area aviation pioneer Wayne Seifert. Unfortunately, the location proved untenable, but in 1929, Seifert and E.R. Kahla obtained land near the present-day Gallatin Field for a second airport. In this photograph, early aviators Jim Stradley, Norma Stuart, and Al Newby of Lynch Flying Service are pictured.

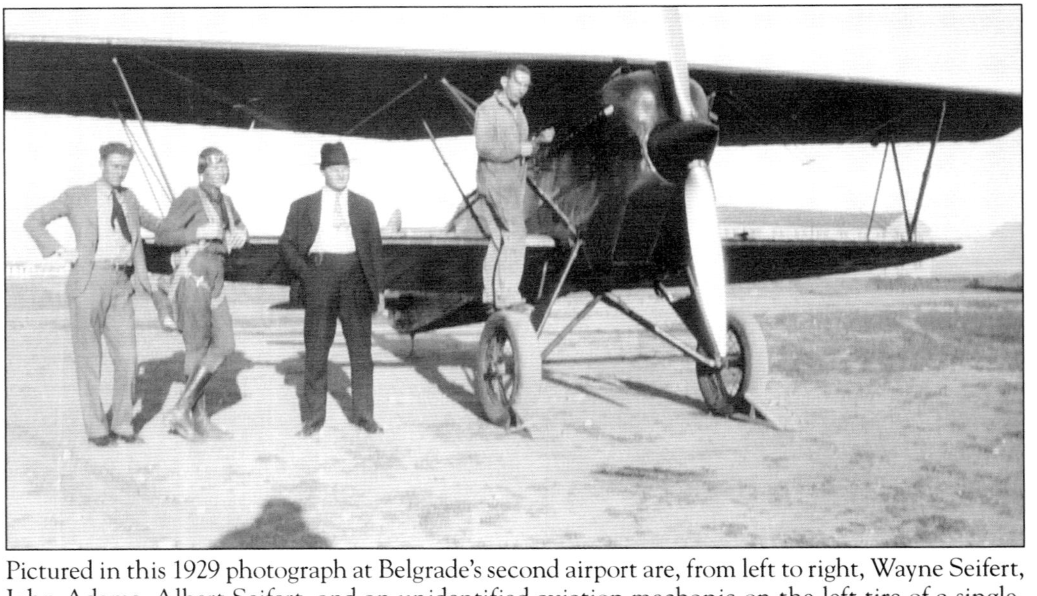

Pictured in this 1929 photograph at Belgrade's second airport are, from left to right, Wayne Seifert, John Adams, Albert Seifert, and an unidentified aviation mechanic on the left tire of a single-prop Alexander Eagle Rock. A half-mile north of Belgrade, the airport opened with six runways. Each runway was 100 feet wide and between 1,200 and 1,300 feet in length.

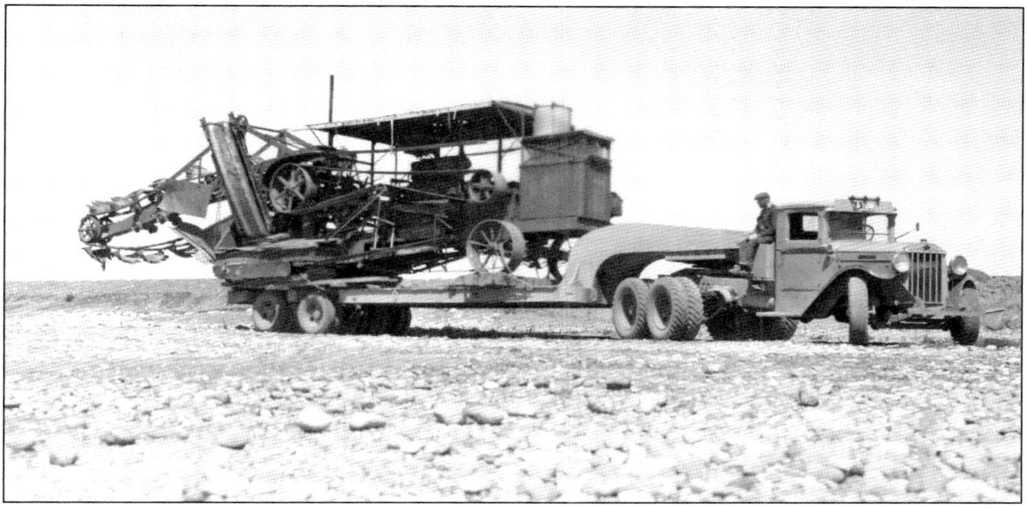

As Gallatin County continued to grow, so did the need for increased air services. In October 1943, the Bozeman Airport Commission was formed. The initial members were Dean Chaffin, Ernest Anderson, Gardner "Pete" Waite, Eric Therkelsen, and Frank Hoey. The commission decided to build a new airport near Seifert Field and set out to obtain land and the necessary finances. By the end of the year, contracts were signed, financing was secured, and early construction began. Pictured here is a trencher used for digging ditches to lay electrical lines for lighting.

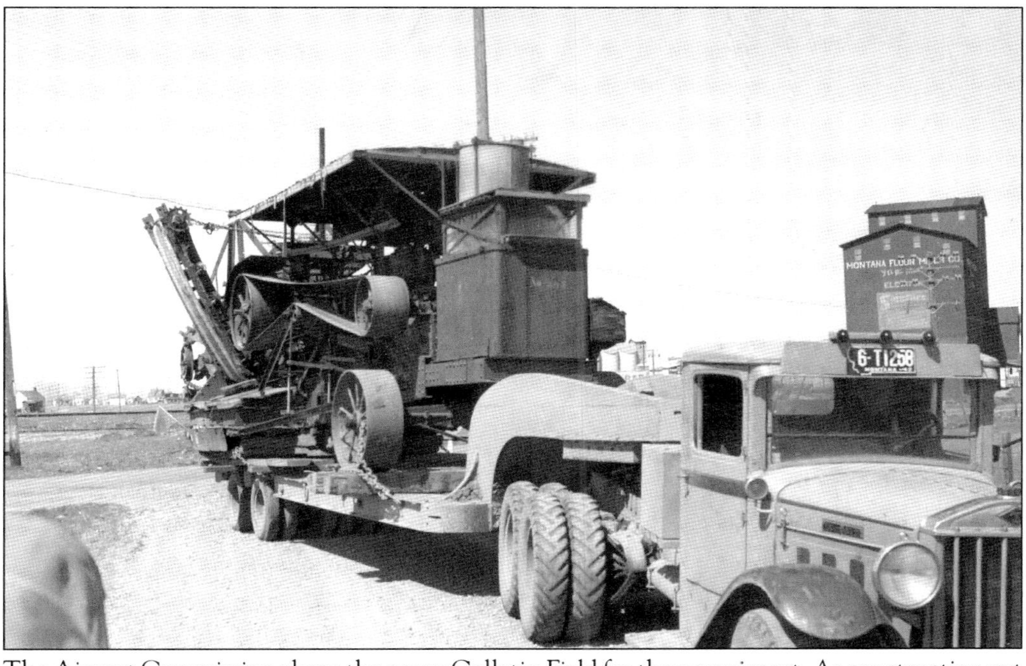

The Airport Commission chose the name Gallatin Field for the new airport. As construction got underway in 1941, World War II raged abroad. Many Americans viewed America's involvement in the war as inevitable. Seeking a place to provide training for pilots, the Civil Aeronautics Administration (CAA) financed construction of Gallatin Field in return for use of airport facilities for the government's Civilian Pilot Training Program (CPTP). Gallatin Field was one of 11 CPTP sites nationwide.

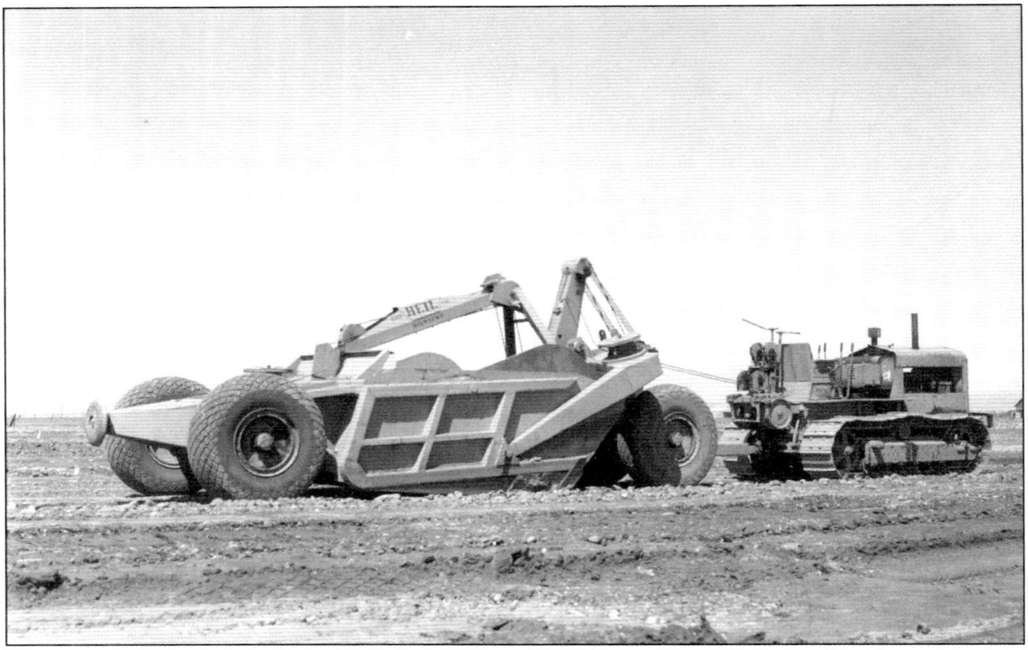

Wayne Seifert was no longer alive when construction began on Gallatin Field. The pioneering aviator had been killed in a 1938 plane crash in Pueblo, Colorado. Reflecting Seifert's legacy, the four runways completed at Gallatin Field in 1941 owed much to his initial efforts to establish air service in the valley.

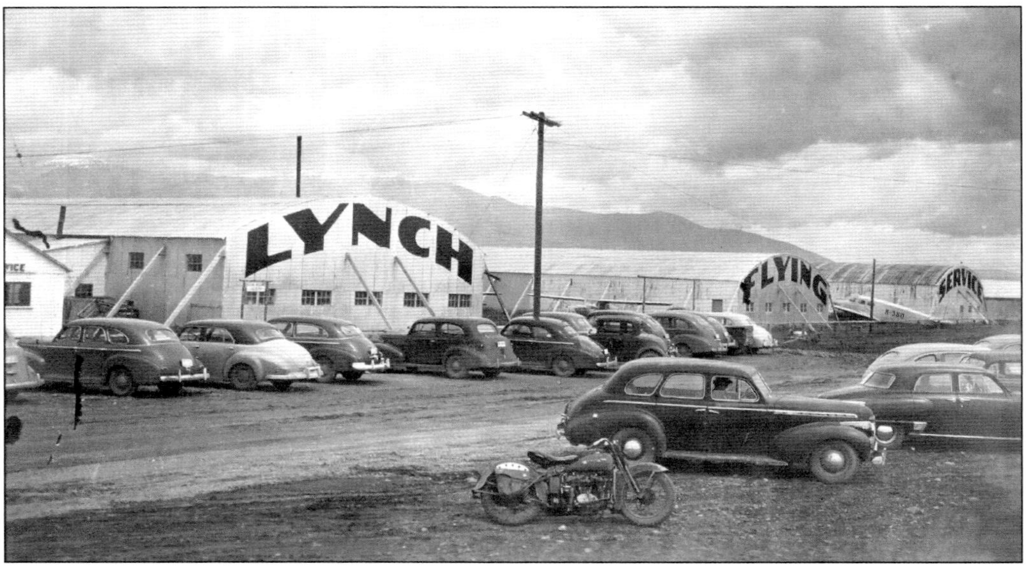

The Lynch brothers—John F., Charles (Chuck), Leonard, and Tom—opened and operated Lynch Flying Service, the first fixed-base operator (FBO) service at Gallatin Field. Opening in conjunction with the arrival of the new airport in 1941, the Lynches became operators of the fastest-growing air school in the state of Montana. The Lynch office is to the left, and Bozeman Aviation is on the far right (the building burned in 1952). A Bobcat twin-engine plane is pictured on the right.

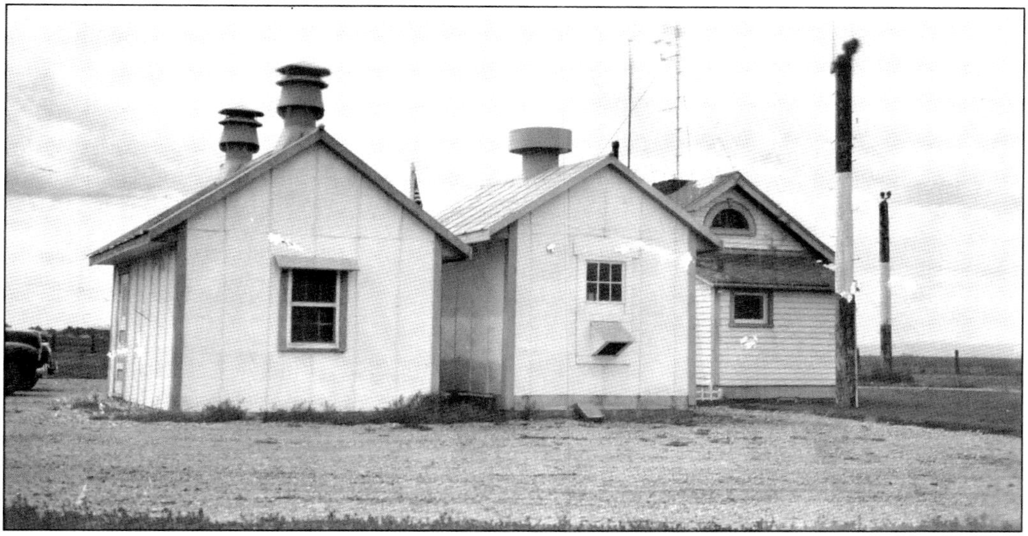

While well received by citizens, Gallatin Field, within the first year of operation, proved more expensive than Bozeman City officials had anticipated. Seeking to enlarge the financial operating base of the airport, Bozeman officials appealed to the county. In 1942, Gallatin County became part owner of Gallatin Field, and the airport in Belgrade became a city-county airport. Pictured in this 1947 image are airport buildings. On the far right is Bozeman Flight Service Station, which housed communications equipment.

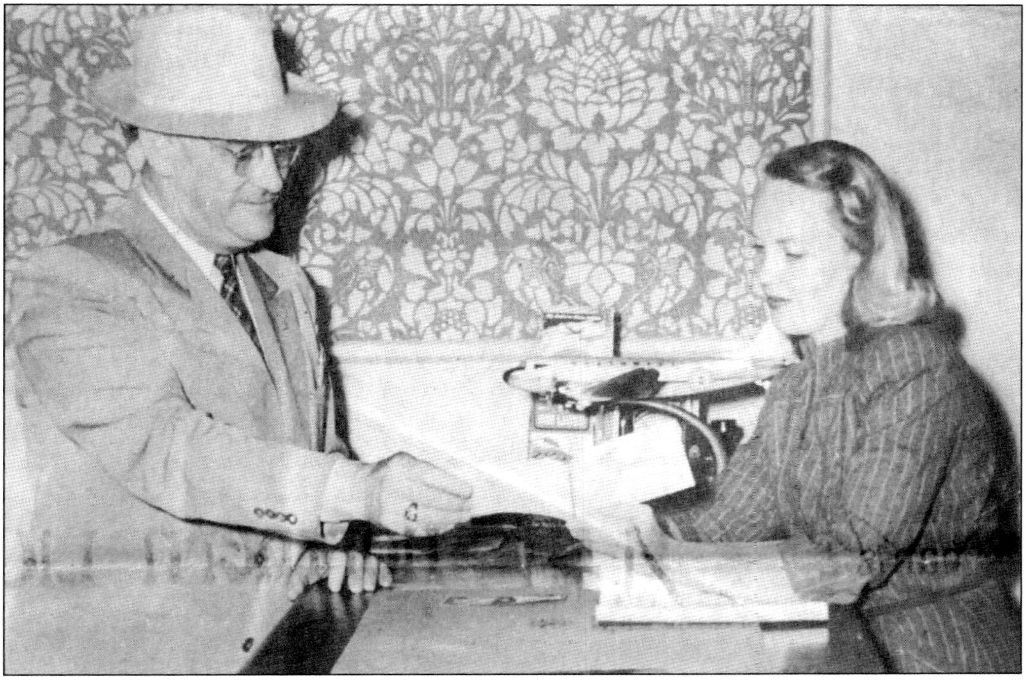

The beginning of scheduled commercial air service from Northwest Airlines (NWA) in 1947 changed the dynamics of Gallatin Field. Northwest's flights offered area residents quick access to the outside world. In this photograph, Dean Chaffin, an original member of the airport's board, purchases the first air passage from Gallatin Field on a Northwest flight. The clerk is Adelai Hansen.

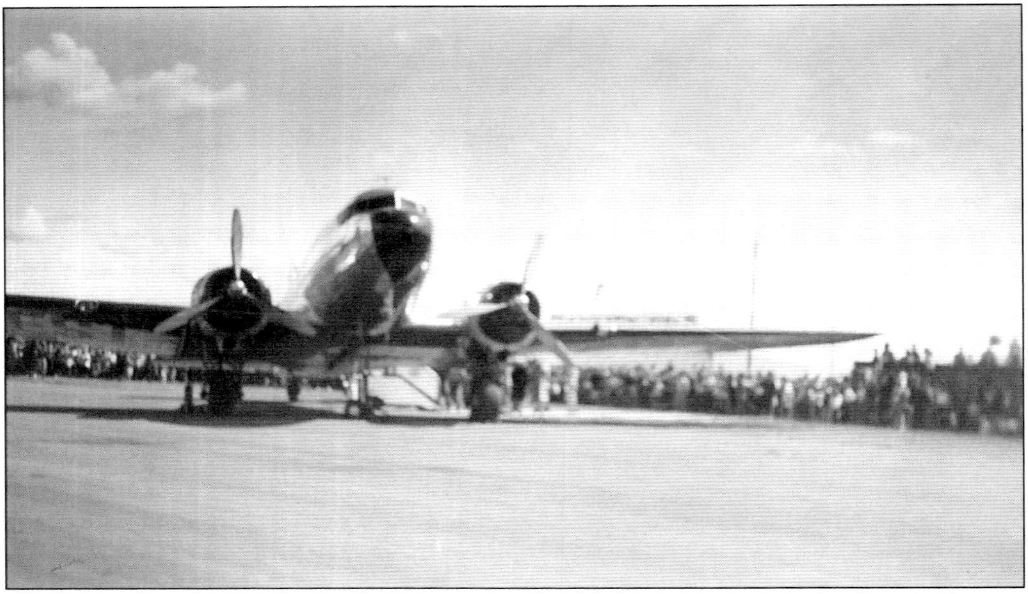

The first scheduled commercial flight into Gallatin Field, by Northwest Airlines, took place on June 22, 1947. Northwest's initial flight into Gallatin County came 20 years after the airline first commenced passenger services. In the larger picture, the post–World War II years witnessed a rapid expansion of commercial air services to many smaller towns and cities across America.

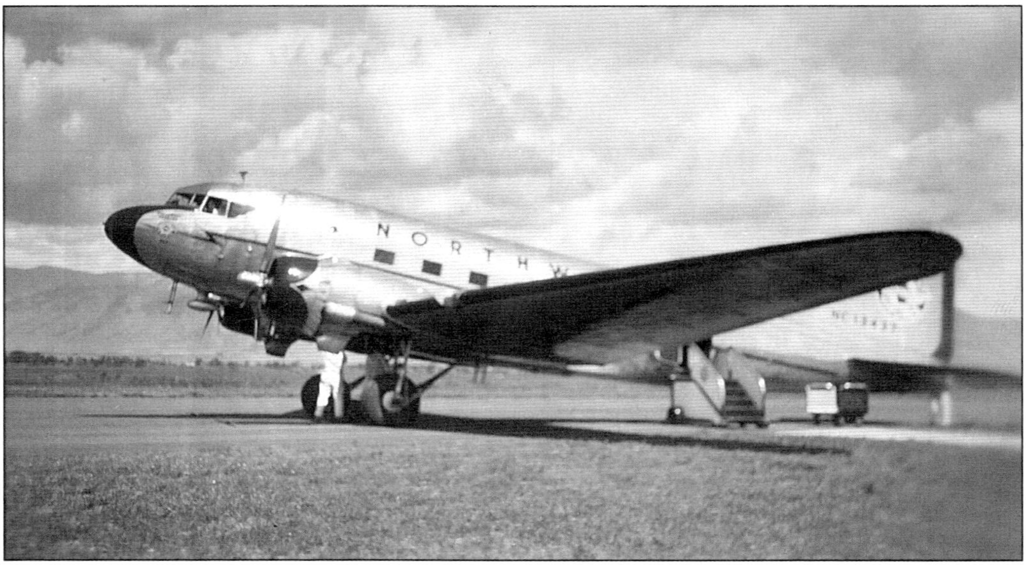

The first commercial flight into Gallatin Field was a DC-3 that serviced Northwest's Minnesota-to-Seattle route. By the time the big airliner touched down, the Belgrade airport featured mile-long runways. Lighting had been installed in order to facilitate evening operations. In addition, a Quonset hut that was 35-feet-by-75-feet served as a temporary depot, or terminal, for Northwest Airlines in the early months of commercial services.

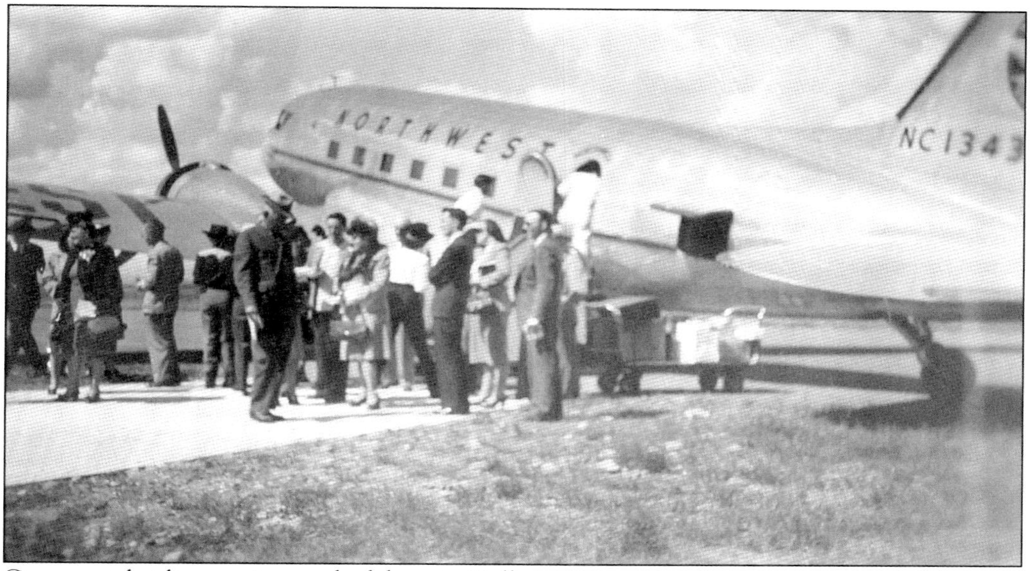

Commercial airline service touched down in Gallatin County at a time when the state of Montana was experiencing a postwar boom. In the midst of population growth and an expanding economy, commercial air services, similar to railroads decades earlier, opened up new opportunities for Belgrade and the county at large; yet, Gallatin Field retained a local touch. For example, Gyp, the airport dog, greeted each arriving Northwest plane and received cookies from stewardesses.

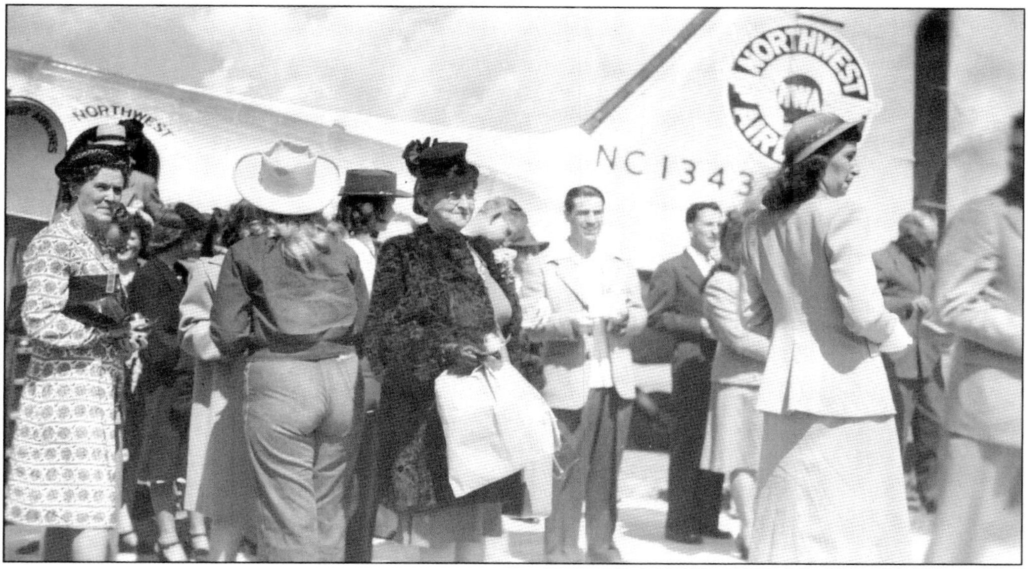

The introduction of commercial flights to Belgrade's Gallatin Field provided a boost to an emerging sector of the region's economy: tourism. Mining, once a driving force of southwest Montana's economy, was fading. For Gallatin County, commercial air service arrived as nearby Yellowstone National Park experienced growing popularity worldwide. Prosperous American and international families now had another transportation option for visiting the world's first national park.

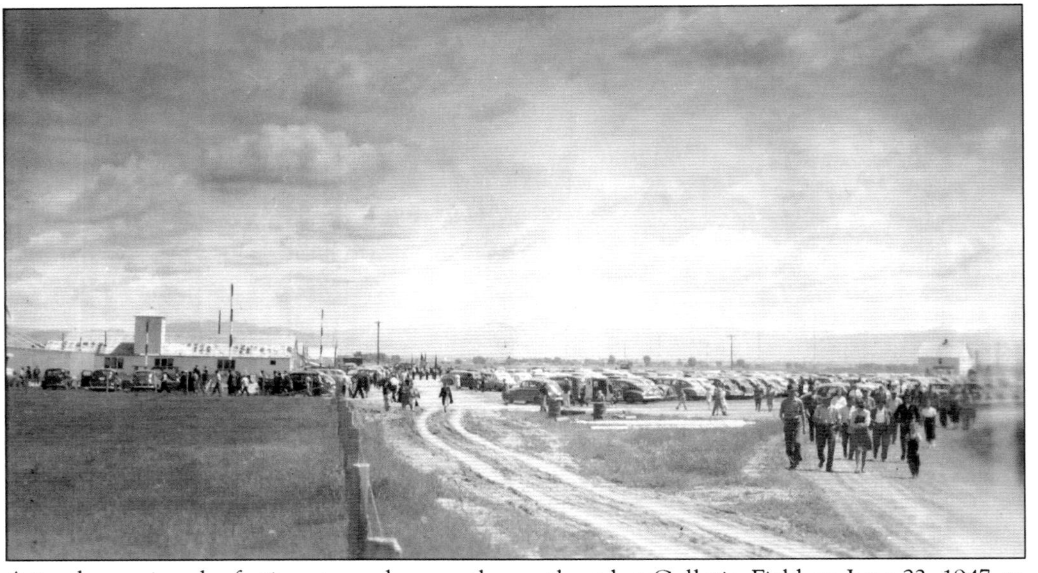

Attendees enjoyed a festive atmosphere as they gathered at Gallatin Field on June 22, 1947, to witness the historic Northwest Airlines flight. Within a short distance of downtown Belgrade, hundreds, if not thousands, of onlookers knew that a new era was dawning. The day became one of the most photographed events thus far in the history of Gallatin County. Lynch Services is pictured on the left, and the airport manager's house is to the right.

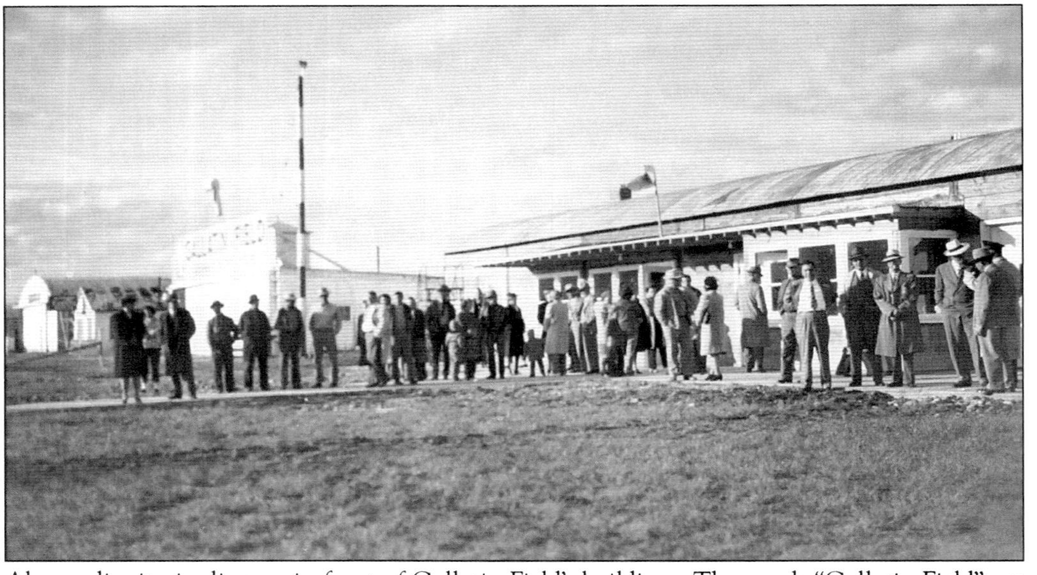

Above, dignitaries line up in front of Gallatin Field's buildings. The words "Gallatin Field" are visible on the airport maintenance shop. As in the 1880s, visionaries eyed new opportunities afforded by a new means of transportation. At the time, one concept in formulation was Bridger Mountain State Park, to the east of Belgrade. While the state park idea eventually fizzled, Bridger Bowl ski resort eventually emerged, attracting skiers from near and far—many of whom traveled by air to Gallatin Field.

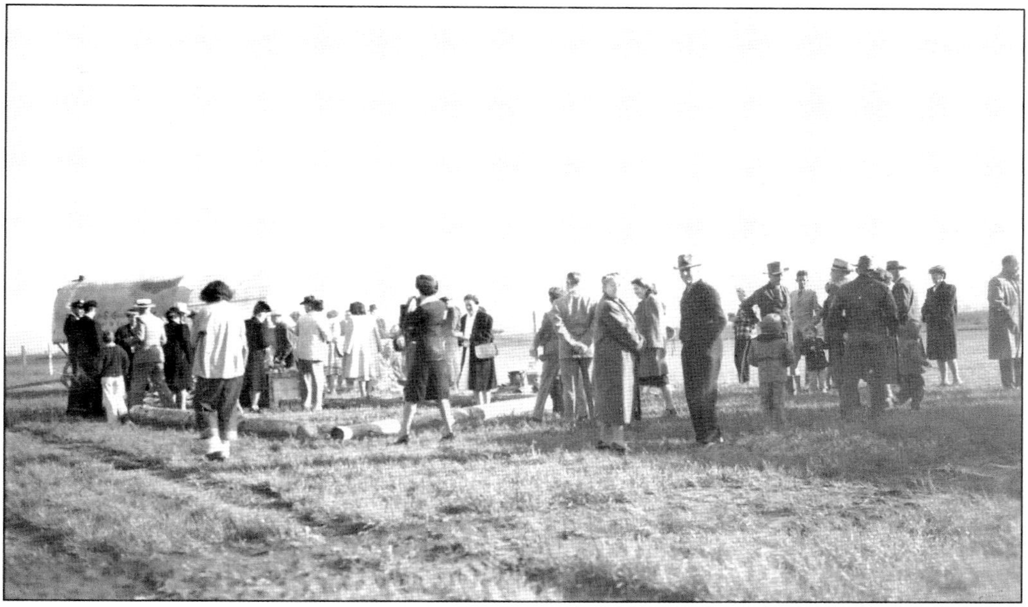

This photograph offers a glimpse as to why Gallatin Field was built alongside Belgrade: an abundance of level space situated a suitable distance from the surrounding mountain ranges. Belgrade provided desirable land and, in return, received increased visibility and improved highway infrastructure in the years following.

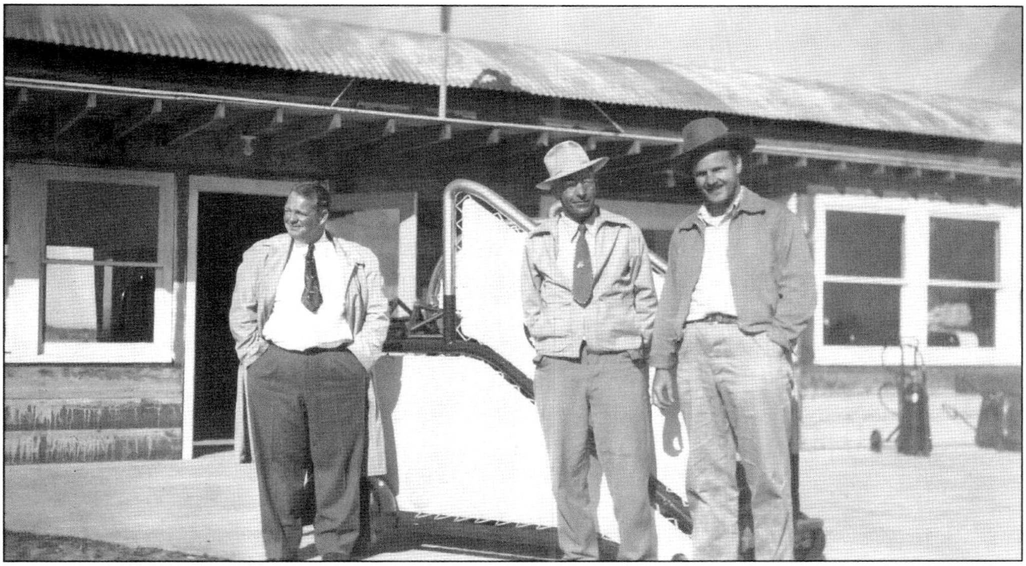

In this image, from left to right, are George Sime of the Montana State Highway Department; Joe Monger, Gallatin Field's first airport director, and an unidentified man in front of a stairway ramp used to load and unload air passengers. In the background is the airport's original Northwest Airlines terminal. Also visible to the right is an ever-present fire extinguisher, necessary because of the highly combustible fuel used by airplanes.

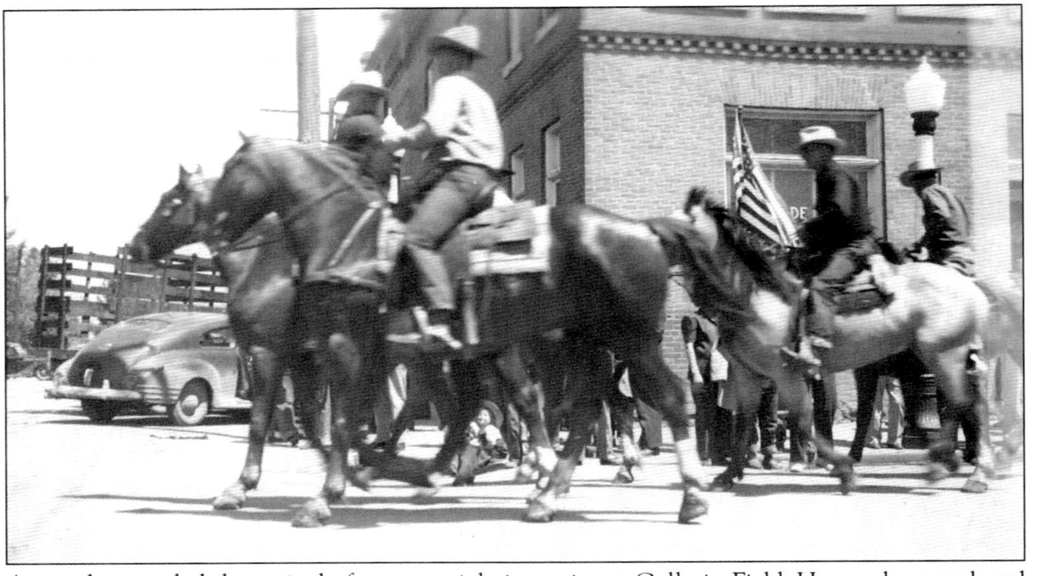

A parade attended the arrival of commercial air service at Gallatin Field. Horses, long replaced as a means of everyday transportation, were still common in the valley and a routine feature at parades and other community celebrations. In this photograph, the airport parade, led by horsemen, leaves downtown Belgrade on the way to nearby Gallatin Field, passing by the bank building.

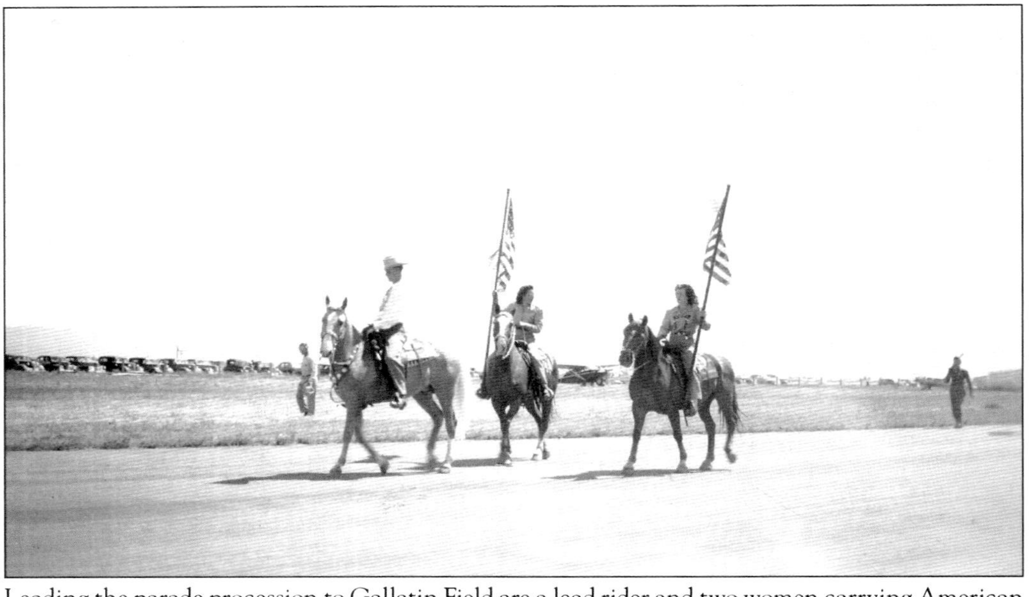

Leading the parade procession to Gallatin Field are a lead rider and two women carrying American flags. Following in the distance is a young serviceman, probably a veteran of World War II. Victory over Hitler and the Axis in the war elevated feelings of patriotism in Gallatin County. A Stinson Station Wagon plane is visible in the background.

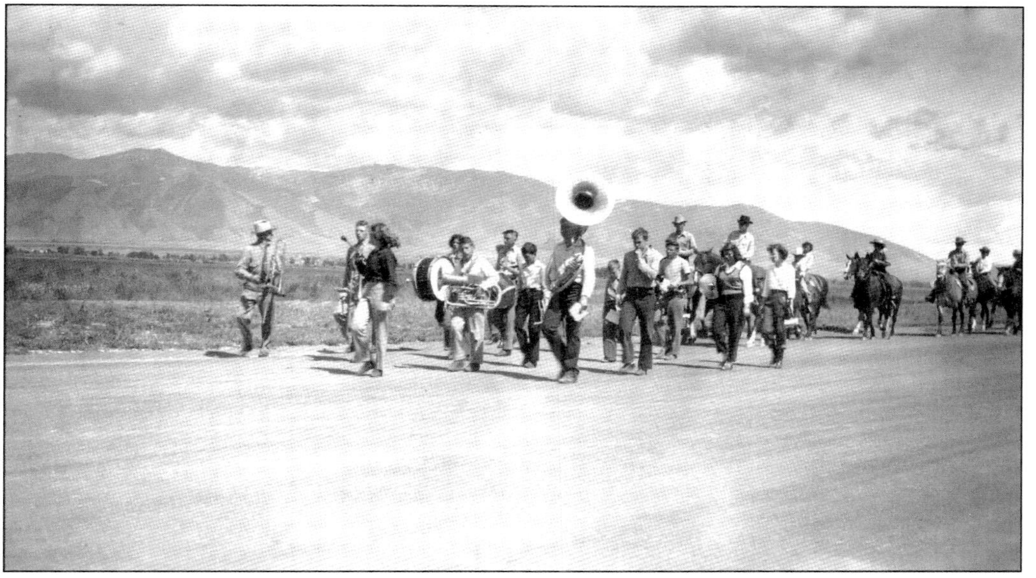

Pictured here are Belgrade High School band members on the way to their performance at Gallatin Field. They are followed by riders mounted on horses, with the Bridger Mountains towering in the background. Gallatin County's mountain ranges dictated the layout of the airport's runways.

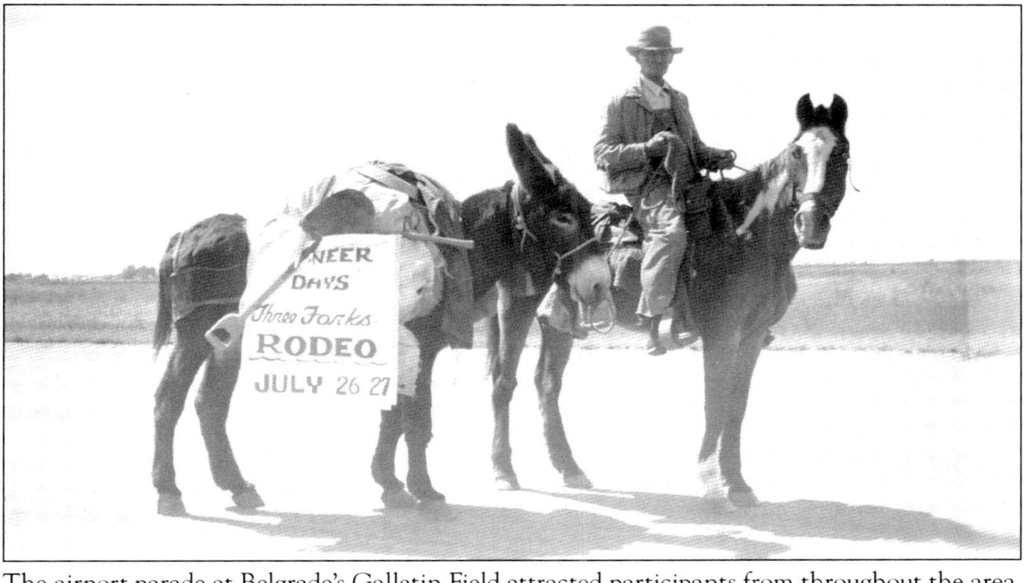

The airport parade at Belgrade's Gallatin Field attracted participants from throughout the area. In this photograph, a weathered rider promotes Three Forks' Pioneer Days and Rodeo. Located about 25 miles to the west, the small town of Three Forks represented the far western edge of Gallatin County. Commercial air service bolstered Three Forks and other area communities.

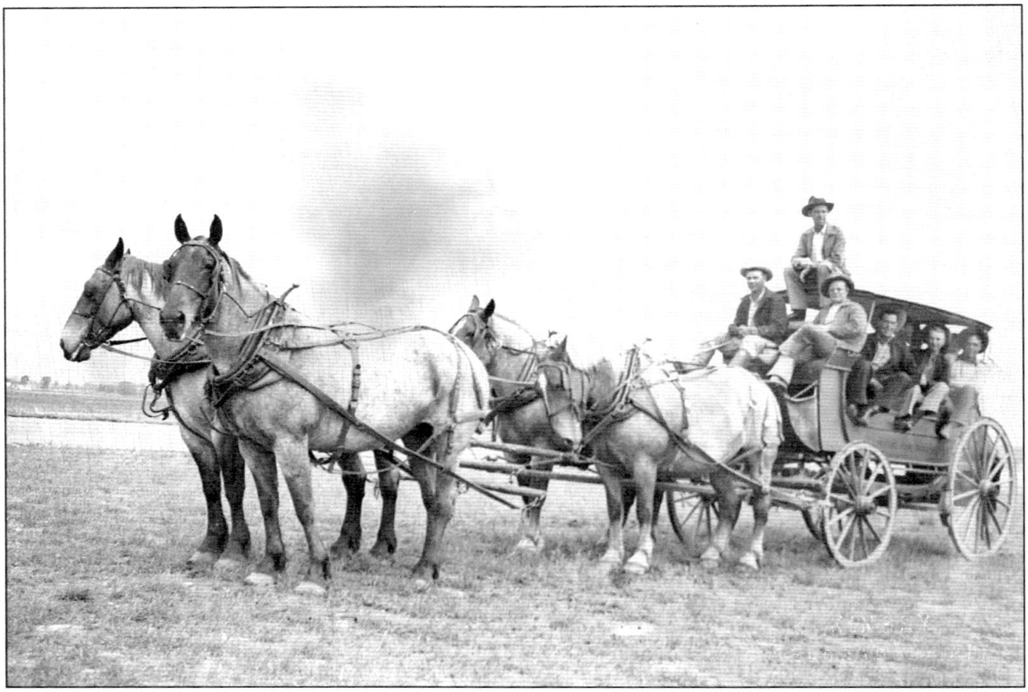

Old meets new at the celebration of Northwest Airline's commercial service. For at least one day, horse transit is not entirely obsolete. In this image, unidentified men mug for the photographer in a horse-drawn carriage. Most likely, the horse and carriage were on hand for the benefit of attendees who wished to experience yesteryear's transportation.

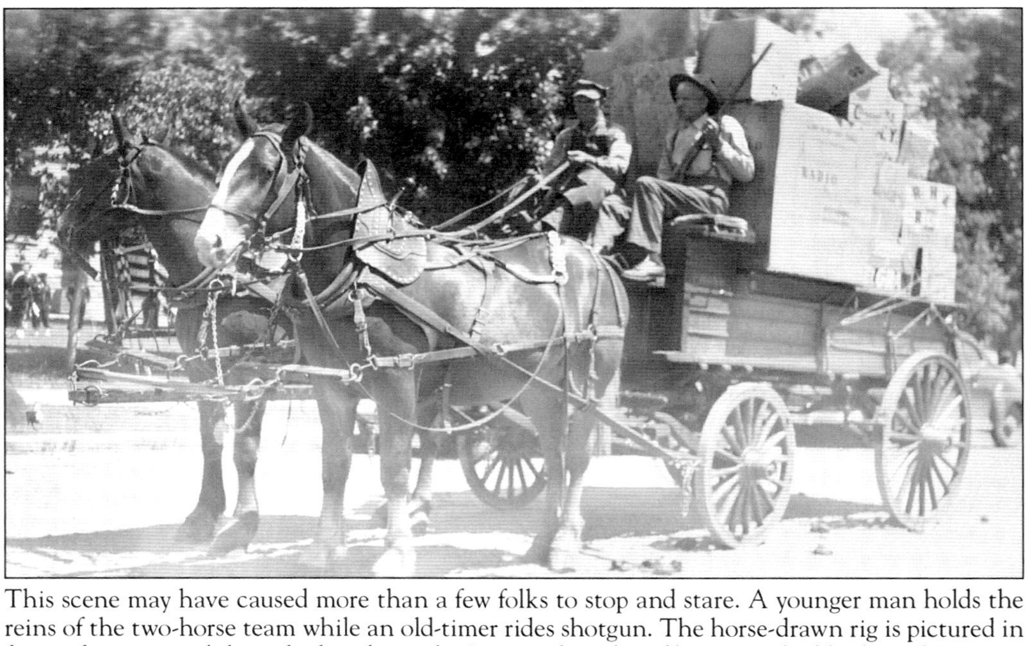

This scene may have caused more than a few folks to stop and stare. A younger man holds the reins of the two-horse team while an old-timer rides shotgun. The horse-drawn rig is pictured in front of an automobile parked at the curb. Among the piles of boxes stacked high in the wagon is a large box containing a new radio.

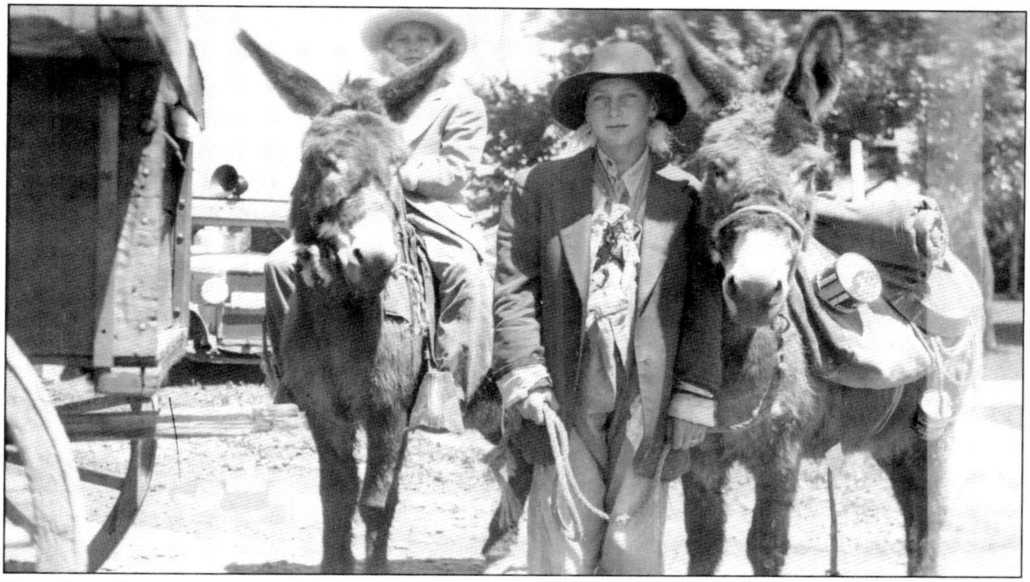

Four-footed transportation was not restricted to older men. Here, two young lads pose for the camera. Packed for an overnight stay, a bedroll and skillet are visible. The rear end of a wagon is visible to the left, and in the background is a parked automobile with a speaker mounted atop the cab.

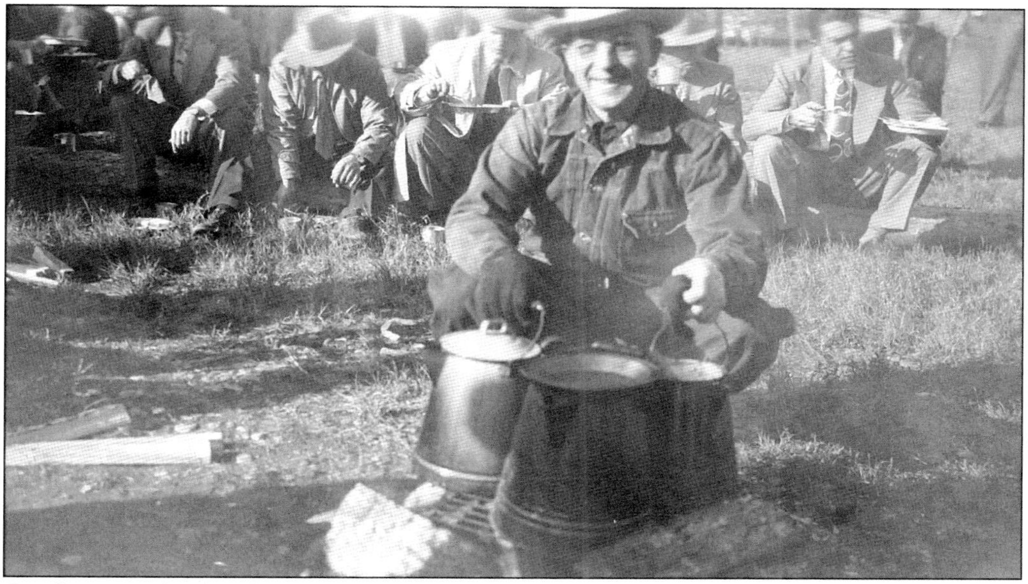

On the grounds of Gallatin Field, vestiges of the Old West are on display in this photograph. Men with suits and ties sitting on a log bench enjoy an outdoor meal as a smiling cook tends to coffee pots over a homemade outdoor grill. A memorable day was had by all.

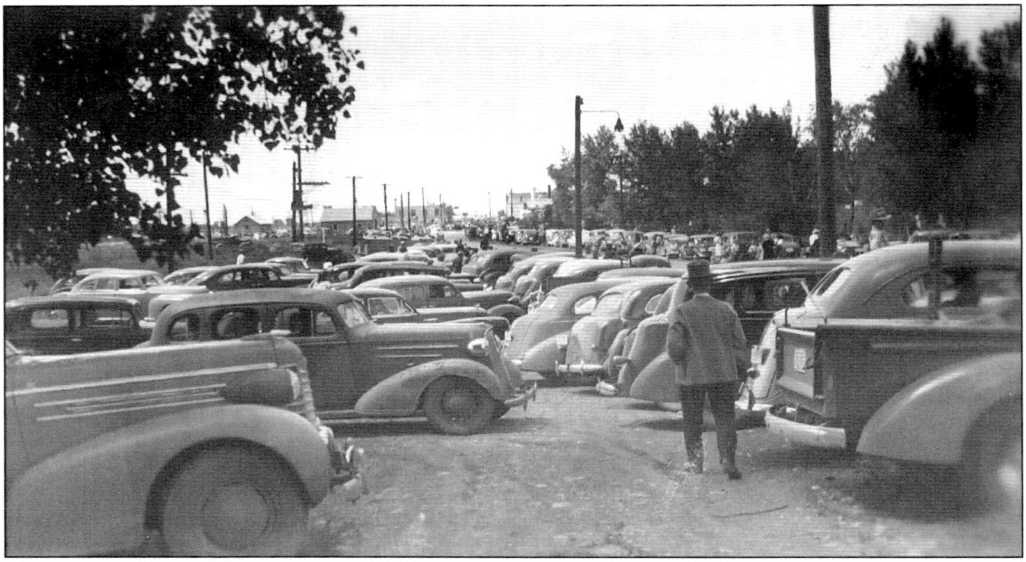

Horses, dogs, motorized carts, automobiles, and planes of various sizes shared Belgrade's Gallatin Field during the celebration of June 22, 1947. This photograph reveals the extent to which automobiles were now a part of everyday life in the Gallatin Valley.

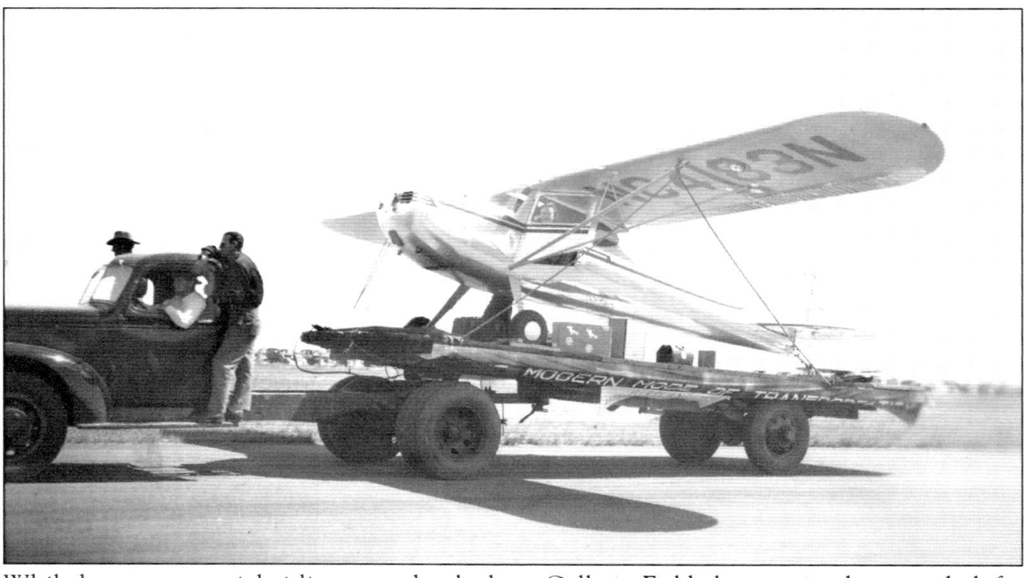

While large commercial airliners awed onlookers, Gallatin Field also remained an area hub for small aircraft. In this photograph, an early version of a Cessna 140 is strapped onto a flatbed trailer. Small craft provided a variety of services, including private flying services and crop dusting. Note the wording on the trailer, "Modern mode of transportation."

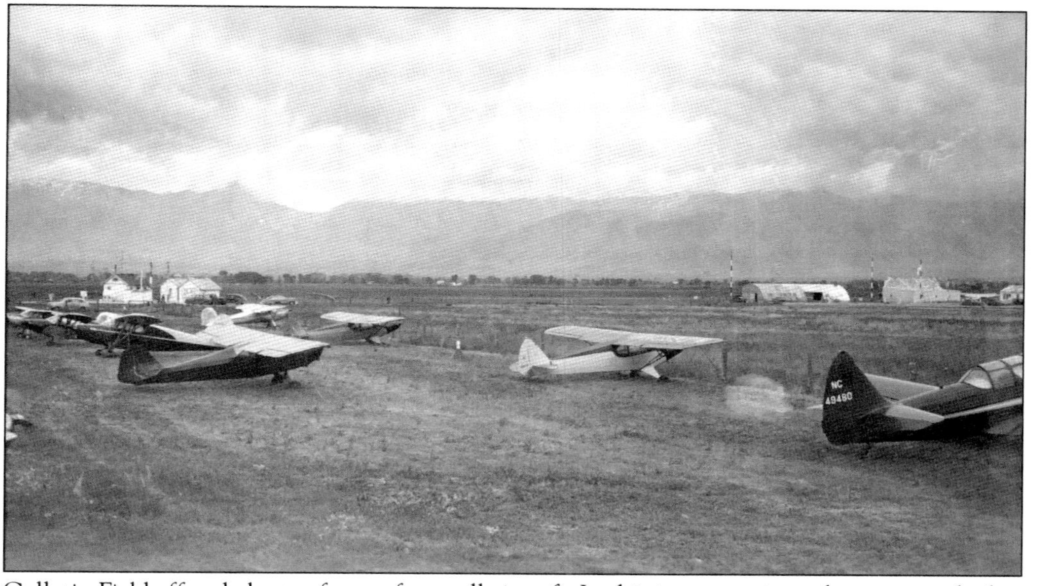

Gallatin Field offered plenty of space for small aircraft. In this image, various planes are parked in the grassy field. Among the craft pictured are Pipers, Stinsons, and Taylorcraft, along with a BT-13 (used for military training) on the right. A few airport buildings are visible in the background, including one under construction. Commercial flights into Gallatin Field sped up the development of the airport, which, in turn, also benefited private aircraft owners and operators.

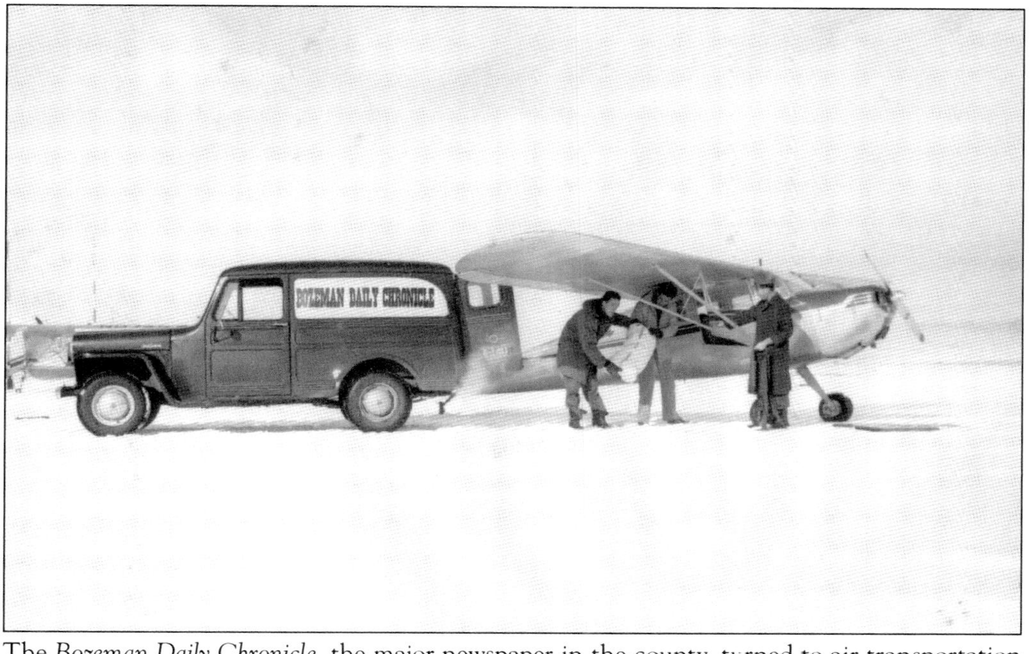

The *Bozeman Daily Chronicle*, the major newspaper in the county, turned to air transportation to deliver the paper to several hundred outlying subscribers. World War II Air Force veteran and Lynch pilot Al Newby flew the paper route. He once dropped a Sunday paper in the lap of a surprised farmer who was riding on his tractor in the middle of a field. Newby and partners bought out Lynch's Bozeman operations in 1956.

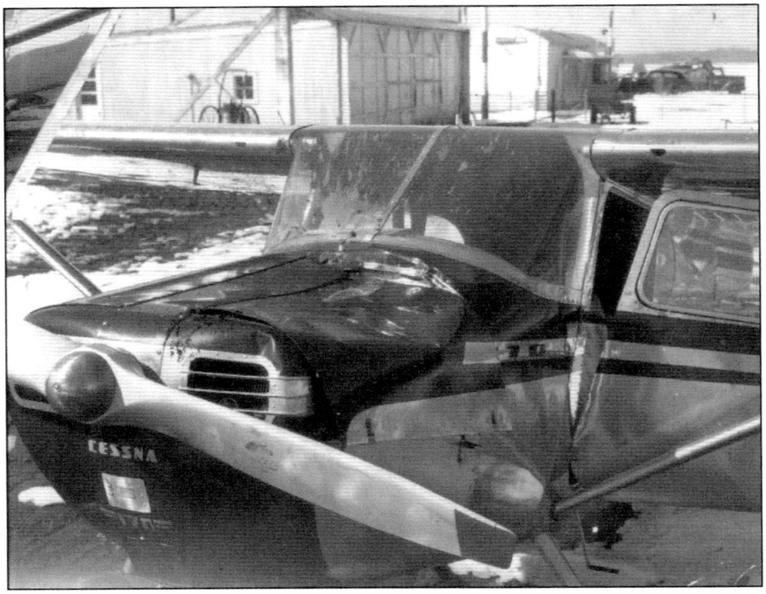

Air travel of the mid-20th century was not without hazards. The smaller the craft, the greater was the likelihood of accidents. Pictured in this 1950 photograph is a Cessna plane piloted by Al Newby that collided with an eagle while looking for lost horses at the Nine Quarter Circle Ranch. The damage is quite noticeable, although the plane landed safely with no injuries to Newby and his passenger.

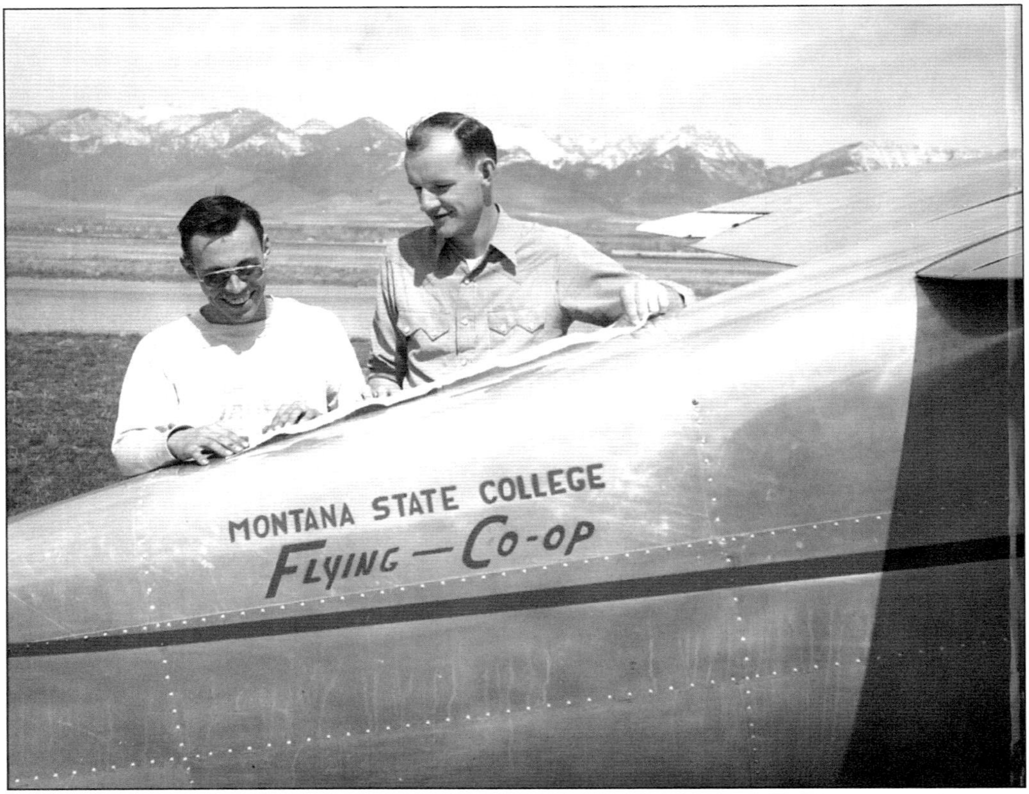

Montana State College (later University) in Bozeman utilized Gallatin Field's services. Pictured here are Jim McPherson (left) and Springhill farmer Bill Wright standing next to a Cessna 120 operated by the Montana State College Flying Co-op. Montana State was formed in 1893 as a land-grant agricultural college.

Three

Manhattan

Amber Waves of Grain

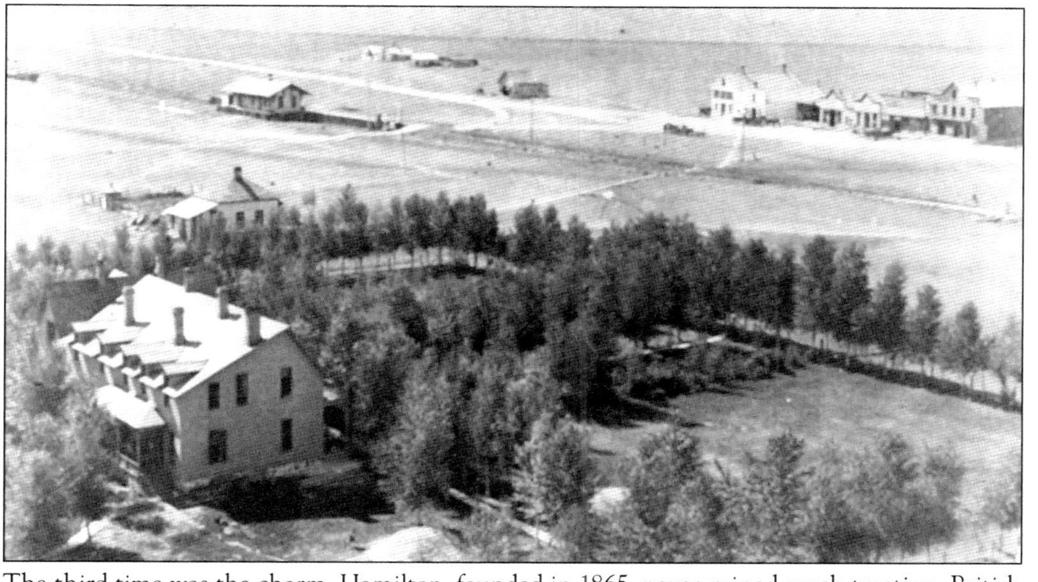

The third time was the charm. Hamilton, founded in 1865, never gained much traction. British horse breeders arriving in the 1880s renamed the community Moreland, but the English families came and left. Barley ultimately offered the community a future. New York businessmen bought land, renamed the town Manhattan in 1891, and recruited Dutch immigrants. This photograph was taken one year later, on August 1, 1892.

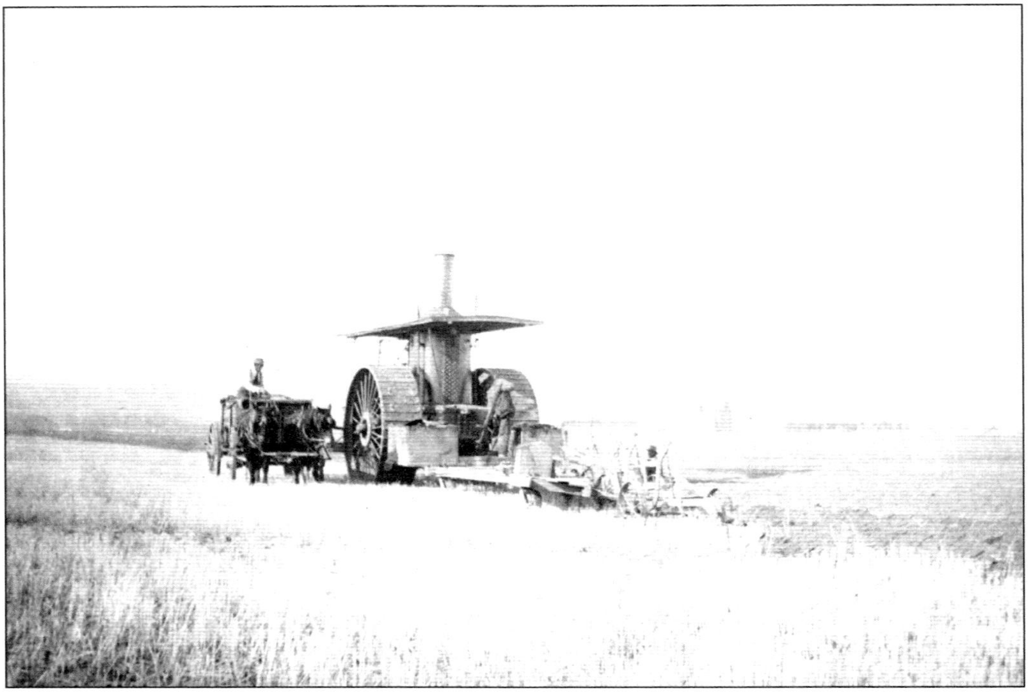

The Manhattan Malting Company, formed by Henry Altenbrand, Jacob Rupert, and partners, built the town of Manhattan in order to have access to the nearby high-quality Saale barley. Saale was the best variety of malting barley. Pictured is an early agricultural operation in the area.

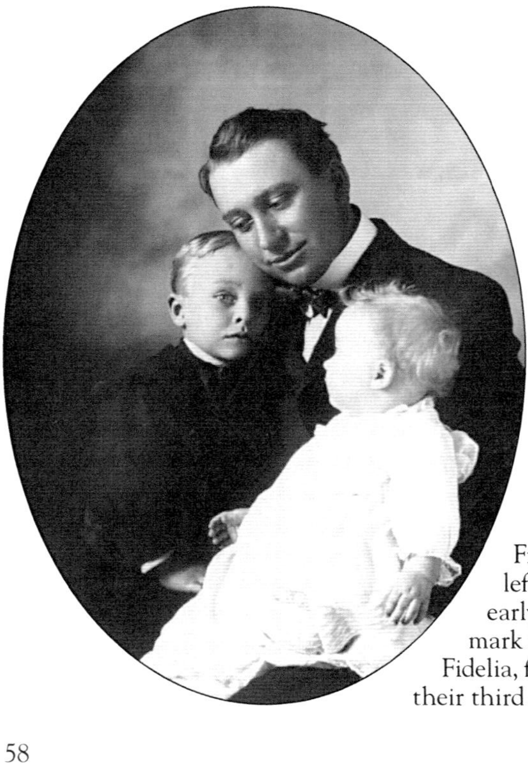

Franklin "Frank" Geiger and his children Delos, left, and Delilah are pictured in this portrait. An early businessman in Manhattan, Geiger made his mark in the newspaper business. Frank and his wife, Fidelia, favored first names starting with the letter *D*, as their third child, Donald, was born in 1909.

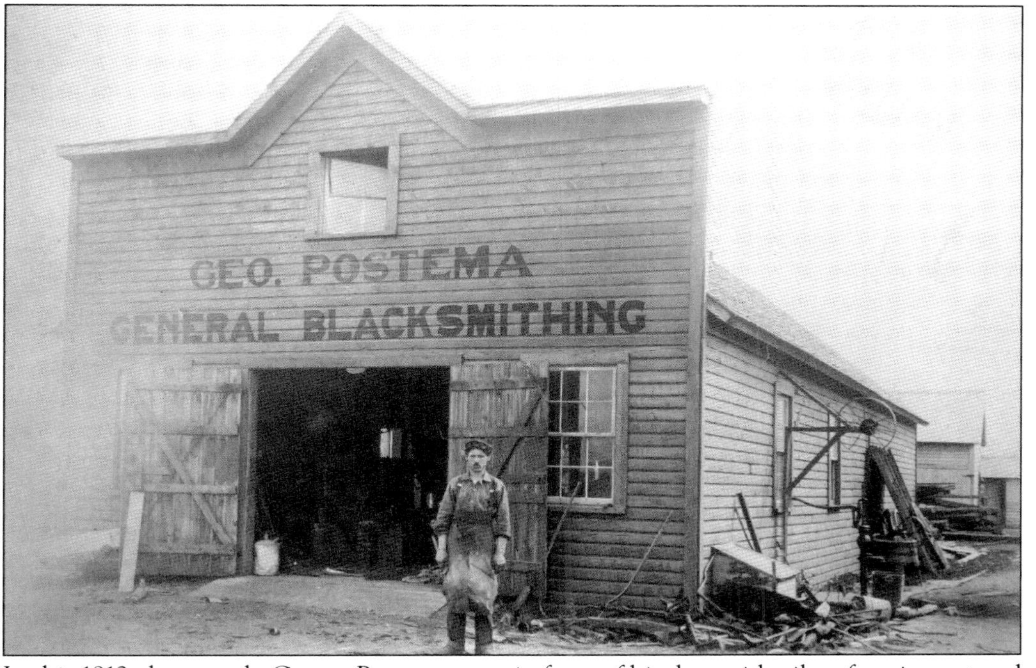

In this 1912 photograph, George Postema poses in front of his shop with piles of equipment and scrap metal to his right. The interior is barely visible through the open doors. Postema's work clothes reflect the fact that blacksmithing was hot, dirty work.

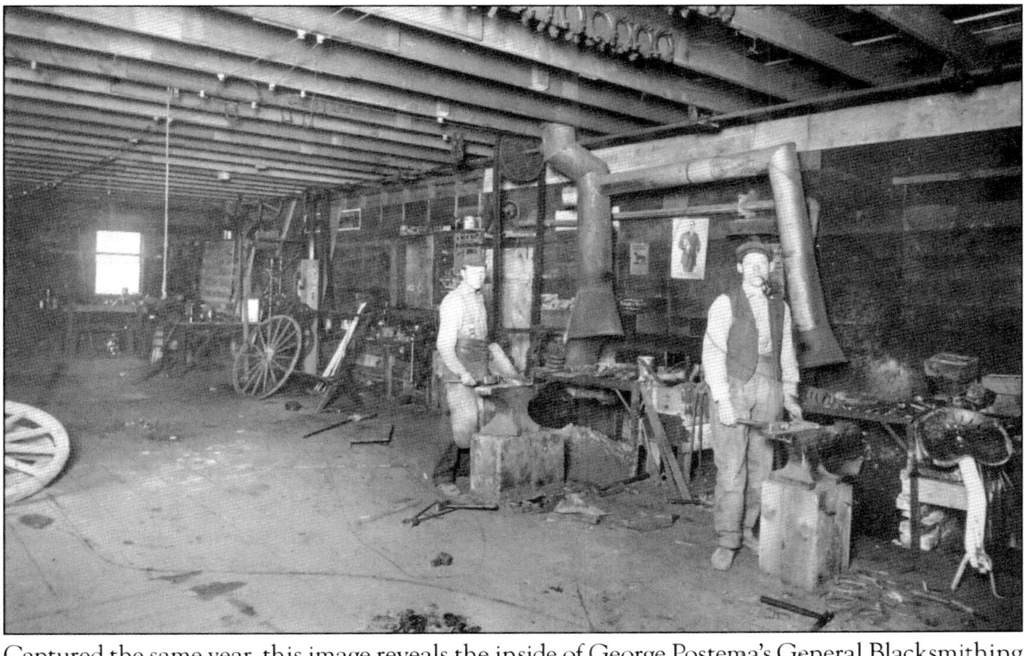

Captured the same year, this image reveals the inside of George Postema's General Blacksmithing shop. Dual anvils and furnaces allowed Postema and John T. Kamp, left, to work simultaneously. Hammers, bars, and tongs litter the room. Postema smokes a pipe while looking up from working on a horseshoe. Overhead, horseshoes are neatly hung from ceiling beams.

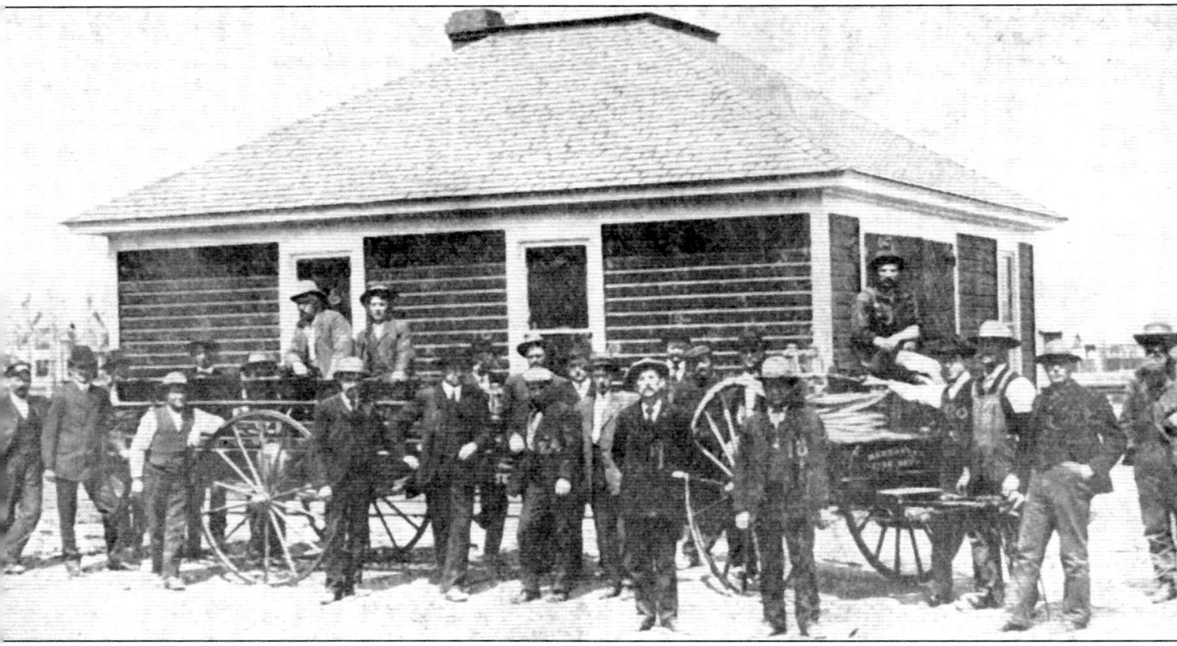

Pictured here is the Manhattan Fire Department in 1906. In the early 20th century, the fire equipment was operated by foot power rather than horses. Fire was always a threat in a town constructed of wooden buildings heated by fireplaces. Volunteer firemen (local businessmen) stood ready on short notice to cart fire hoses to the scene of a blaze. Pictured from left to right are Tom Gray, Fred Campbell, S.L. Farmer, Dave Johnston, Jack Sherven, Still Huling, John Hoffman, Ed Yoder, F.D. Geiger, Jay Curtis, Iven Verwolf, Harry Altenbrand, Tom Johnston, Judge Odell, James Veltkamp, Myron Bond, George E. White, George Kellogg, Ed Connell, Lou LeLacheur, Jess Nelson, Charles ?, Frank Van Ness, and Abner Littlefield.

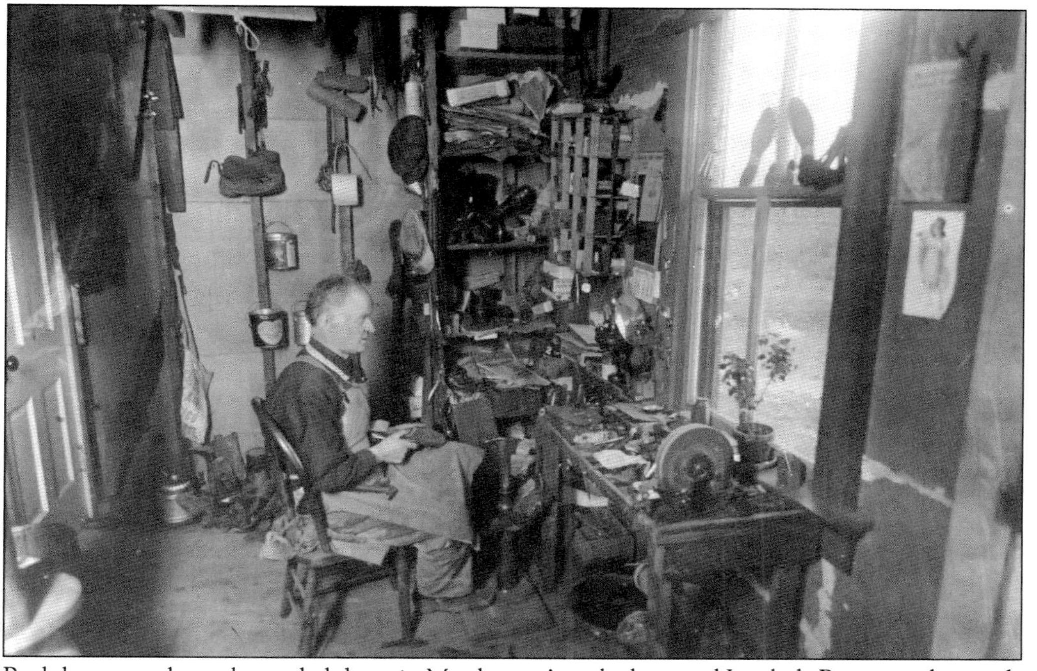

Both horses and people needed shoes in Manhattan's early days, and Jacob de Ruig met the needs of the latter. One of many Dutch immigrants settling in Manhattan in the early 20th century, Ruig arrived in town in 1911 and operated his shoe shop until 1931.

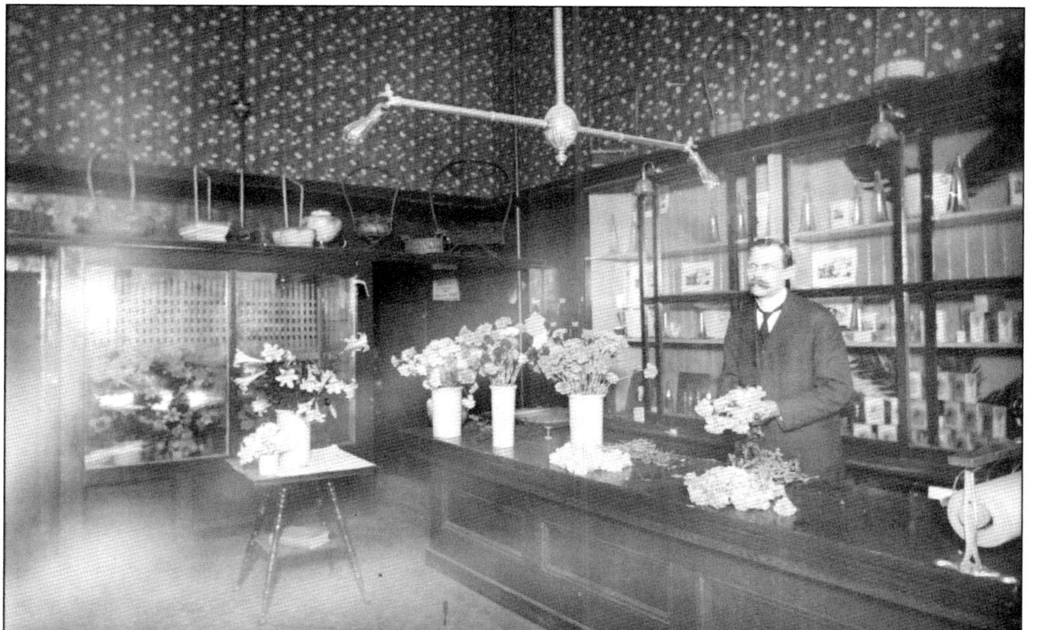

Early Dutch settlers in Manhattan brought a love of flowers with them. Tulips were a favorite of Hollanders, and the Netherlands led in the worldwide flower trade. Pictured here is the interior of a Manhattan flower shop, displaying wares that brightened life in the Gallatin Valley.

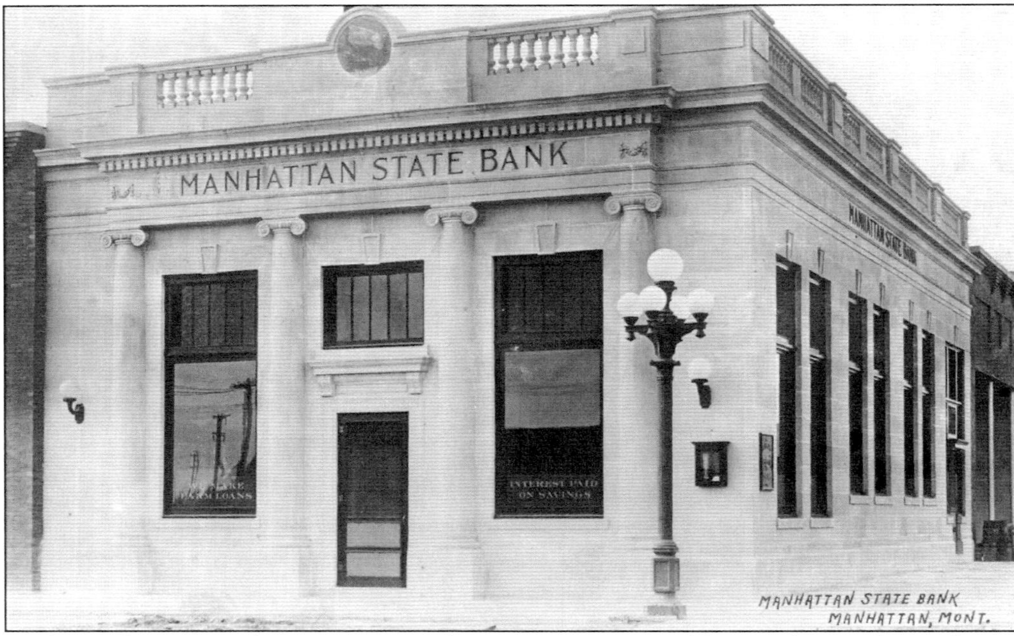

With population growth came an expanding economy. Pictured here is the stately Manhattan State Bank building that opened in 1916. Organized in 1905, the bank began operations before telephone and electricity arrived in town, and until 1913, it was the only bank serving the Manhattan area.

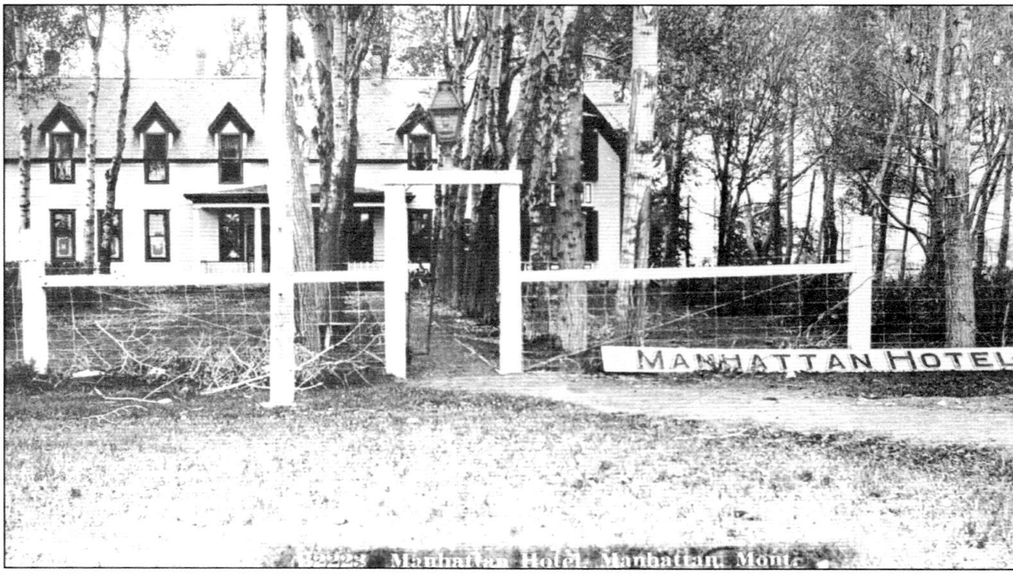

The Manhattan Hotel, nestled in a grove of poplar trees, was built in 1891 by the Manhattan Malting Company. A nice hotel for its day, it was primarily intended for use by company stockholders and their families visiting from New York City. A few other hotels also existed in the town's early days, serving tourists and businessmen.

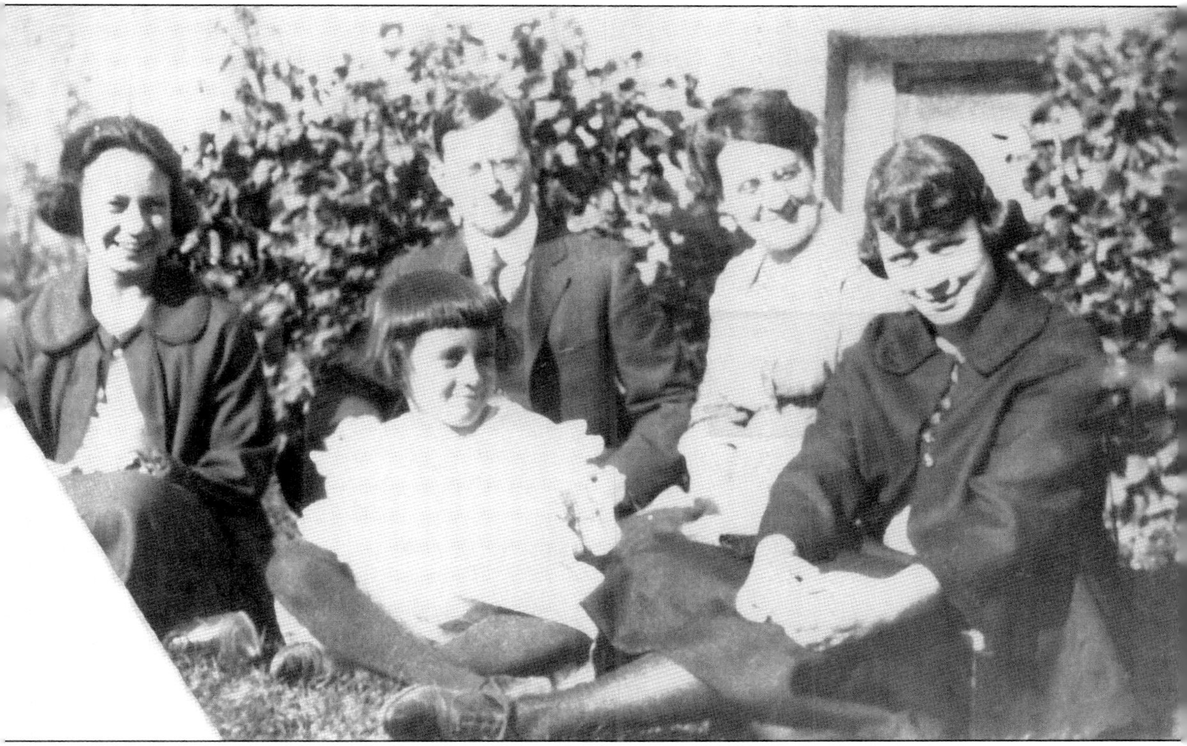

In this October 1921 portrait, the Phelps family is seated on the lawn beside their Manhattan residence. A portion of the Phelps' house is visible in the background. By the 1920s, family portraits were becoming more common. Tucked inside of one of the children's Sunday school Bibles and forgotten about, this photograph was eventually rediscovered by the family.

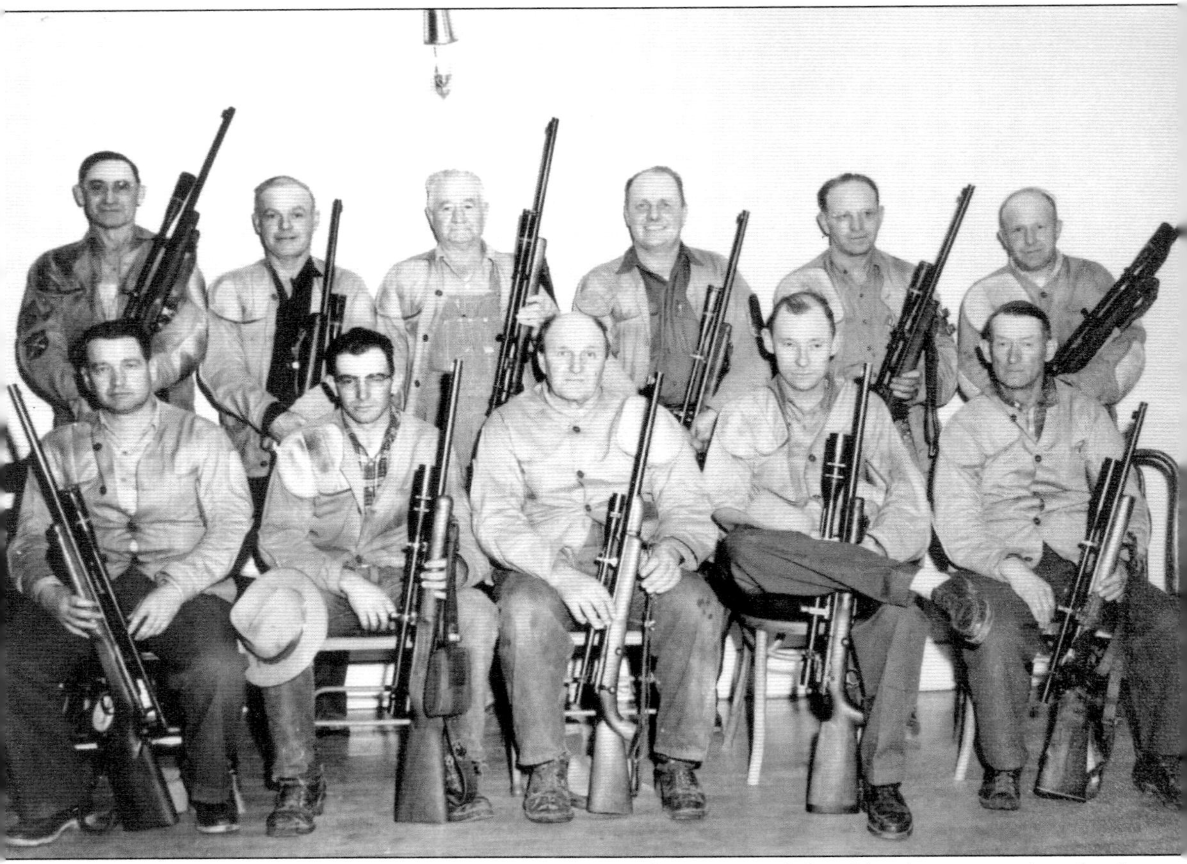

In the early 20th century, the community of Manhattan was defined by the surrounding land. Fertile fields produced the best Saale barley in the nation during Manhattan's early years and wheat and seed potatoes from the 1920s onward. Meanwhile, the nearby hills and mountains offered abundant wildlife to help supplement the diets of area families. While the era of the Wild West had passed by this time, guns remained vital on the remaining western frontier, whether for hunting for meat or shooting varmints that threatened livestock and livelihood. Pictured here are 11 members of the Manhattan Gun Club. Each man holds a bolt-action rifle with a high-powered scope. Most are unidentified, but Doctor Hathway is located in the front row center.

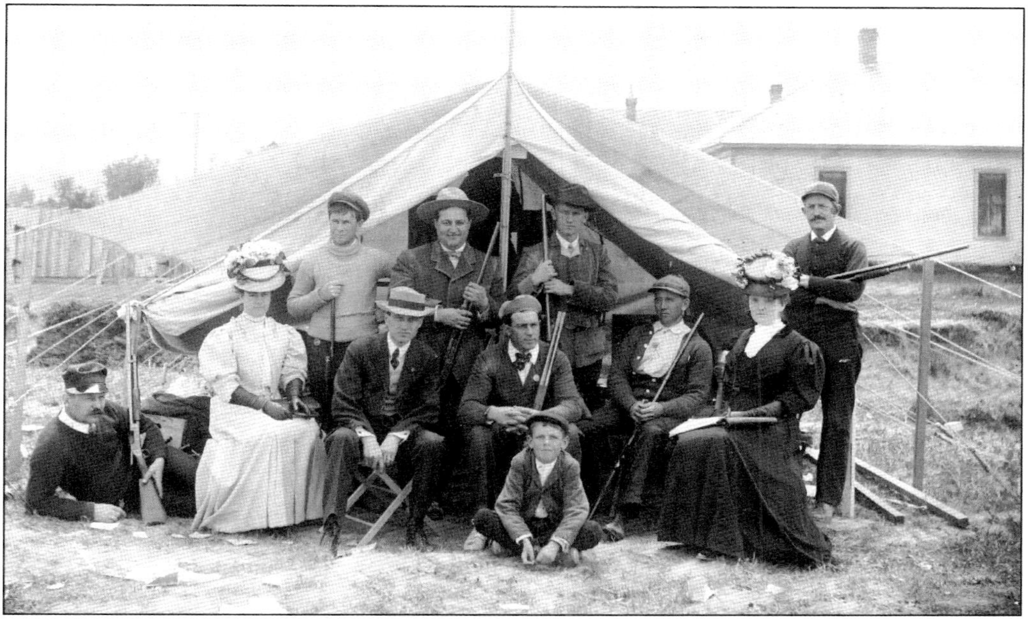

In this 1906 photograph, area residents with rifles lounge in front of a large tent. Pictured in no particular order are Etha Story, Roy Martin, Albert Schlechten, Henry Altenbrand Jr., Gus Steffens, Armilla Martin, Claude Steffens, Bud ?, and Joe Westphal.

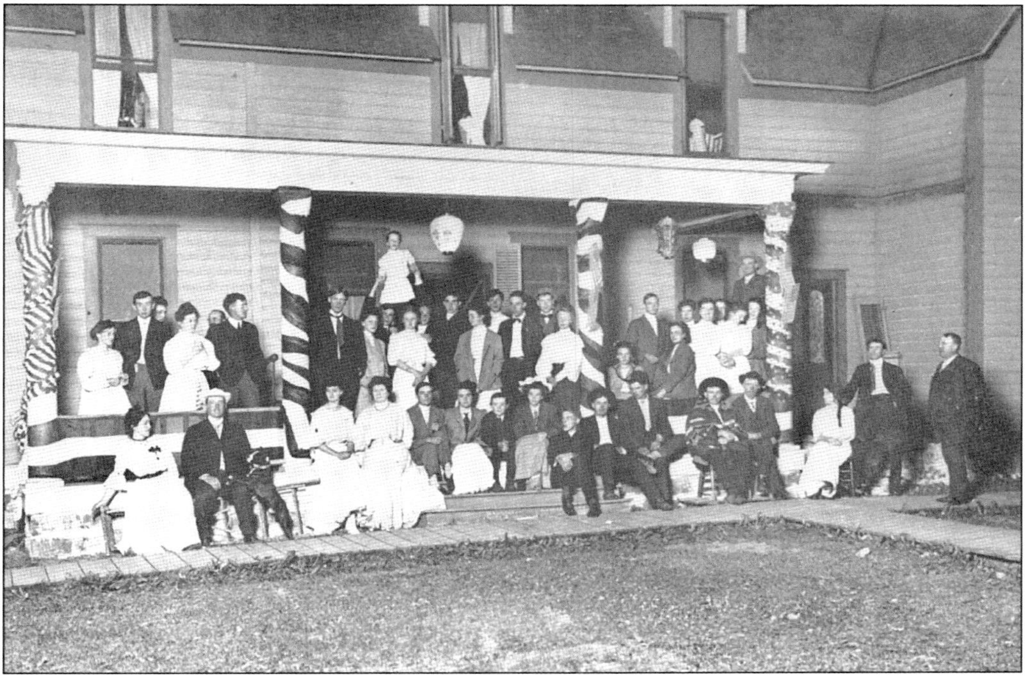

Horses also remained integral to life in early-20th-century Montana. While typically used for transportation and working the land, horses also spurred recreational opportunities. The Manhattan Riding Club, pictured in this 1906 photograph, offered members the opportunity to cultivate and display their riding skills.

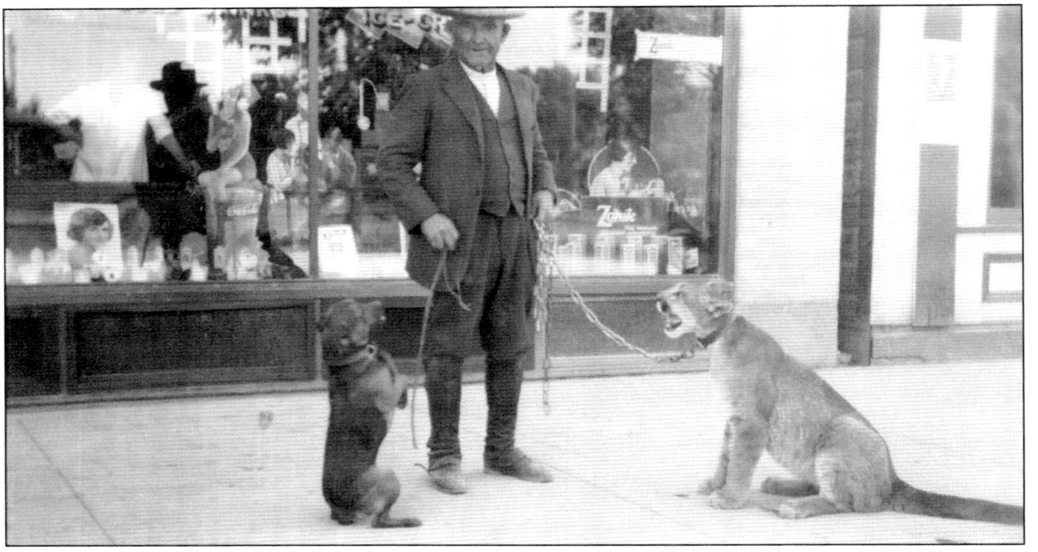

Although a small town, early Manhattan did not lack for entertainment options. At the forefront of the local entertainment industry was David "Kid" Johnston, ex-prizefighter, entrepreneur, and animal trainer. Pictured here is Johnston on a city sidewalk with his trained and collared mountain lion in one hand and his well-trained dog in the other. Johnston's mountain lions sometimes pulled a cart, and a few appeared in Hollywood movies. At one point, Johnston also owned a trained grizzly bear.

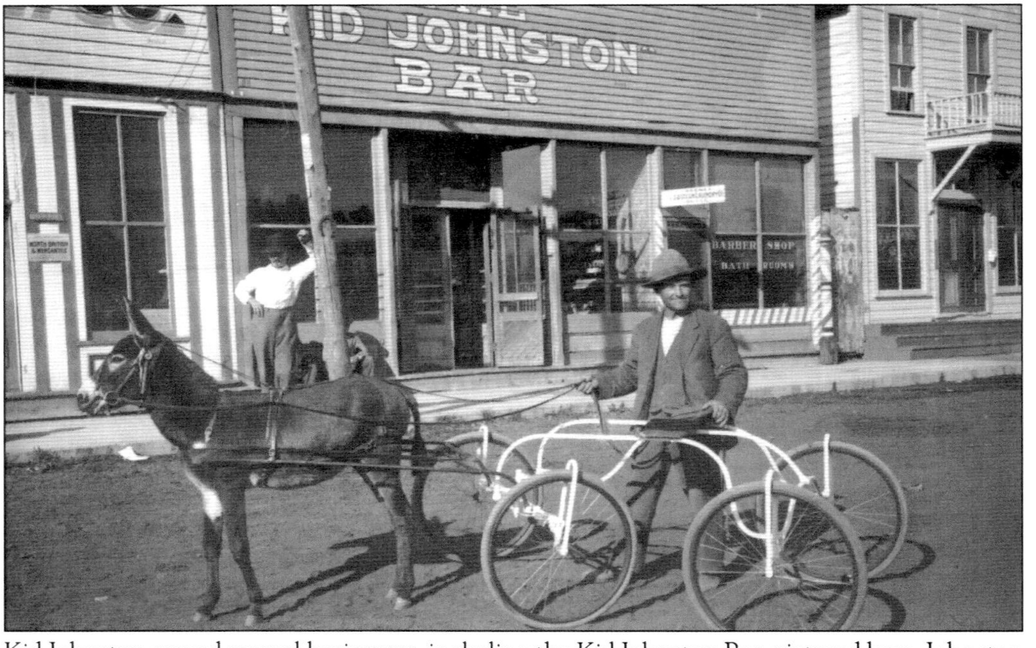

Kid Johnston owned several businesses, including the Kid Johnston Bar, pictured here. Johnston also owned the Kid Theatre, one of two electric theaters in town. In addition to movies, Johnston's theater, constructed in 1915, featured Saturday night dances, basketball games, wrestling, and boxing matches. High school graduations were also held in the theater until the completion of a new high school in 1923.

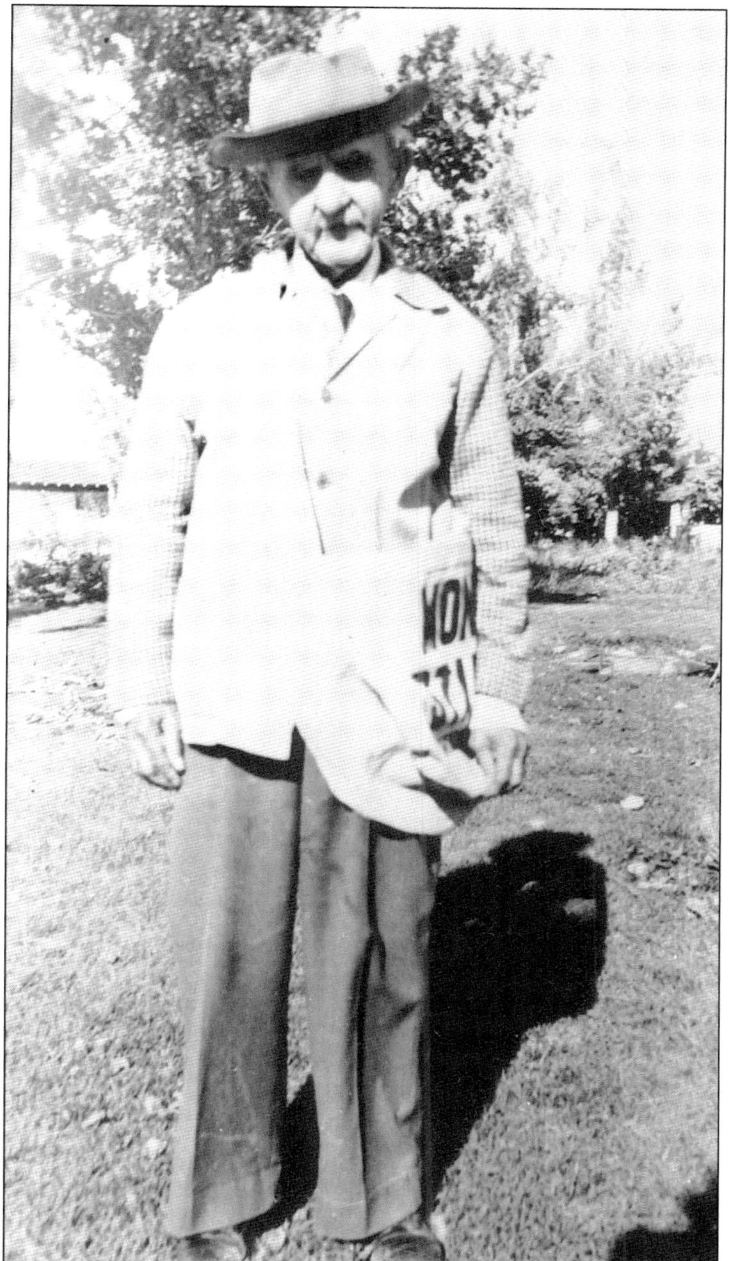

Before the advent of radio and television, newspaper carriers were a lifeline to the outside world for Manhattan-area residents of the late 19th and early 20th centuries. Braving the elements of the often-harsh Montana weather, newspaper carriers were hardy souls. Pictured here is smartly dressed William Krause, longtime deliveryman, holding a paper. In this 1930s photograph, Krause is 95 years old, one of the oldest residents in Manhattan at the time. In the late 19th and early 20th centuries, several newspapers served the Gallatin Valley, including *Montana Pick and Plow* (1869–1870), *Bozeman Avant Courier* (later *Bozeman Daily Chronicle*), *Gallatin Farmer-Stockman*, *Belgrade Journal*, and *Manhattan Record* (founded 1906).

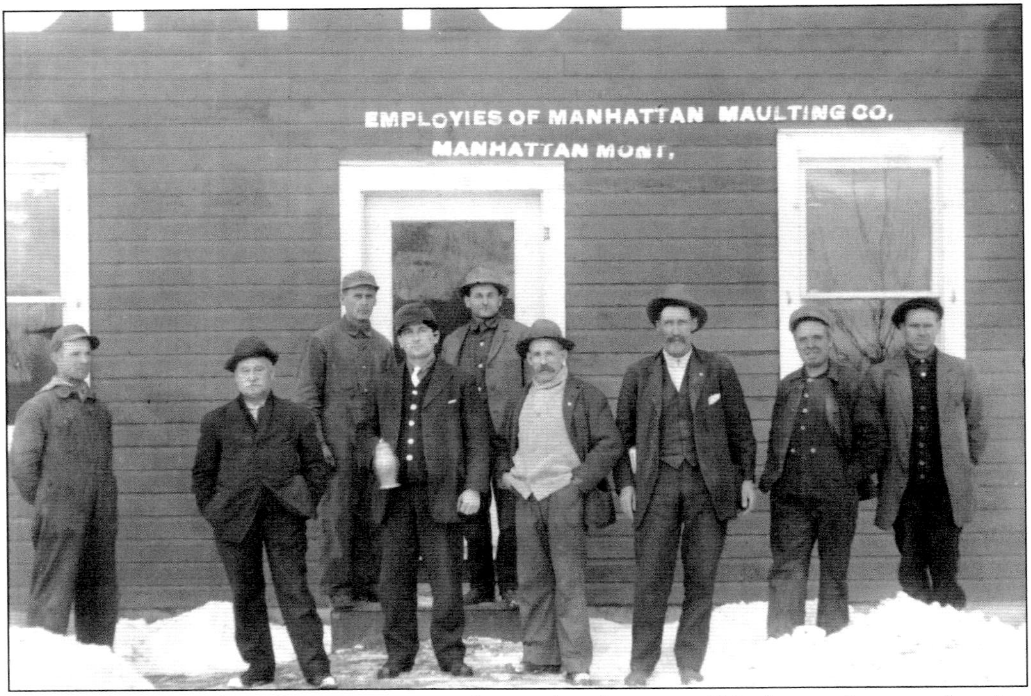

The Manhattan Malting Company remained central to the town of Manhattan for many decades. Pictured above in 1915 are company employees standing outside of an employee building during the winter months. Years of company profits dried up during Prohibition in the 1920s, while area farmers diversified into seed potatoes, wheat, dairy, and beef cattle.

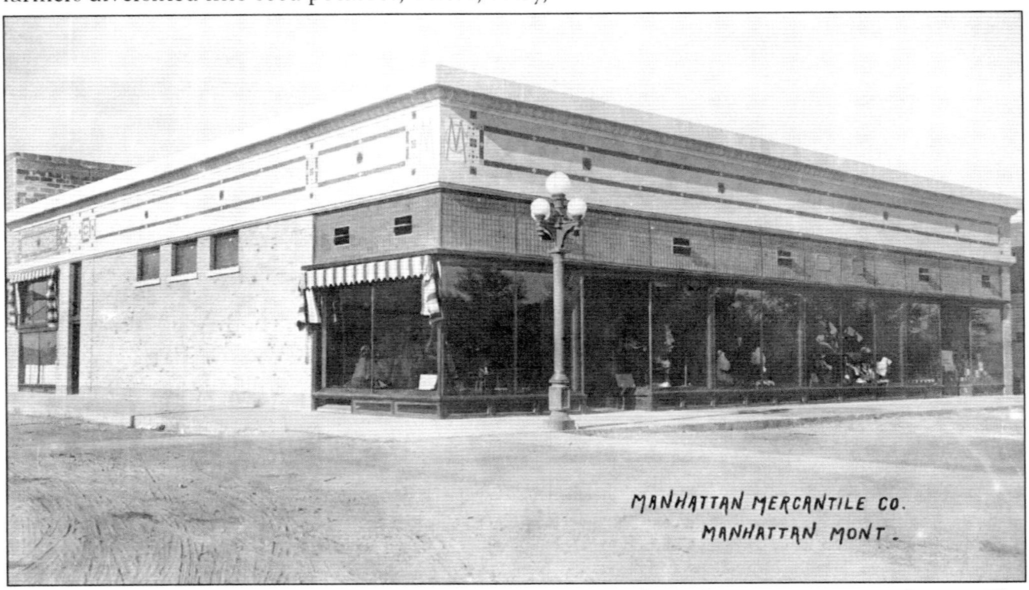

The fortunes of the Manhattan Malting Company were reflected among town merchants. The Manhattan Mercantile Company, built about 1916, offered all manners of merchandise to area residents. Displayed in the storefront windows are clothing and other items. The streetlamps were relatively new, as electricity had arrived only six years earlier.

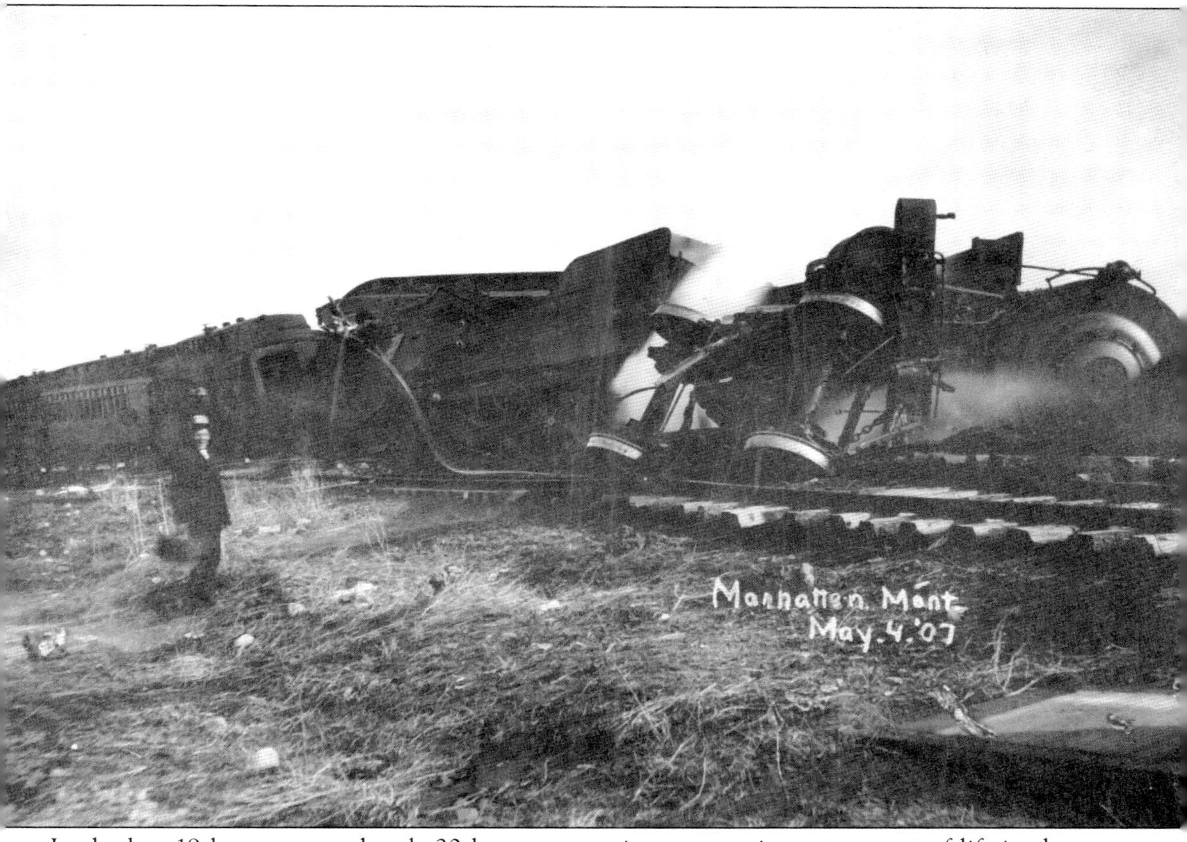

In the late 19th century and early 20th century, trains were an important part of life in the Gallatin Valley, transporting commodities and passengers to and from other parts of the state and nation. Yet train accidents, such as collisions, derailments, and explosions—like the May 4, 1907, accident near Manhattan, pictured here—were commonplace, particularly during the era of steam engines. The engine, noticeably mangled in this photograph, conveys the seriousness of this particular Northern Pacific Railway accident. This accident, though, was a bit unusual. The train struck a handcar sitting on the tracks, and the engine was somehow thrown off the rails. The fireman was killed, and 25 passengers were hurt. During the first decade of the 20th century, there were at least four other deadly train accidents in the state of Montana.

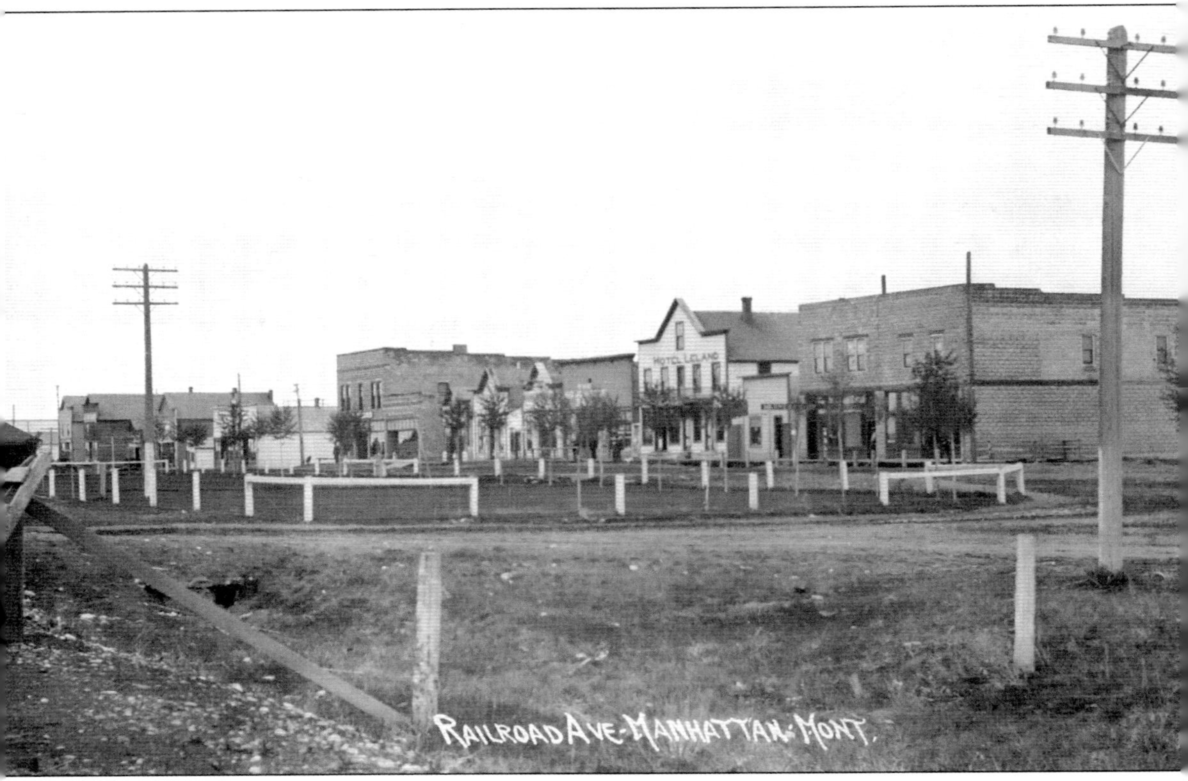

In this undated photograph, Manhattan storefronts are pictured along Railroad Avenue across from grassy empty lots. Prominently pictured is the Hotel Leland. To the left of Hotel Leland is the aforementioned Kid Johnston Bar. A number of unidentified individuals can be seen walking or standing on the boardwalk by the storefronts, but neither horses nor cars are visible. Manhattan's tree-lined streets were spacious, and the town was platted alongside the railroad. Critical to the Manhattan Malting Company's success, the rails in the late 19th and early 20th centuries brought new settlers to town and shipped malt to the east (little of the malt was brewed locally). In addition, some New York–based Manhattan Malting Company executives built summer homes in the area and utilized the rails for traveling back and forth.

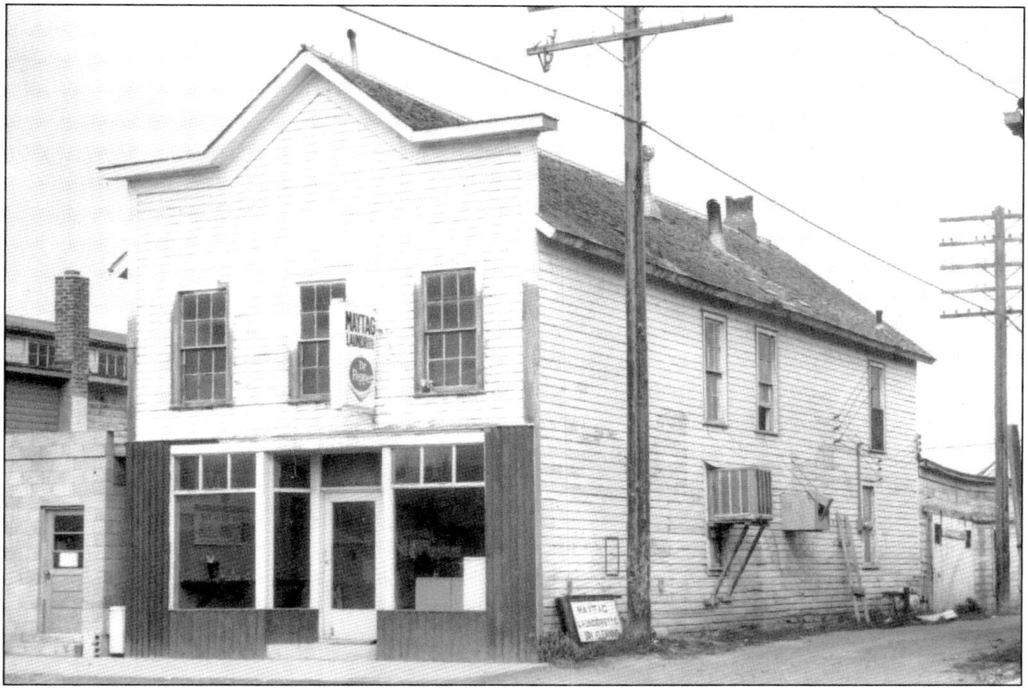

When the town of Hamilton moved closer to the railroad and was renamed Moreland (and later Manhattan), John Potter's General Store moved with the town in the winter of 1883–1884. In this undated photograph, Potter's store has been turned into a Maytag Launderette and Dry Cleaners. The Dr. Pepper advertisement represented competition for the soda market, dominated by the Coca-Cola Company. Dr. Pepper was created in the 1880s in Waco, Texas.

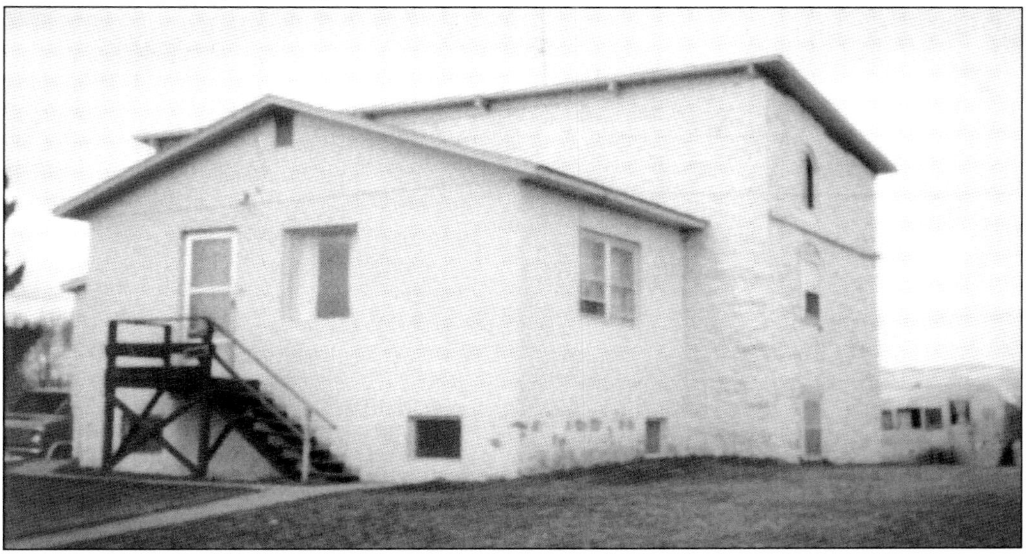

Pictured here is the Manhattan Paper Mill office. The paper produced in Manhattan was a byproduct of barley production. The straw, unused in the malting process, provided the raw material for the mill. However, the paper mill was short lived, as the silicon-heavy straw resulted in a product of lesser quality than the market could sustain.

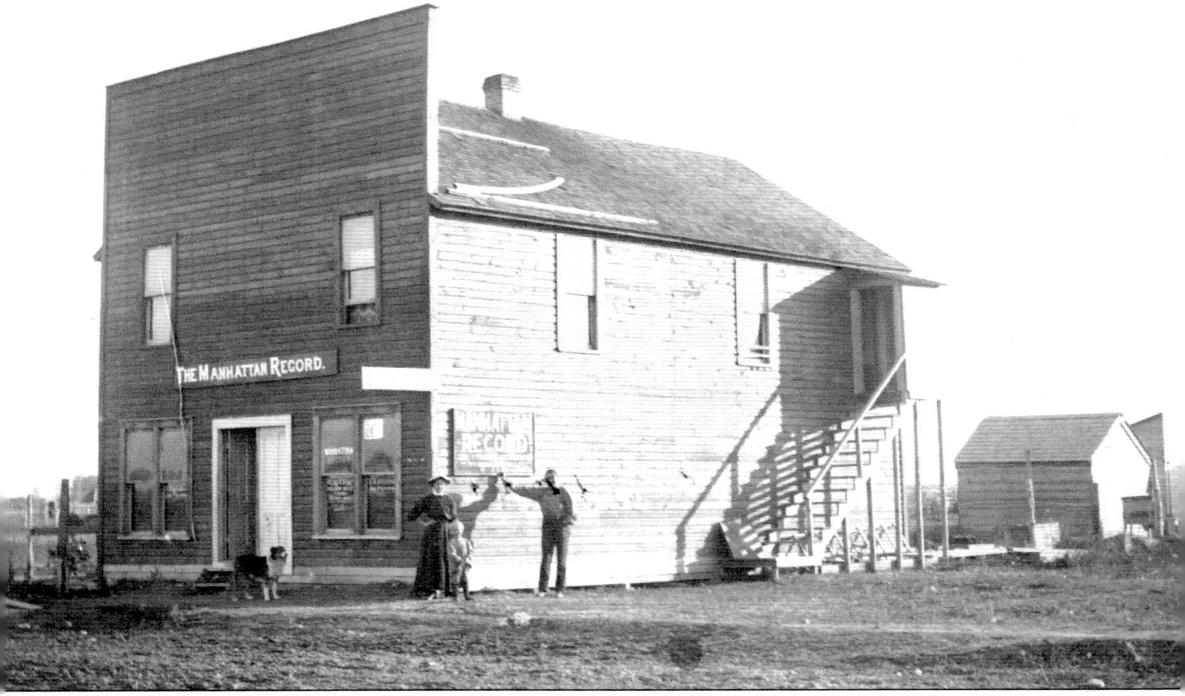

In the undated photograph seen here are the offices of the *Manhattan Record*, the town's local newspaper. Founded in 1906, the independent *Manhattan Record* was owned and edited by Franklin Delos Geiger, originally from Independence, Iowa. The paper was published weekly on Thursdays. Standing in front of the building are Miss Hoyt, Frank Geiger, and Frank's son Delos (born 1904), as well as Gyp the dog to the left. In the building's windows are signs advertising real estate opportunities. Small-town newspapers flourished in early-20th-century America, although the news operations were typically small and, often, family-operated businesses. The *Manhattan Recorder* competed with many other Gallatin Valley newspapers, demanding much of Geiger's writing, marketing, and entrepreneurial skills in order to stay afloat.

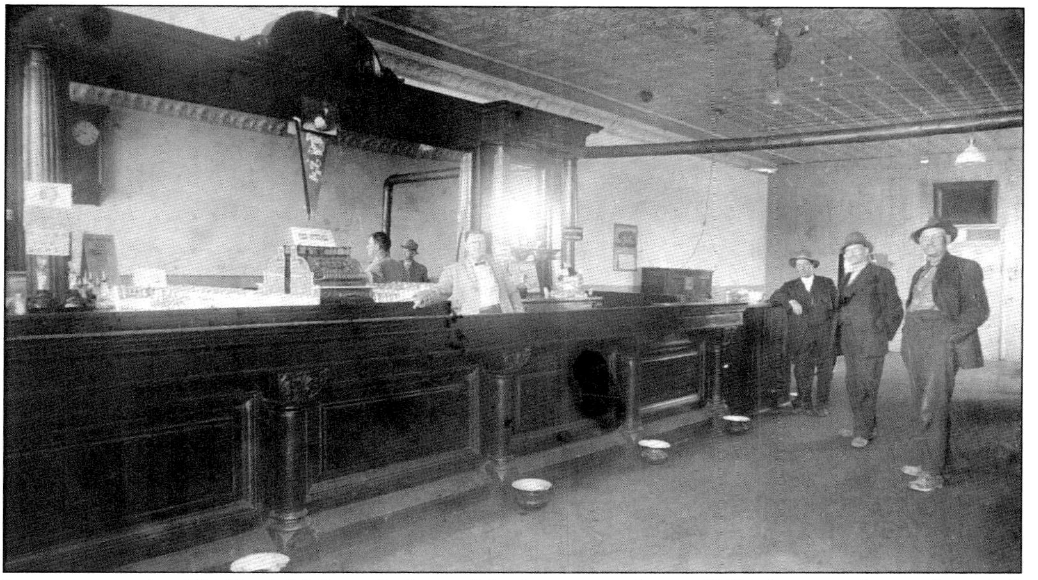

Lounging at the Old Faithful Beer Parlor in Manhattan in this c. 1937 photograph are, from left to right, Charley Stenley (bartender), Willie Davis (owner), and Frank and Martin Dunbar. Note the spittoons on the floor. A sign over the cash register reads, "Free Buttermilk." This image was captured immediately after the end of the Prohibition era. Other than during Prohibition, saloons and bars were a focal point of and gathering place in many rural, late-19th- and early-20th-century Montana communities.

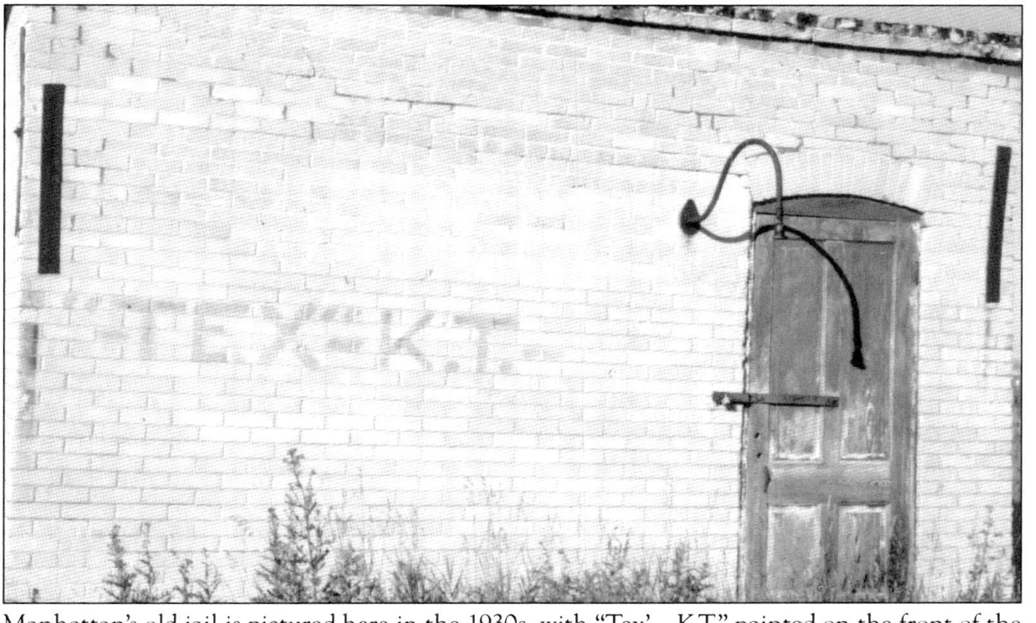

Manhattan's old jail is pictured here in the 1930s, with "Tex'—K.T." painted on the front of the building. Tex was locally known as the King of Tramps (K.T.) during the 1930s Depression era, with his legend stamped onto the jail. As in many other rural communities across the nation, Manhattan suffered during the Great Depression, although to a lesser degree than urban areas. The railroad brought despondent outsiders, such as Tex, to town in search of food and shelter.

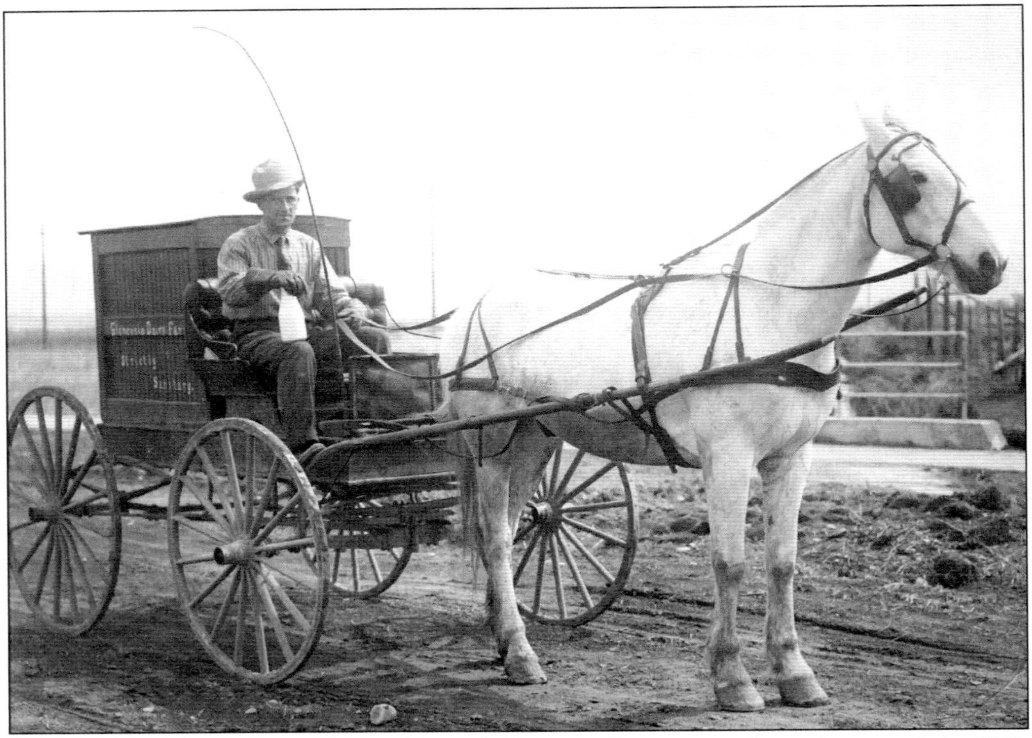

Lawrence Niven and a horse named Jim of Glencosie Dairy pause for a photograph in 1913. The Glencosie operation recognized customer demands for healthy milk at a time when food production was frequently unsanitary. Niven, attired in a dress shirt and tie, balances a quart of milk between his knee and gloved hand. Writing on the side of the carriage proclaims, "Glencosie Dairy Farm. Strictly Sanitary."

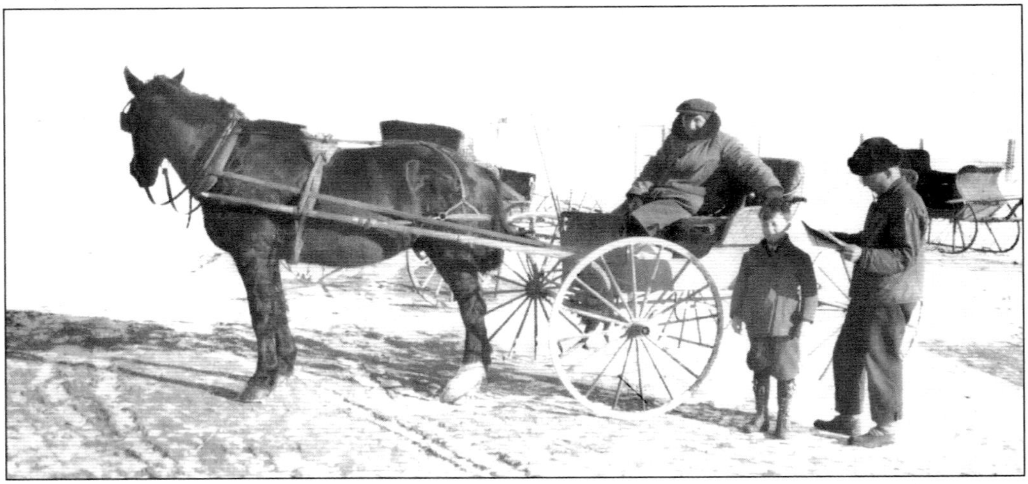

Horses remained a common means of transportation into the third decade of the 20th century. While increasingly popular, automobiles did not yet fully rule the road in Manhattan. Rough terrain remained unsuitable for cars on some mail routes. In this 1921 image, postal carrier Henry Becker delivers mail during the winter season. Note the horse sleds parked in the background to the right.

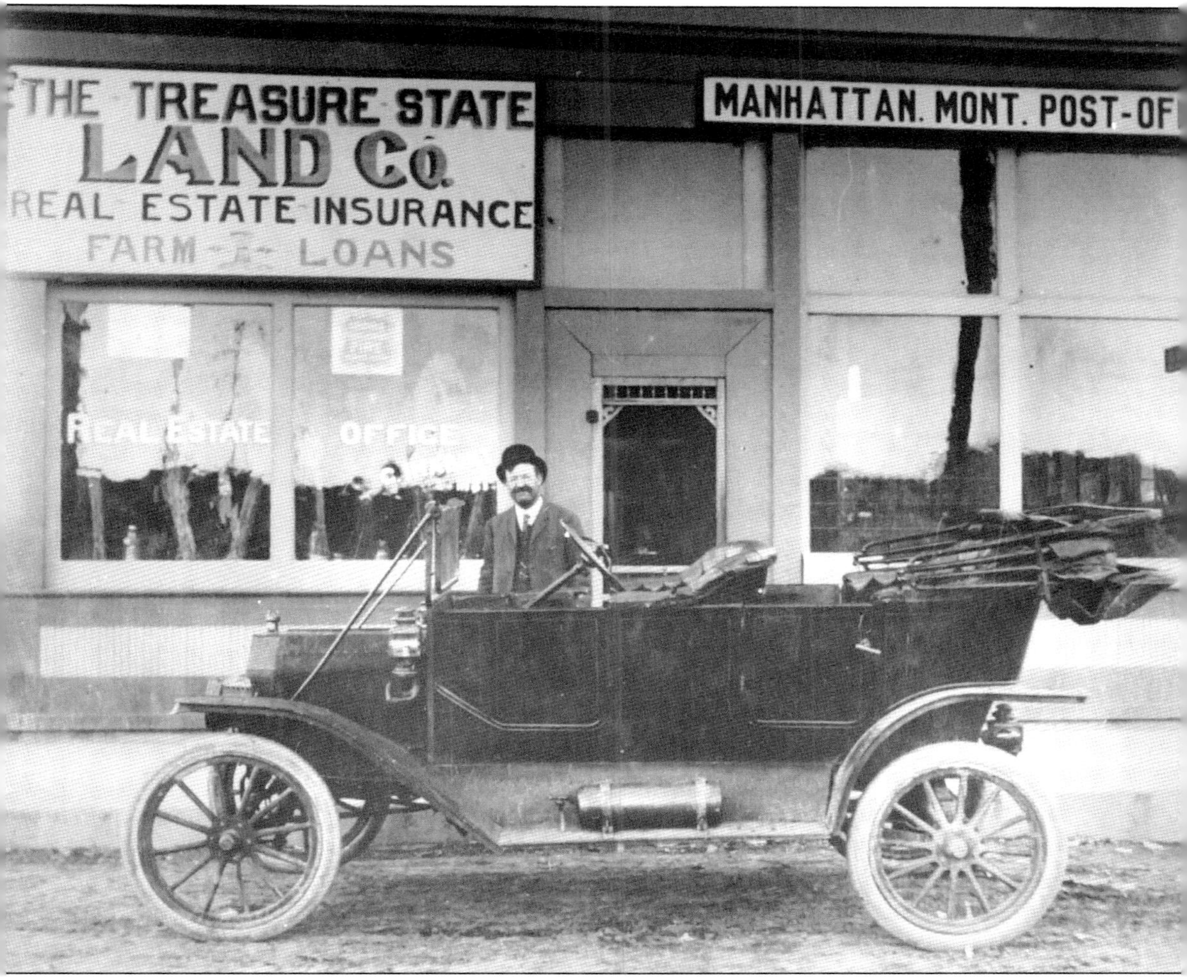

Born in Somerset, Kentucky, in December 1863, Cephus Inabnit settled in Manhattan, where he lived until his death in January 1929. Here, Inabnit stands beside a 1913 Model T. Ford in downtown Manhattan. Behind Inabnit is Manhattan's Treasure State Land Company and the Manhattan Post Office. The 1920s and 1930s witnessed periods of boom and bust for the area's economy, of which land was the focal point. While some years of prosperity emerged in the 1920s, Prohibition and drought ravaged the agricultural markets and led to the decline of the Manhattan Malting Company. In turn, many families and local businesses fell upon hard times; however, the 1920s were but a prelude for what came next in America. Inabnit died months before a stock market crash steered the nation down the road to the Great Depression.

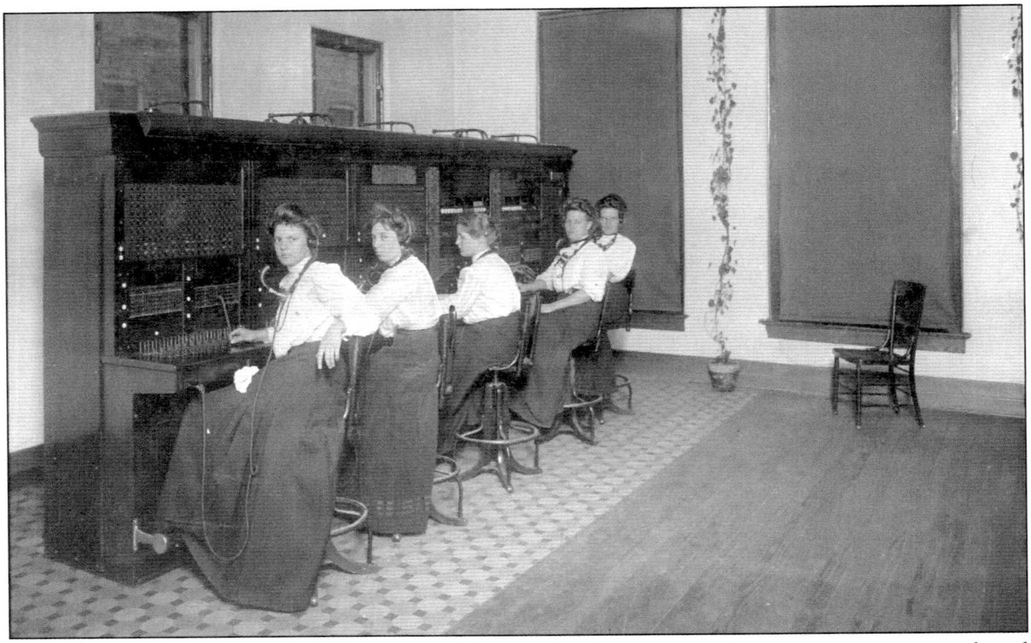

Telephone service came to Manhattan in 1909, nearly 25 years after phone service was introduced in nearby Bozeman. In this undated photograph of the Manhattan telephone exchange, five women operate telephone switchboards in an otherwise sparsely furnished room. One year earlier in 1908, a new phone facility had opened in Bozeman, also with room for five operators.

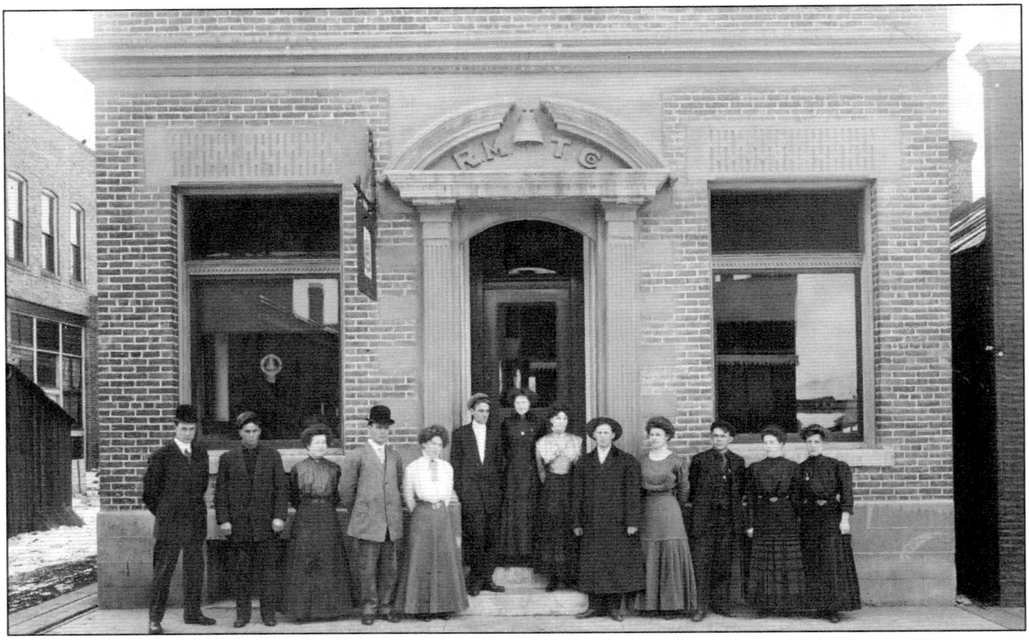

In this undated photograph, the 13-member crew of the Rocky Mountain Telephone Company's Manhattan facility stands in front of the telephone exchange. Though phone service did not take firm hold in the Gallatin Valley until the early 20th century it was indispensable for most families and businesses by mid-century.

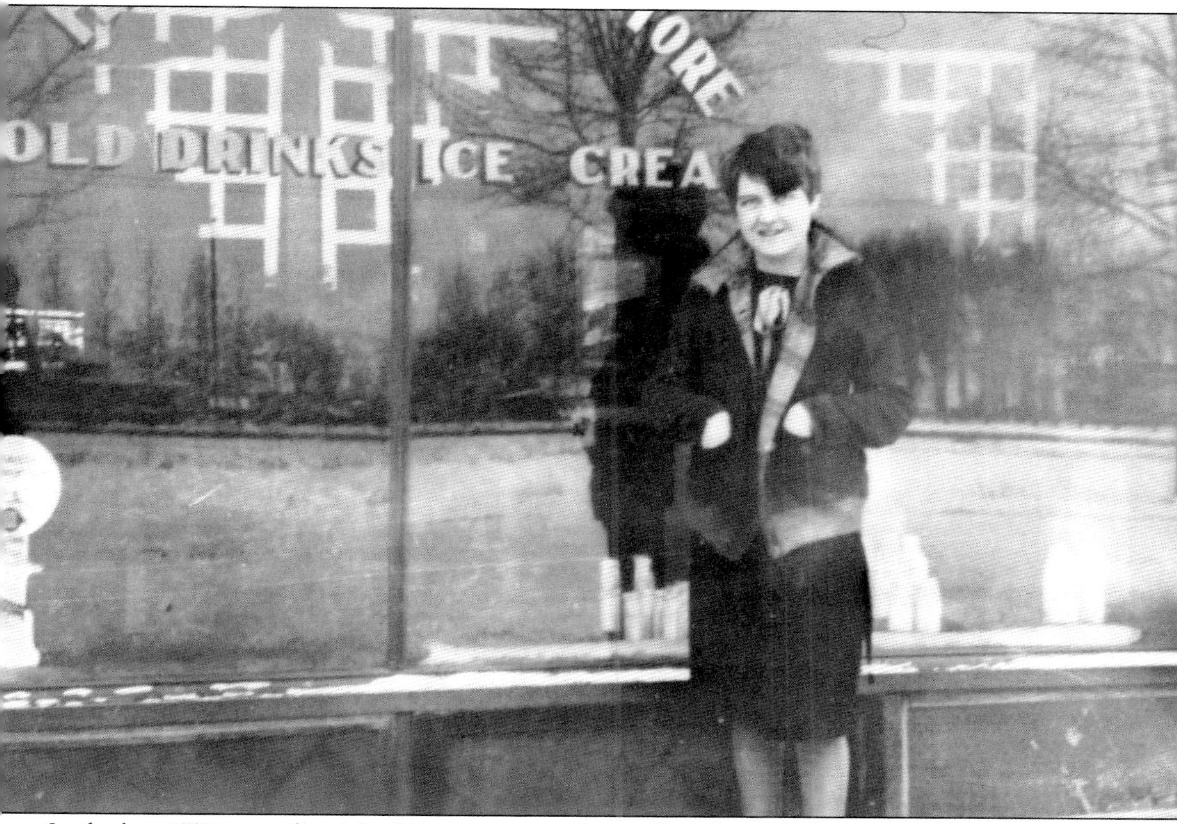

In the late 1920s, a smiling Mae Higgins poses in front of Manhattan's drugstore. The origins of drugstores are obscure, going back to at least the 1820s and possibly decades earlier. The Civil War not only sent waves of settlers westward to Montana and other western territories, but also popularized Army dispensatories in response to the injuries and illnesses that ravaged military ranks. It was not until the 1890s that the storefront drugstore, as pictured here, appeared on the American scene. Initially, drugstores narrowly focused on filling prescriptions. Prior to the 1920s, soda fountains and sandwich counters were not common in drugstores. Prohibition, however, witnessed the widespread expansion of drugstores to include the serving of cold drinks, ice cream, other snacks, and even meals, a trend reflected in Manhattan's drugstore. As such, adults and children both frequented the drugstore, perhaps more often for drinks and treats than to fill prescriptions.

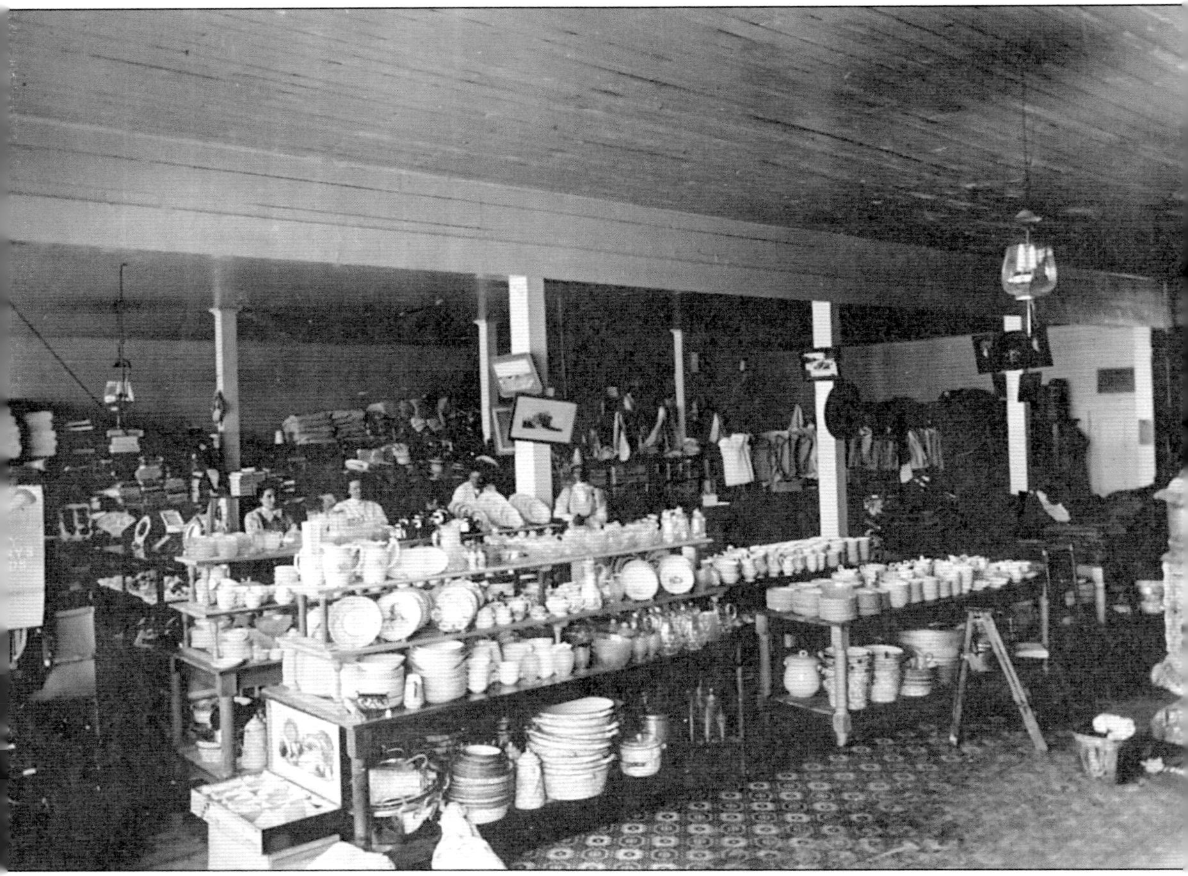

Pictured here is McLeod's Store in Manhattan around 1908. In the early 20th century, general stores offered a wide range of merchandise and played an important role in the life of small, rural towns where shopping options were limited. Bozeman, some 20 miles distant, was too far away for many Manhattan families to routinely frequent during the pre-automobile era. Large stacks of fine and everyday china, as well as ordinary kitchenware, are front and center in McLeod's Store. A closer look reveals seeds, clothing of various kinds, linens, books, framed photographs, trinkets and other items visible in the background. Four unidentified persons stand in the store, and a wood stove is visible in the bottom right-hand corner. Despite the signs of modernity on the shelves of McLeod's, telephone and electricity had yet to arrive in town.

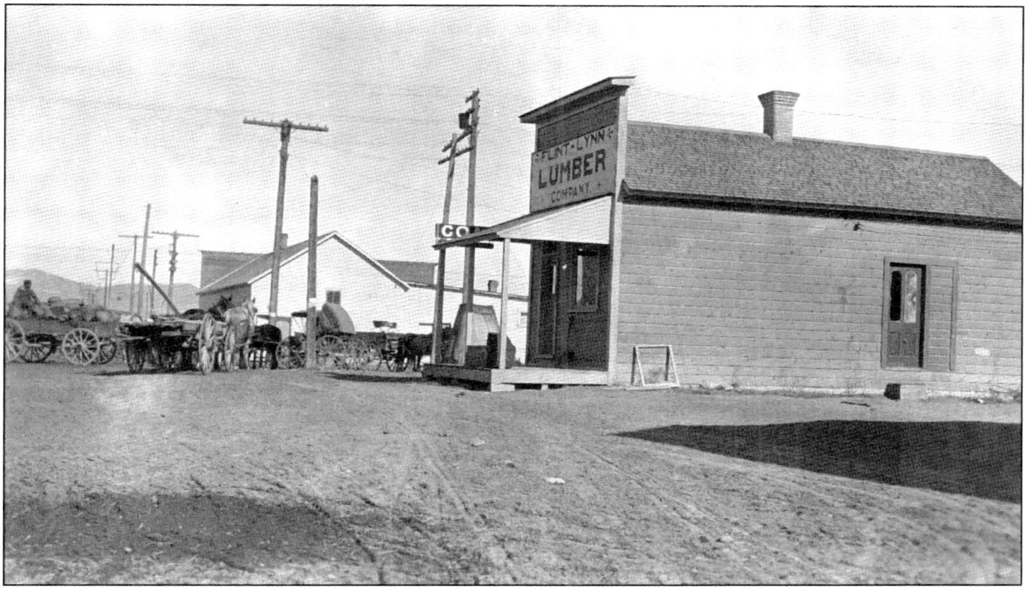

In addition to agriculture, natural resources helped spur Montana's growth in the early 20th century. Pictured in this early photograph is the Flint–Lynn Lumber Company, sellers of wood products, as well as coal. Teams of horses and wagons and one buggy are parked near the store. A huge chunk of coal sits on the porch, and telephone and electrical lines are prominent.

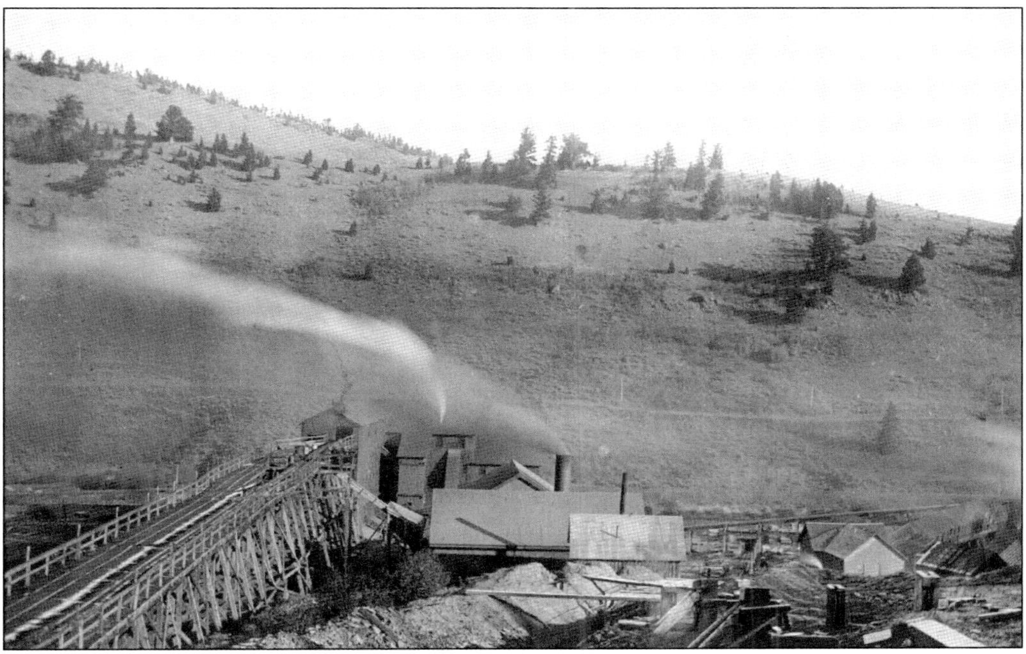

Home to many coal deposits, Montana was earnestly mining the substance for heating homes and powering steam engines by the late 19th century. A number of coal mines operated east of Bozeman, with the heyday of coal taking place during 1890 to 1910. The Kountz Coal Mine in the vicinity of Manhattan, pictured here about 1900, operated briefly in the shadow of more well-known operations.

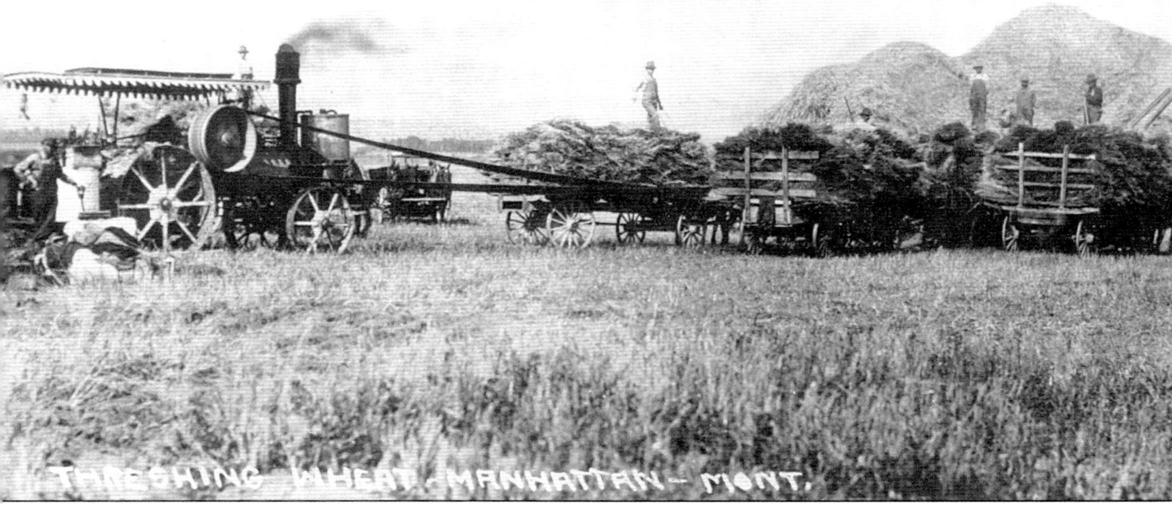

The Prohibition era of the 1920s and 1930s led area farmers to look to crops other than malting barley. For some, wheat proved to be a viable alternative. In this 1925 photograph, the wheat harvest looks promising. Modern threshing machinery enabled farmers to more quickly and easily separate the grain from the stalks and husks. While the first threshing machine was invented in 1784, early versions were very small, hand fed, and powered by horses. The same basic design was used through the 19th century with some improvements. By the close of the 19th century, threshing machinery utilized a cylinder and a concave (curved cylinder) to beat the grain and a series of sieves to separate the cleaned grain from the chaff and incomplete grain. The machine pictured here is operated by diesel. Nonetheless, horses still played a role at harvest time. A close look reveals that the wagons are pulled by teams of horses.

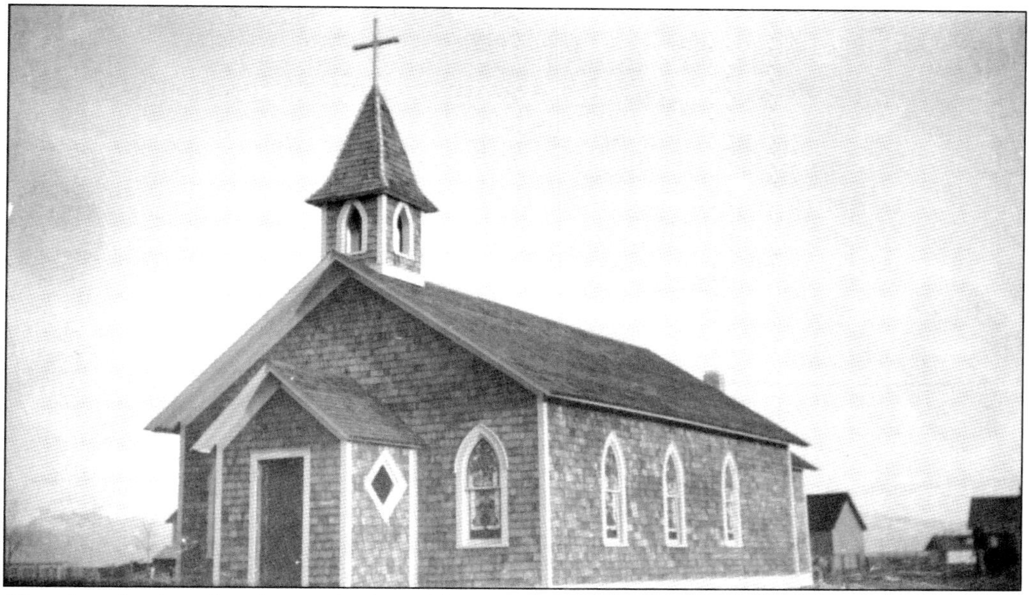

Churches developed and grew slowly in Montana due to the harsh nature of the western frontier and the distance from established religious structures. Pictured above is the Gethsemane Episcopal Church of Manhattan, an early church in the area. Episcopal worship services began in Hamilton at John Potter's General Store, led by Bozeman priest Thomas E. Dickey.

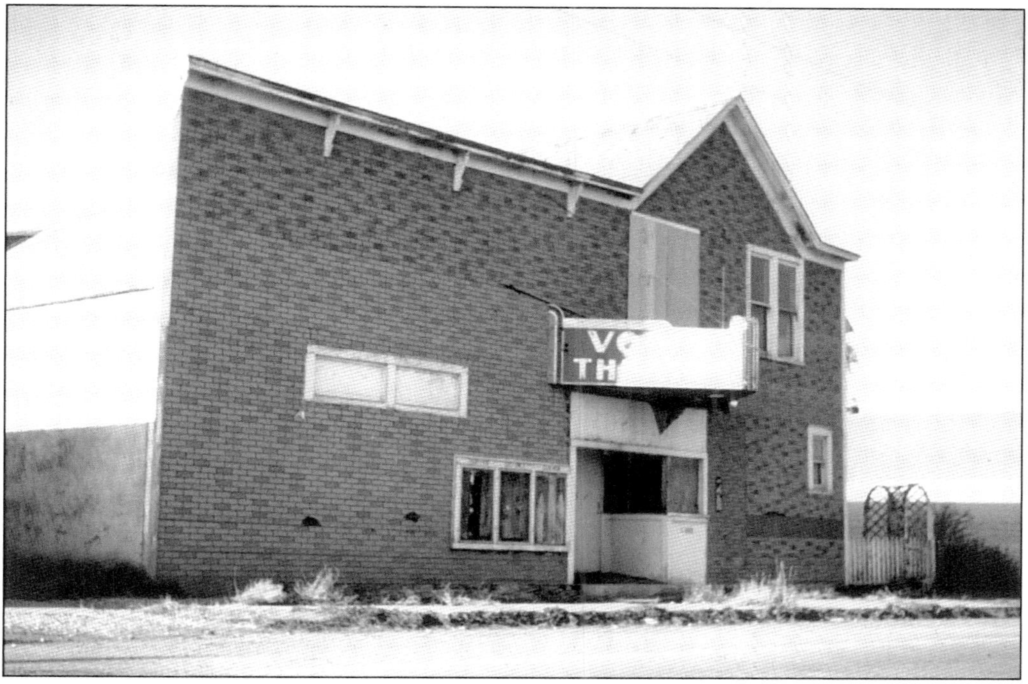

The Manhattan Theater building, seen here, offered a variety of movies to the community, often showing several movies during a given week. Introduced in America in the early 20th century, by the mid-century, movies had become a staple of American entertainment in communities large and small.

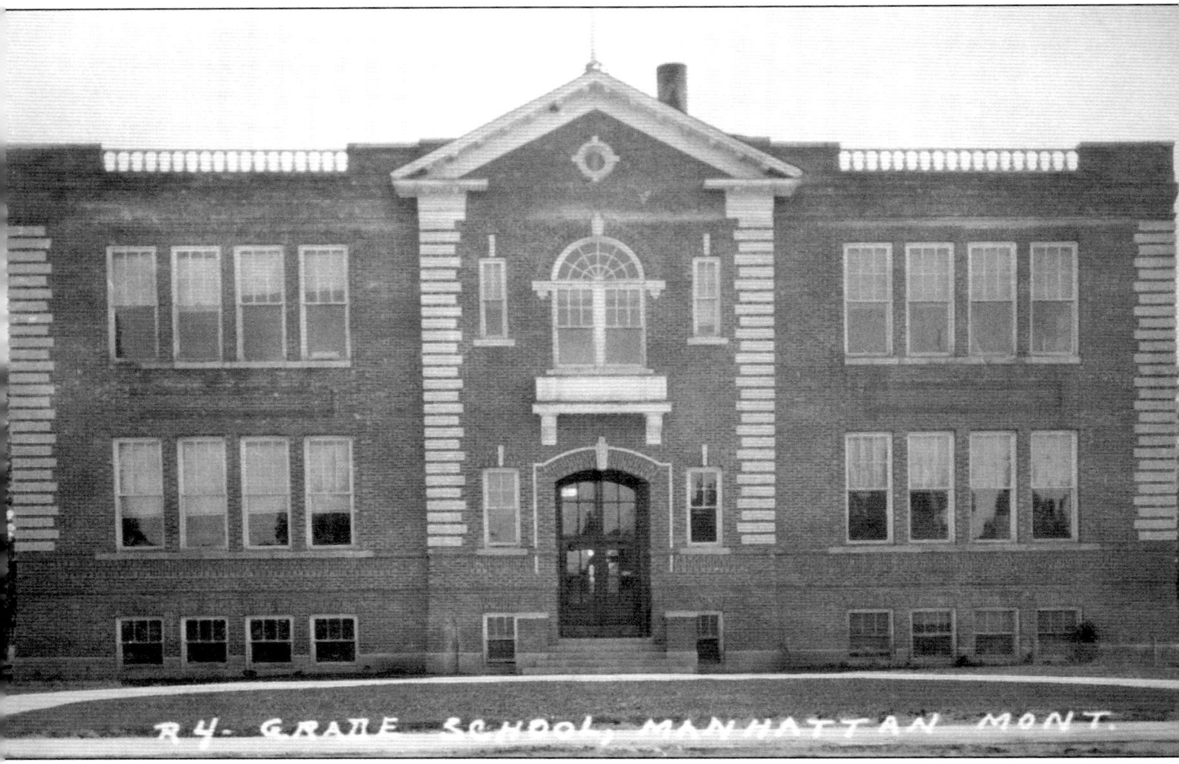

Education of children was a concern and priority of Manhattan's families, even before the town obtained its name from New York investors. The town's first public school, a small wooden building, was built in 1890. Rapid growth quickly made the small school obsolete, and in 1896, a second building was completed on property owned by Henry Verwolf. By 1914, yet another, bigger school building was needed, and that year, the town's third school opened. Unlike the previous two schoolhouses, the new facility was constructed of brick at a cost of $32,000.

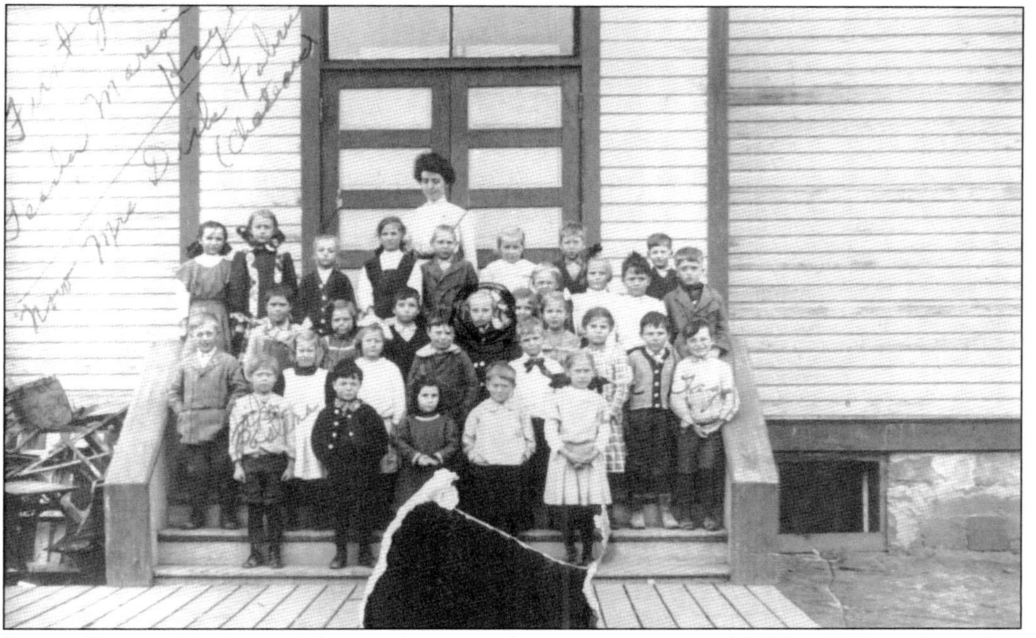

Pictured here is Manhattan's first grade class, taken sometime around 1911 or 1912, with teacher Marian Hoyt (also known as Mrs. Dick Fabrick). Reba Grover is circled in this photograph, while Tony Grover is marked far right in the second row. The children are standing in front of the town's second school building.

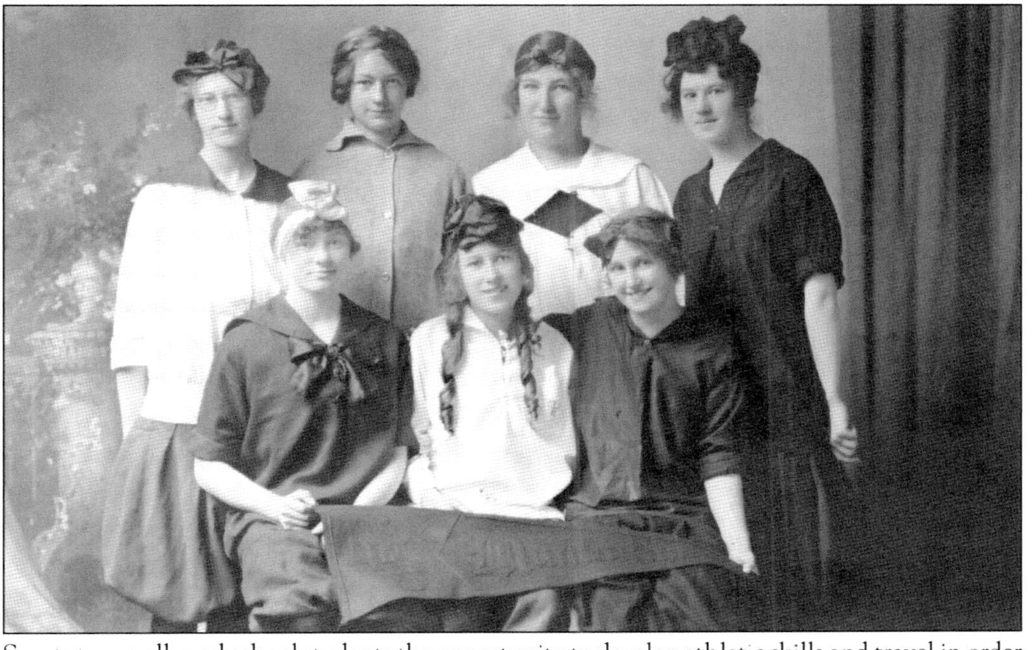

Sports teams allowed school students the opportunity to develop athletic skills and travel in order to compete against other schools. Pictured above is Manhattan's first girls' high school basketball team. High school basketball, played indoors during the winter season, became a favored sport in many Montana communities of the early 20th century.

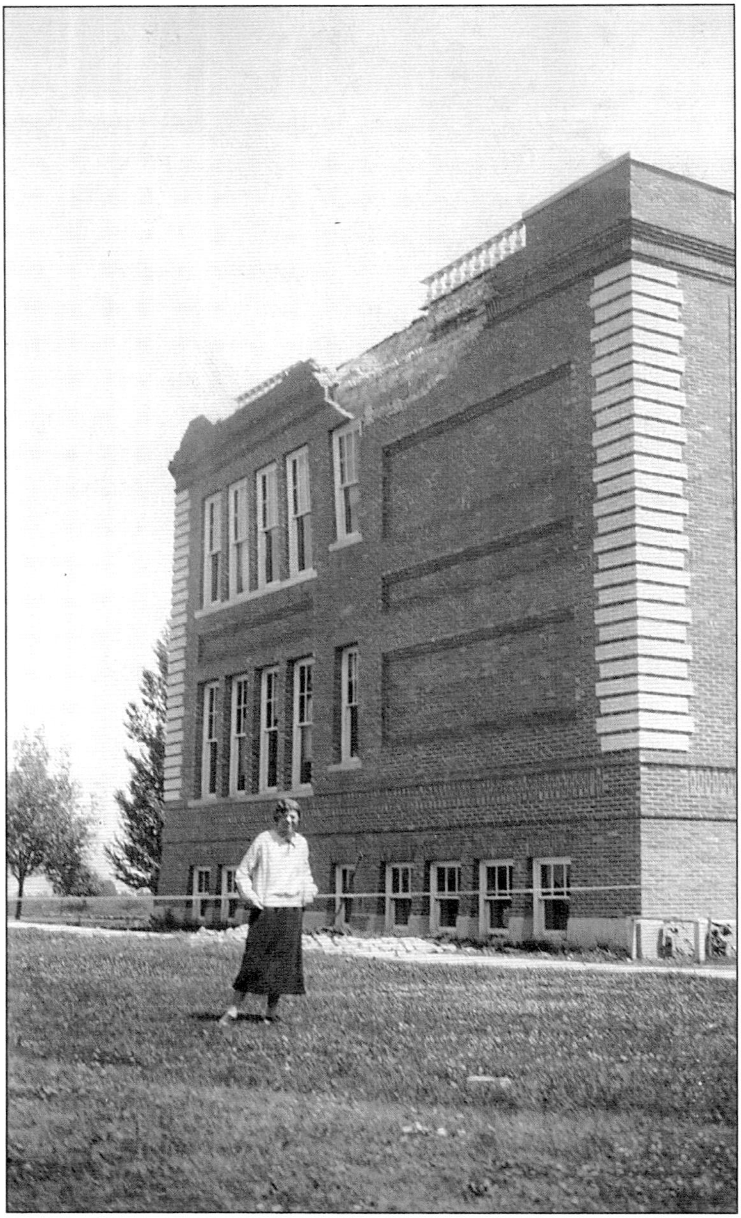

Montana is a seismically active state. The first major earthquake in Montana of the 20th century occurred on June 27, 1925. That day, a 6.6-magnitude quake struck southwestern Montana. Felt over a 500,000-square-mile area that stretched from North Dakota to Washington State, and from Calgary, Alberta (Canada), to central Wyoming, the quake caused damage in a 1,000-square-mile area. The towns of Manhattan, Logan, Three Forks, and Lombard suffered the greatest damage. Among the buildings most affected were school buildings. By 1925, many of Montana's schools were constructed of unreinforced brick. While seemingly sturdy, they proved susceptible to the ground movements caused by earthquakes. The Manhattan Public School, pictured here, crumbled during the 1925 quake. In the image, school superintendent Lucille Quaw inspects damage to the school building.

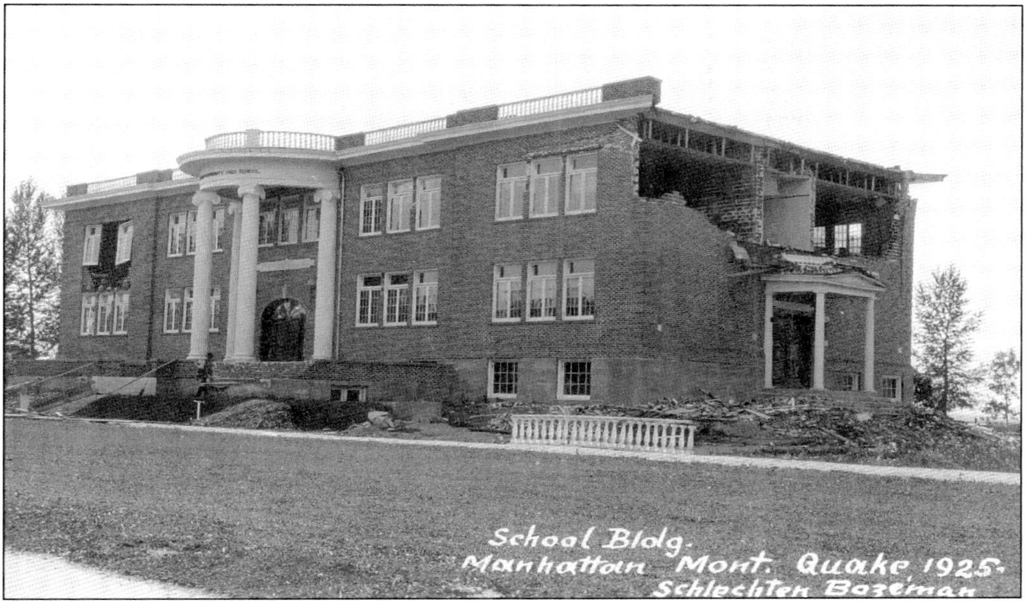

The Manhattan High School building sustained extensive damage during the earthquake on June 27, 1925. From this distance shot, a large portion of the upper wall has collapsed, as well as a smaller section of wall to the far left. Many windows are shattered, and debris litters the schoolyard.

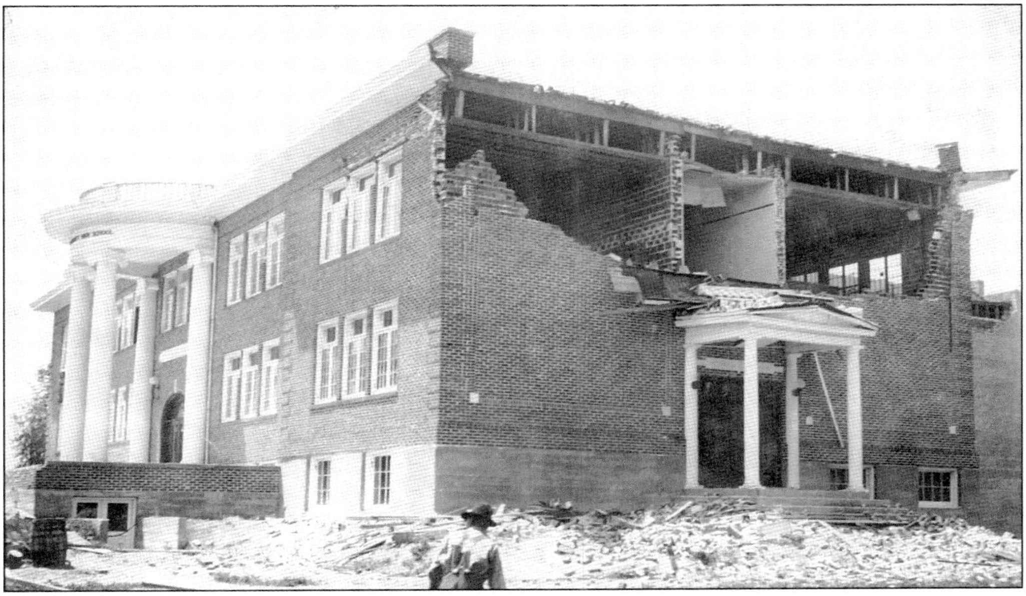

Upon closer inspection, the damage to the high school comes into greater focus. Much of the interior of the building is exposed, while additional damage can be seen to the upper far right, and a crack runs along the front of the building. Also, the debris on the ground is several feet deep. An unidentified man examines the damage.

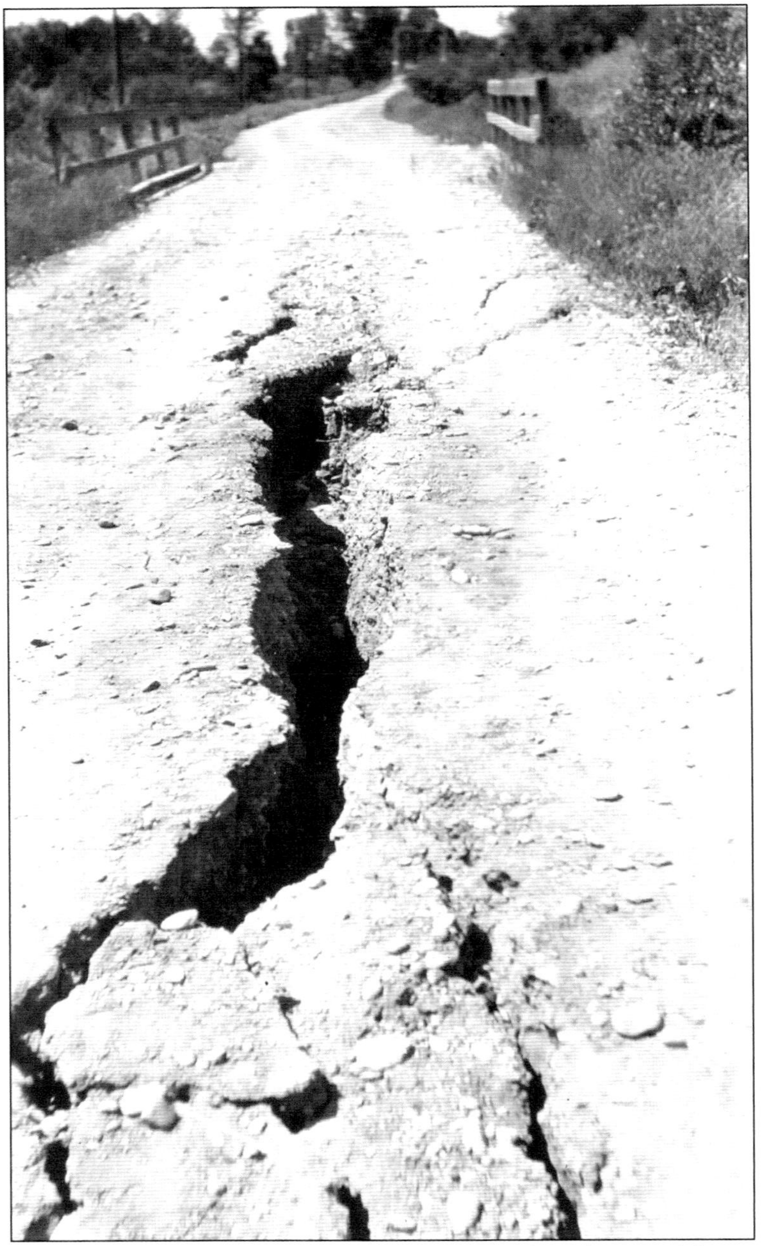

Centered between Bozeman and Helena, the June 27, 1925, earthquake caused damage throughout the town of Manhattan and the surrounding area. Prior to the quake, a lightning storm raged across Helena, and the force of the electrical bolts knocked six people to the ground. Many chimneys toppled from the shaking, and brick and mortar structures were damaged. Graded and filled roads, as well as pavement, cracked from the movement of the earth. Total damage to buildings in Manhattan and other towns was estimated to be from $150,000 to $300,000. The earthquake ranks among the worst in the United States during the 20th century in terms of damage to school buildings. Luckily, no deaths were reported, thanks to the timing of the quake, which took place while schools were out for summer break.

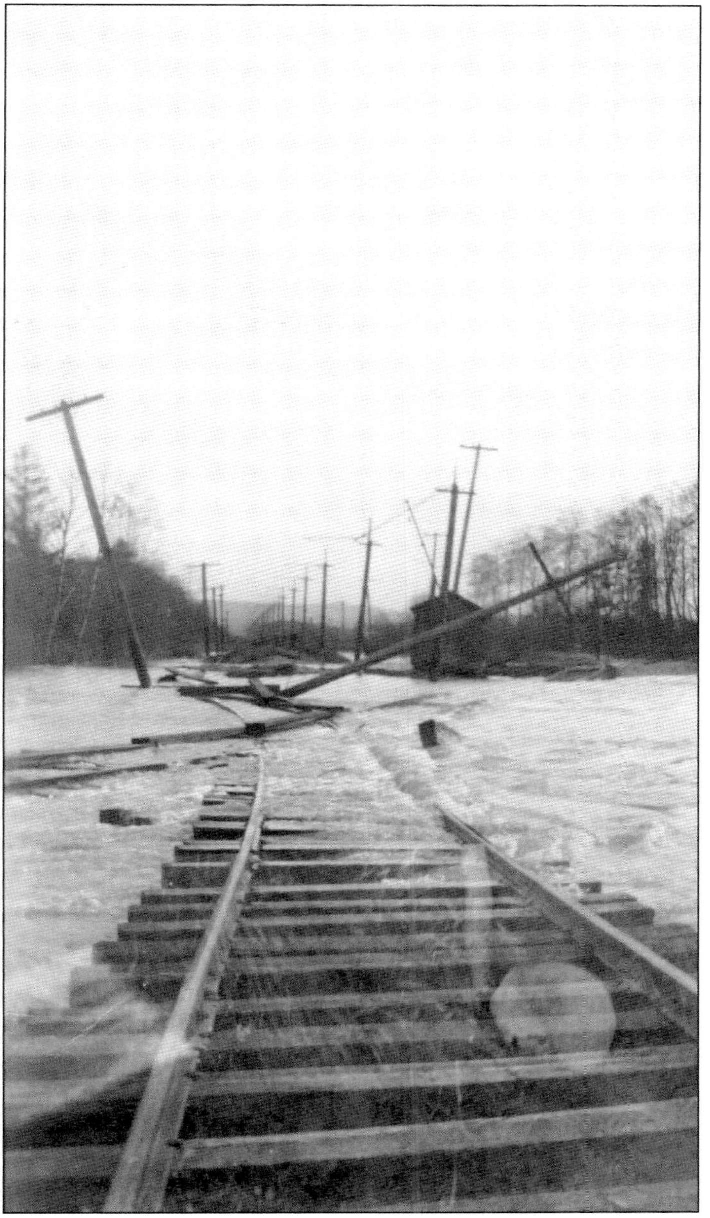

Rock falls and landslides also accompanied the 1925 earthquake. Some of the slides covered roads and blocked railroad tracks. In at least one instance, falling boulders narrowly missed a passing train, while in other cases, trains were forced to a standstill because of damaged tracks. Stretches of railway buckled, as evidenced in this photograph. The damage to the rails was extensive, requiring about $1 million in repairs. While the quake, centered 5.5 miles underground, is believed to have occurred along the Clarkston Valley fault, post-quake investigations were unable to identify the primary surface fault rupture. The repercussions of the earthquake were immediate. The day following, the first earthquake policy in Montana was written, taken out by the First National Bank of Missoula. Within a week, damaged Manhattan railroad tracks were restored.

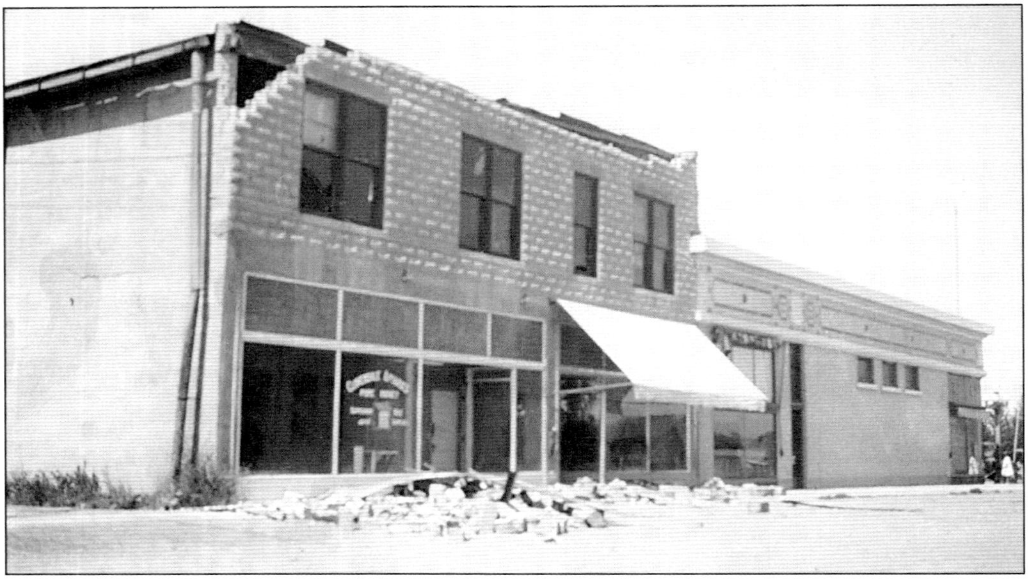

The 1925 earthquake also damaged a number of stores in Manhattan. Pictured here is the Cloverdale Apiary, from which chunks of the building fell to the sidewalk and street below; several windows were also shattered. In addition to selling "pure honey" to Manhattan residents, the apiary also sold beekeeping supplies to area folk.

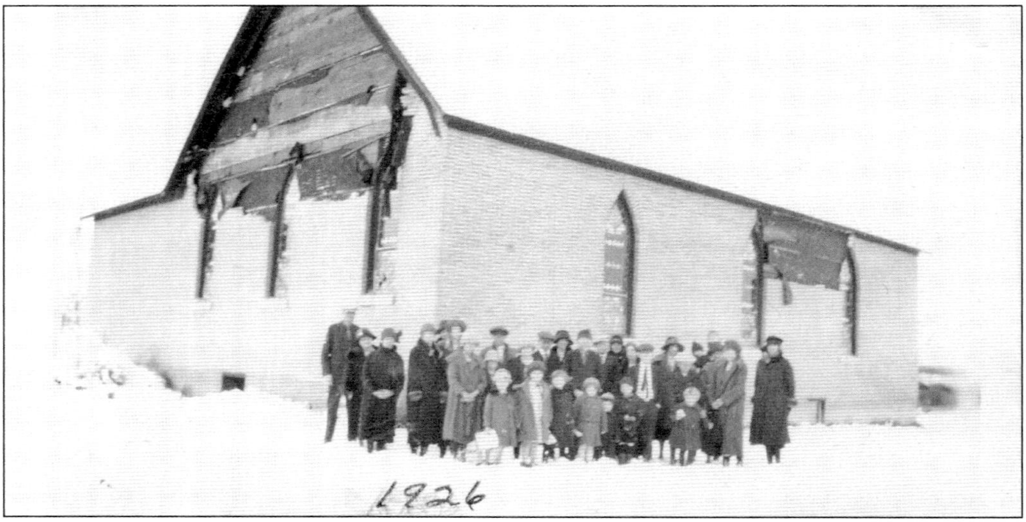

Churches throughout southwestern Montana, many of which were constructed from brick, were also damaged in the earthquake. In this image, members of Manhattan's Baptist Church, dressed in Sunday attire and standing in the snow, pose in front of their damaged church building months after the quake. Large chunks of the church's brick exterior fell away from the structure during the quake.

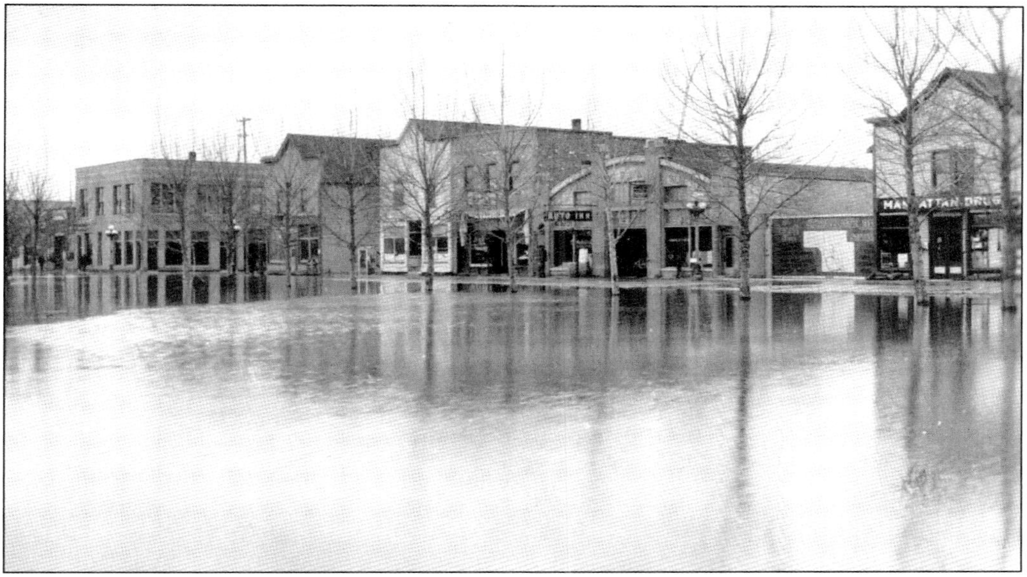

While frightening and capable of causing extensive damage, earthquakes were rare and less troublesome than spring flooding, which could disrupt the lives of residents any given year. One such flood occurred on March 9, 1928, deluging the streets of Manhattan. The bank is to the far left of this photograph, the Manhattan Drug Company to the far right, and the Auto Inn in the middle.

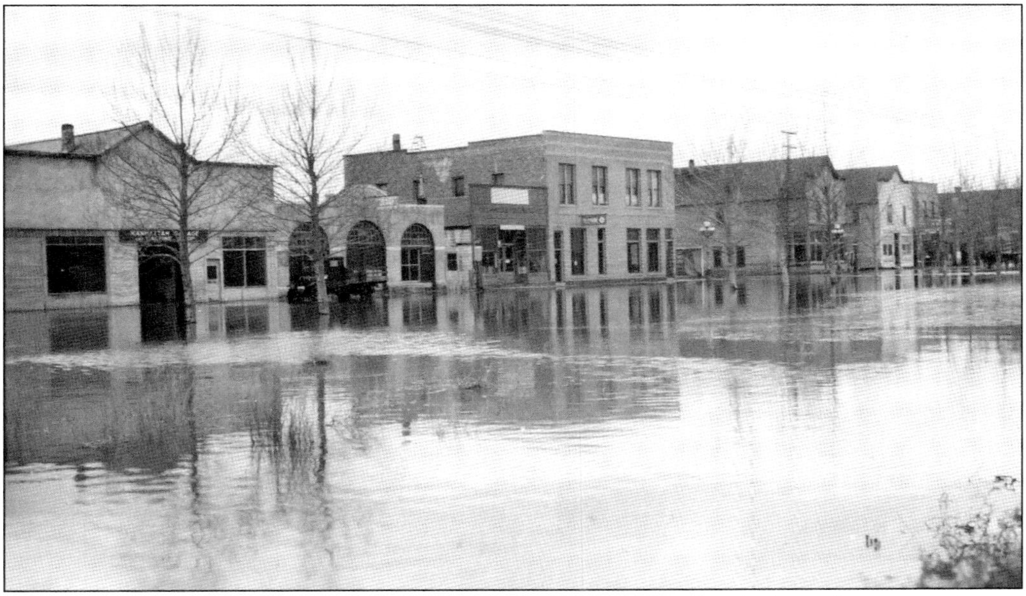

A rapid warming spell and the resulting snowmelt triggered the flood of March 9, 1928. Here, a lone automobile is parked near the Manhattan Garage as floodwaters cover the street. The scene otherwise appears devoid of life. Visible in the middle is the Manhattan telephone building. A number of storefront buildings were flooded.

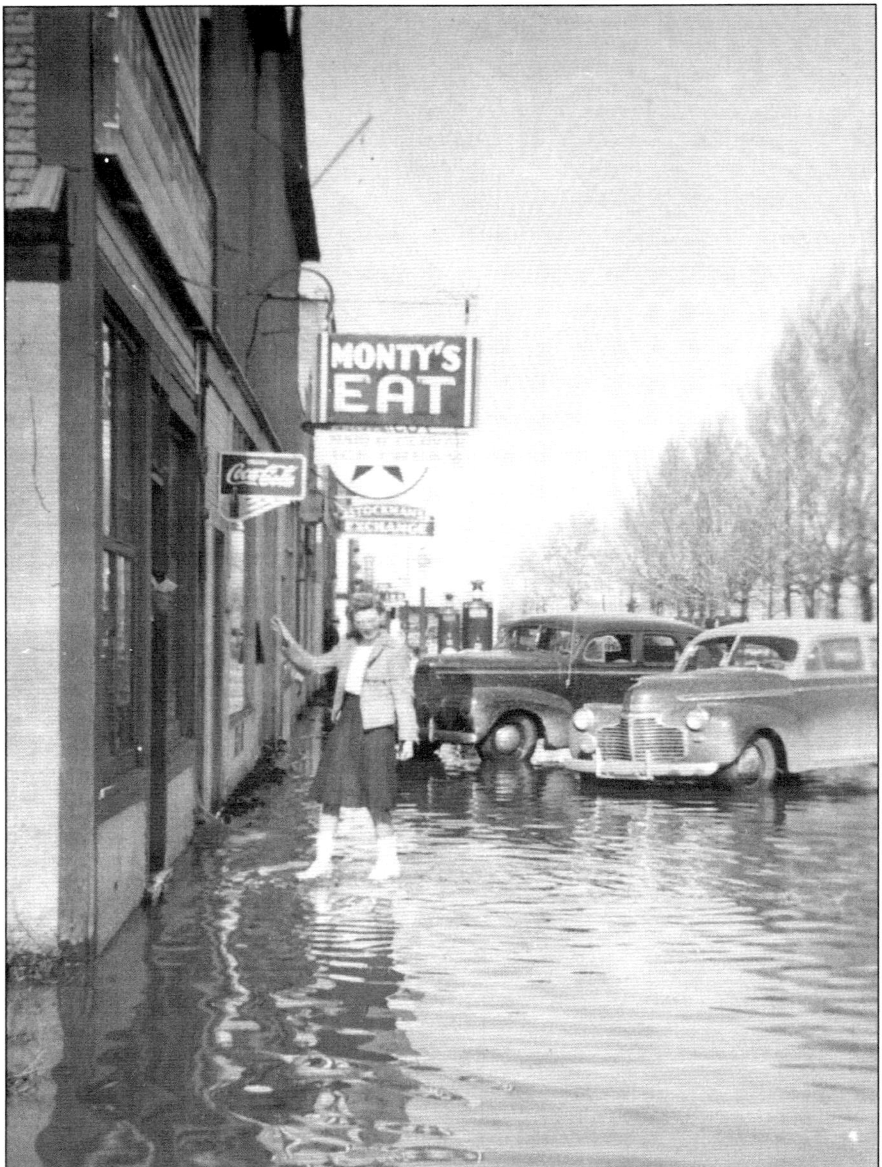

Pictured here is another flood in the town of Manhattan, this one taking place in 1945. Several inches of water cover the street and sidewalk as an unidentified woman walks through the water wearing rain boots on her way to Monty's restaurant. Beyond the cars parked at the curb is the Stockman's Exchange, as well as several Texaco gas pumps. During the mid-century, spring floods continued to be a problem in the Gallatin Valley. Another notable flood in the region had occurred in 1938, and the decades following would witness numerous other flooding events. Deep snowpacks in the nearby mountains, while potentially portending a good stock of summer water for crop irrigation and fish populations, could quickly turn treacherous if several weeks of unusually warm weather hovered over the region between the months of March and early June. While deaths from flooding in Montana were rare, damage to homes and businesses were common.

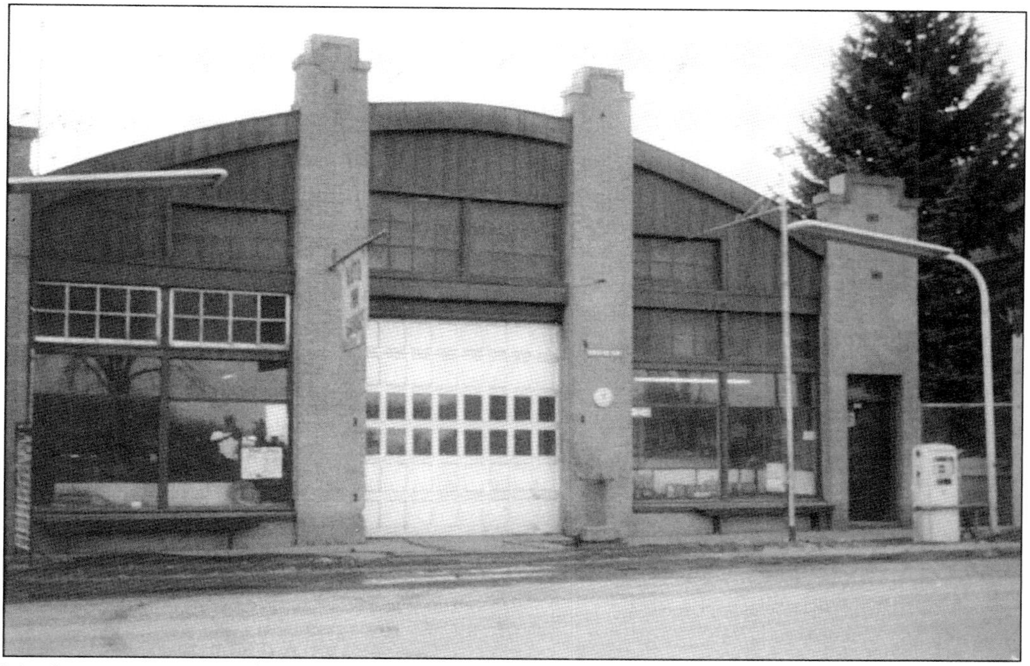

Manhattan's Auto Inn, founded in 1915, underwent several incarnations over the decades. Central to the life of Montana's communities by the 1930s, automobiles provided both transportation and new business opportunities for Manhattan entrepreneurs, of which automobile repair, maintenance, and fueling were the most common. In a similar fashion to the Auto Inn, other buildings in Manhattan housed a variety of businesses during the course of many years.

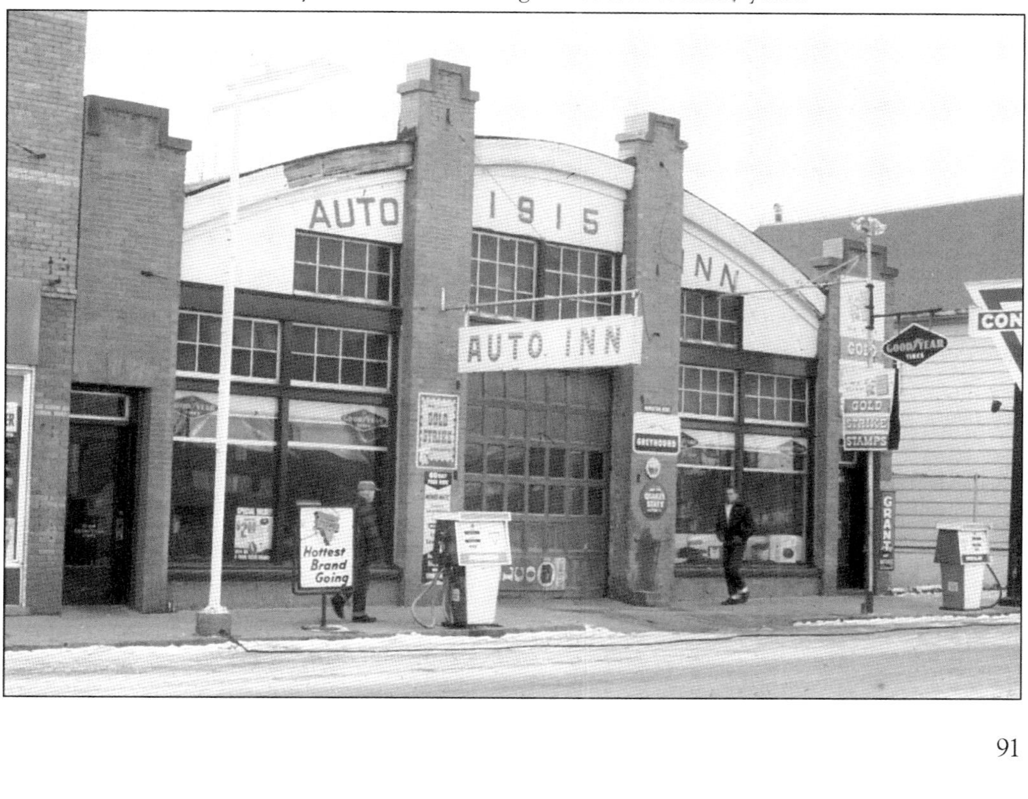

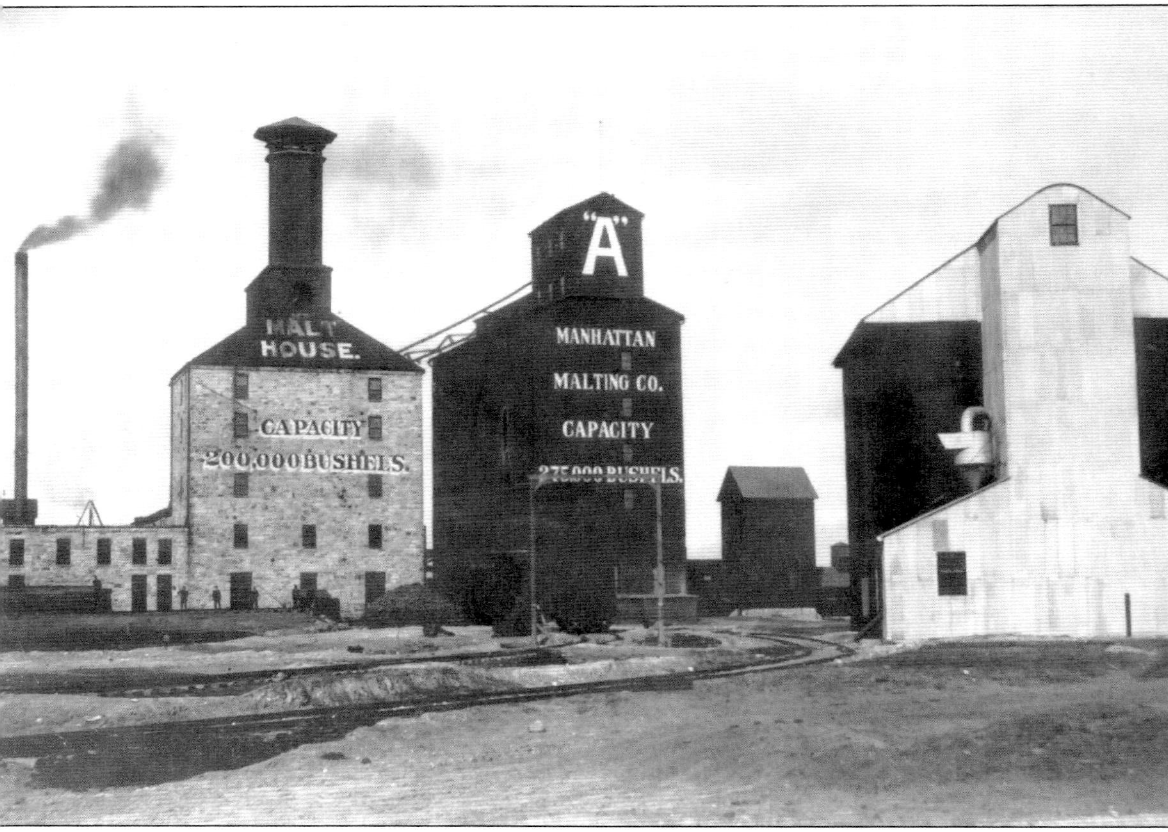

Pictured here are the facilities of the Manhattan Malting Company, the business that built the town of Manhattan. The New York City principals of the company were Henry Altenbrand Sr., president and a maltster; Jacob Rupert, vice president and owner of the largest brewery in the world; John C. Gillig, treasurer; Frank Merges, secretary; and George Kinkel Jr., manager and son of the owner of the New York Yankees baseball team. Most of the officers were members of New York City's Democratic Manhattan Club, hence the reason for their changing the name of the town from Moreland to Manhattan in 1890. The first grain elevator was completed in 1892. The malting plant, completed in 1893, was built with granite blocks quarried near Butte.

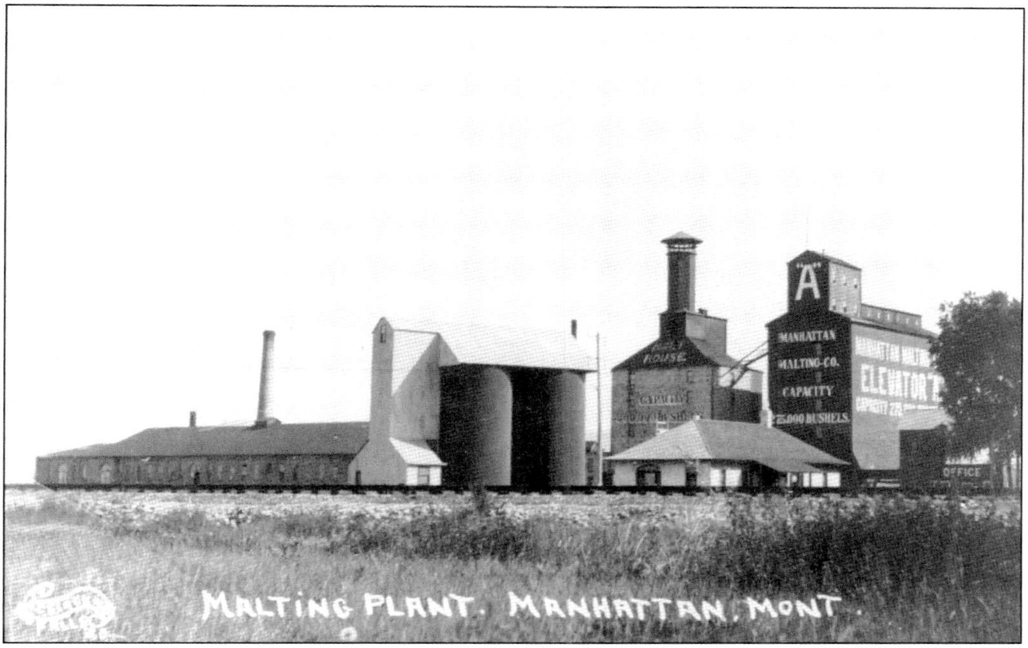

By the time this 1910 photograph was taken, the Manhattan Malting Company was comprised of three elevators that could store 625,000 bushes of grain—525,000 for barley storage, with the remaining capacity for wheat. The elevators pictured on the far right were for storing barley, while the wheat elevator is pictured in the center. To the forefront and center right is the residence of company president Henry Altenbrand.

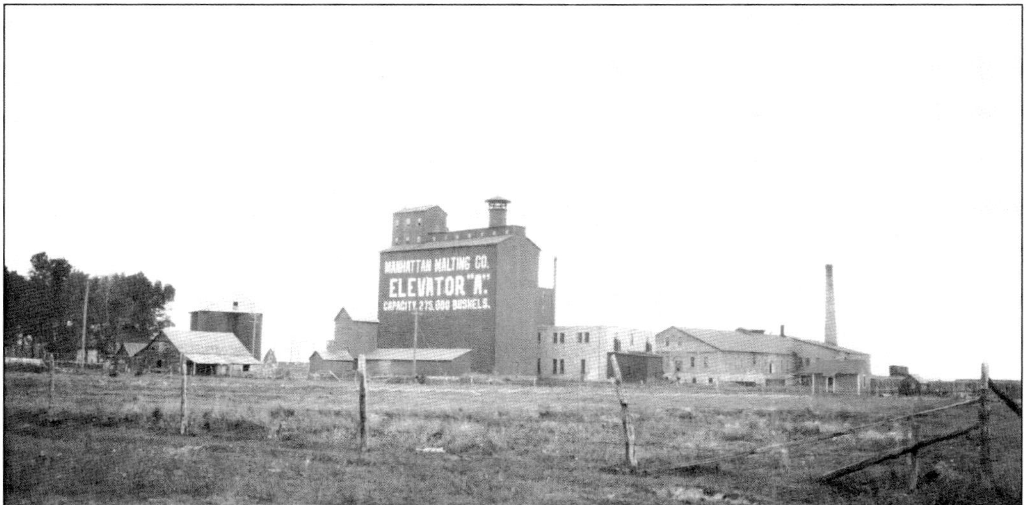

In the center of this picture is one of the barley elevators. Barley was processed in the malting plant. Hosed with water and placed in drums that rotated every 55 minutes, the barley was eventually heated to 240 degrees Fahrenheit in order to dry it out. Operating with a 10-man crew, the malting house produced 225,000 bushels of malt annually, shipping the final product throughout the country and to Europe and Australia; however, most of the barley was shipped from Manhattan in raw form to destinations worldwide.

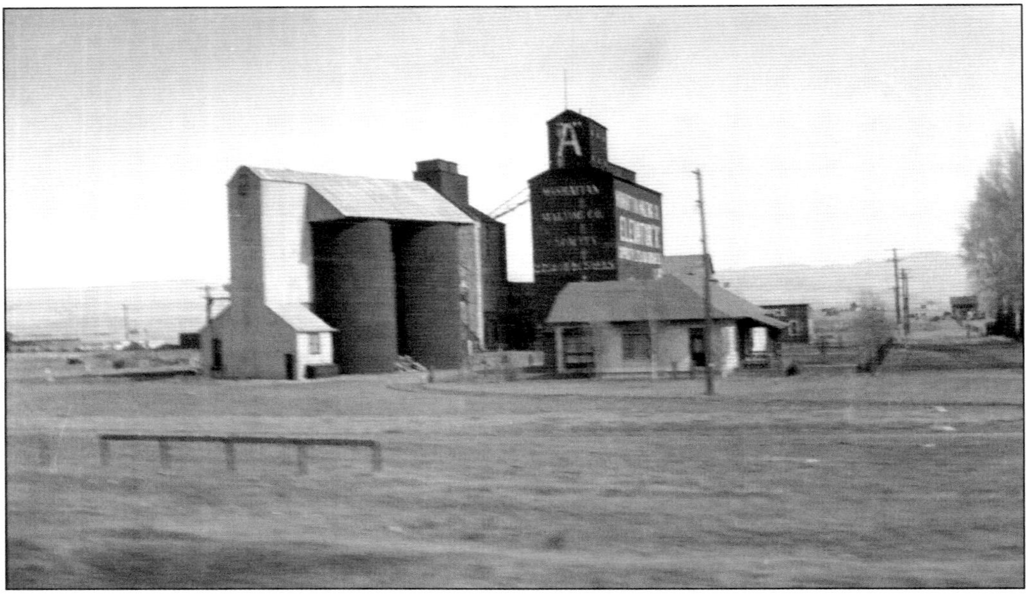

By 1907, the Manhattan Malting Company processed 36 million pounds of barley and oats. Barley remained the primary crop, and malt was the largest export product until Prohibition. The malting plant closed in 1915 in the wake of the nearby states of Idaho, Oregon, and Washington adopting Prohibition. After alcohol was banned on the federal level in 1919, the Manhattan Malting Company shut its doors entirely. The 1925 earthquake damaged the malt house, after which the building was torn down.

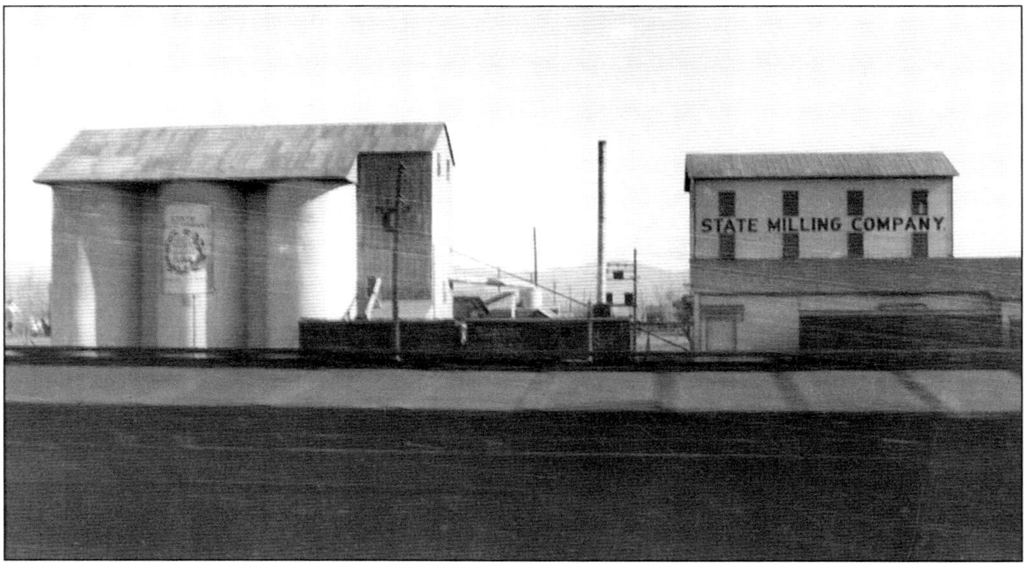

Wheat grew in importance in the wake of the demise of the barley market. Grain remained integral to the life of Manhattan and the surrounding area. Pictured here is the State Milling Company.

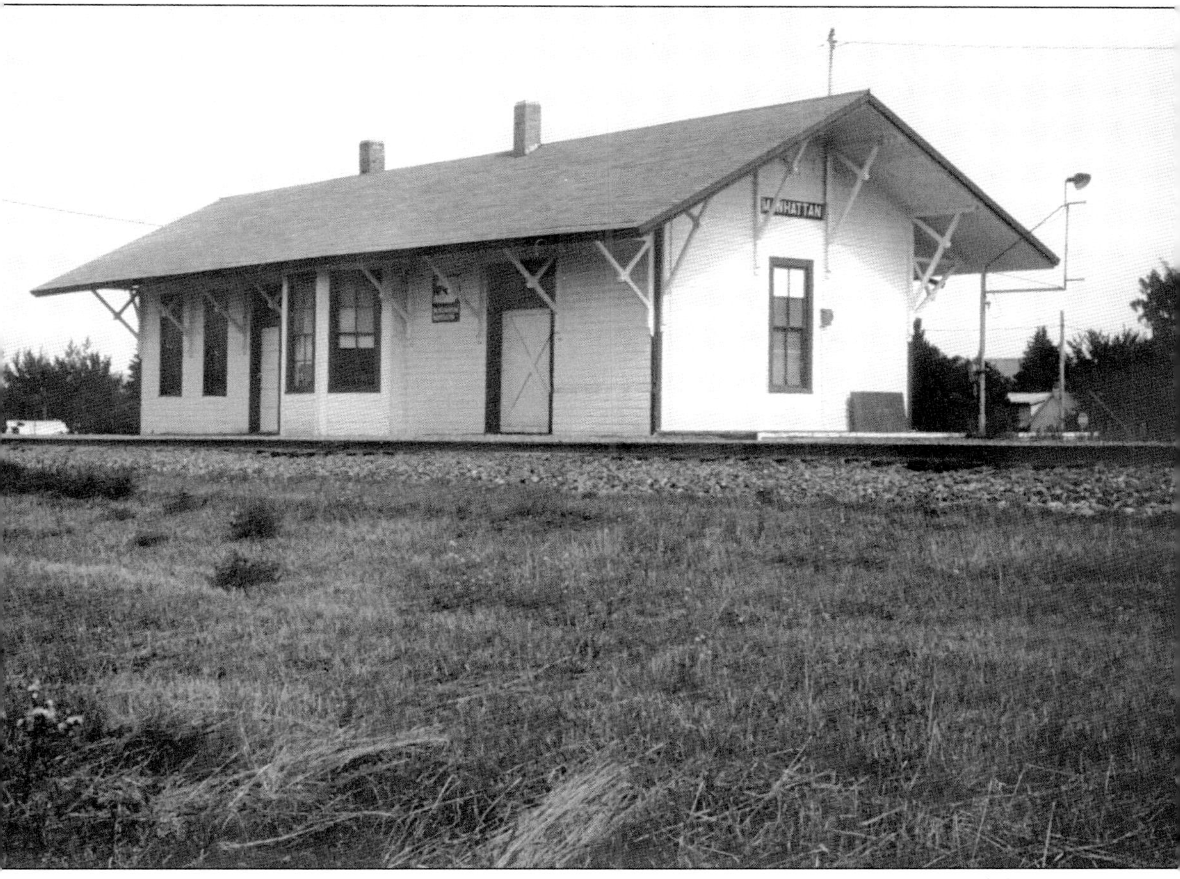

The Northern Pacific Railway built and maintained a depot in Manhattan, one of several depots in the area, including Belgrade to the east and Three Forks to the west. While Manhattan itself was not a popular tourist destination, many visitors en route to or from Yellowstone or Glacier national parks traversed the rails through town.

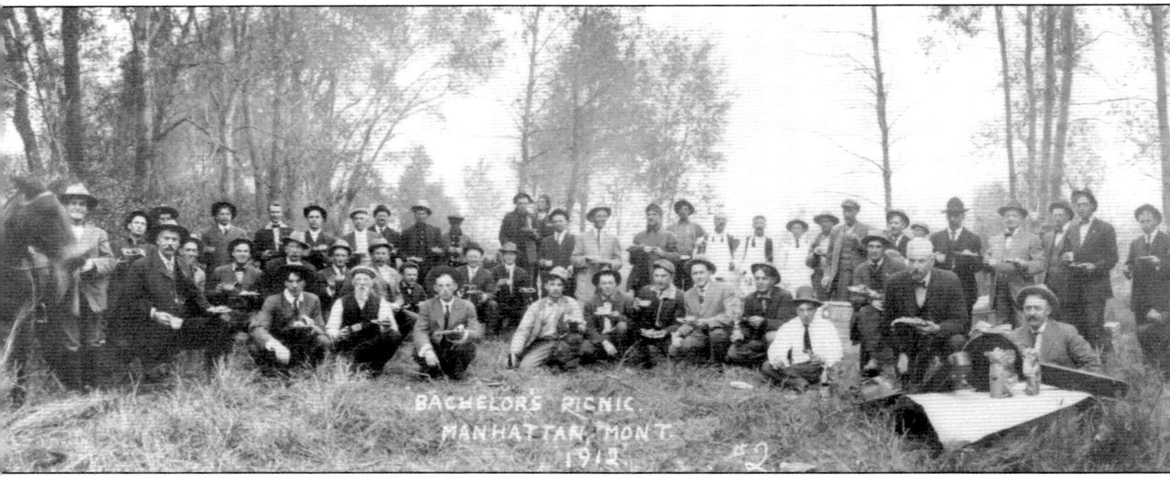

Life in rural areas on the western frontier remained rugged into the 20th century, attracting many single men. In 1910, Manhattan's Bachelor Club held its first picnic, attended by 61 eligible men. This 1912 photograph is of the second club picnic, at which some 50 men were present. Note the contrast of the wooded setting and the formal attire.

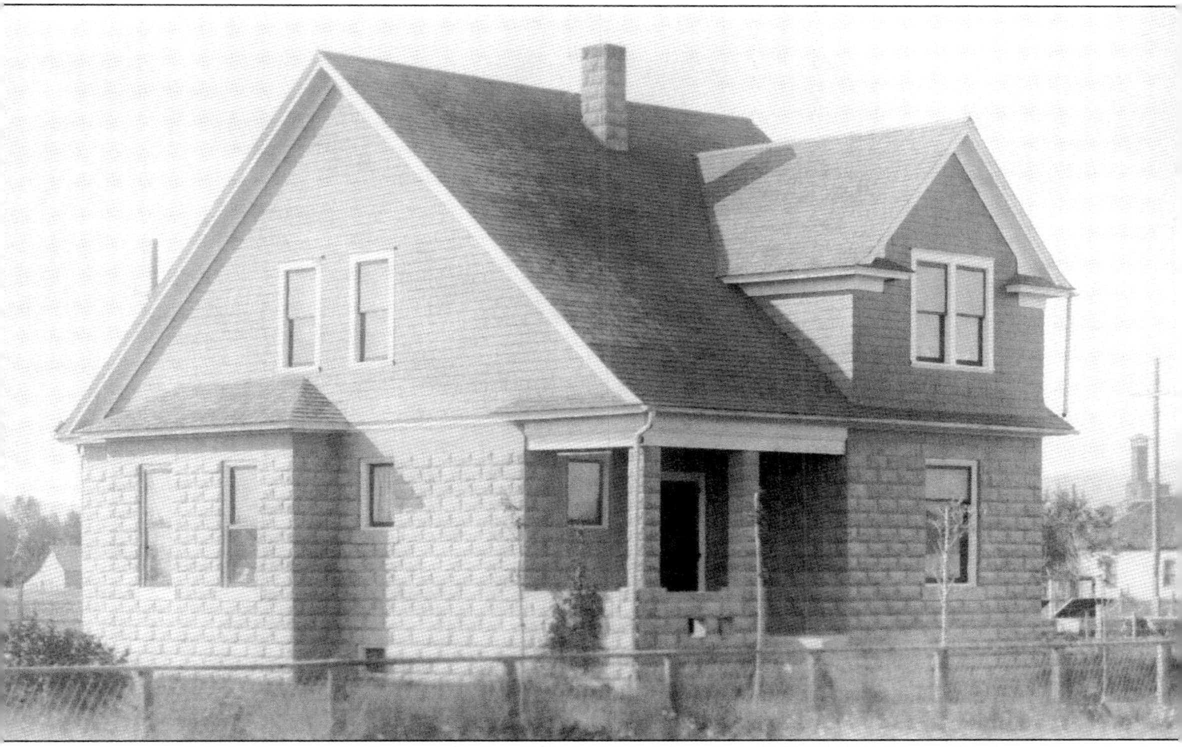

Pictured here is the home of Harry and Elva White, located on South Fifth Street in Manhattan. Harry, an early resident of the Gallatin Valley, grew up in the community of Hamilton, Manhattan's predecessor. A humorous story about Harry revolved around Kid Johnstone, the aforementioned colorful Manhattan character. Unknowingly lured into one of Johnstone's lion's cages, he was recruited to assist Johnstone in pulling the lion's eyeteeth. The Whites purchased the two-story, concrete-block house on May 18, 1912.

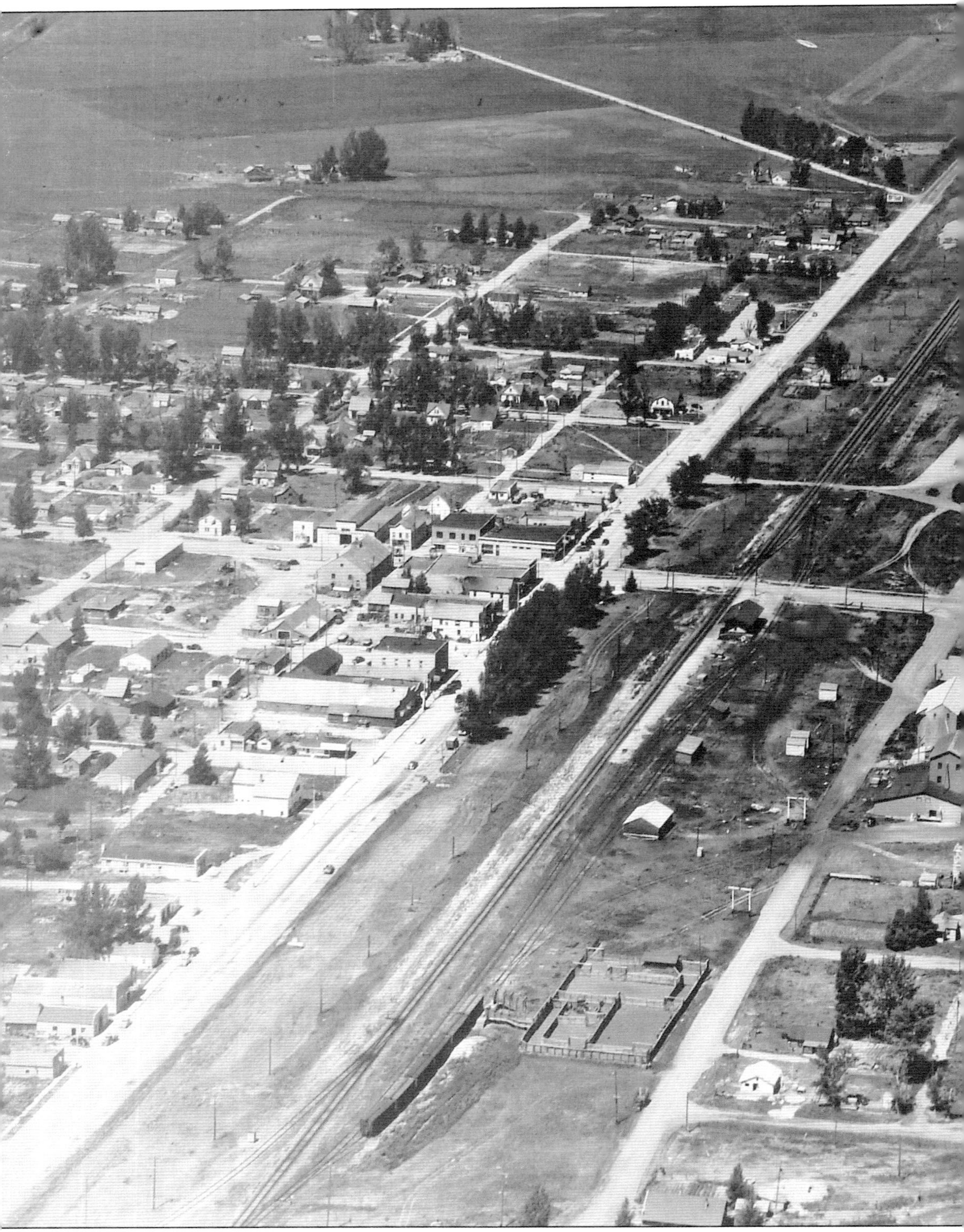

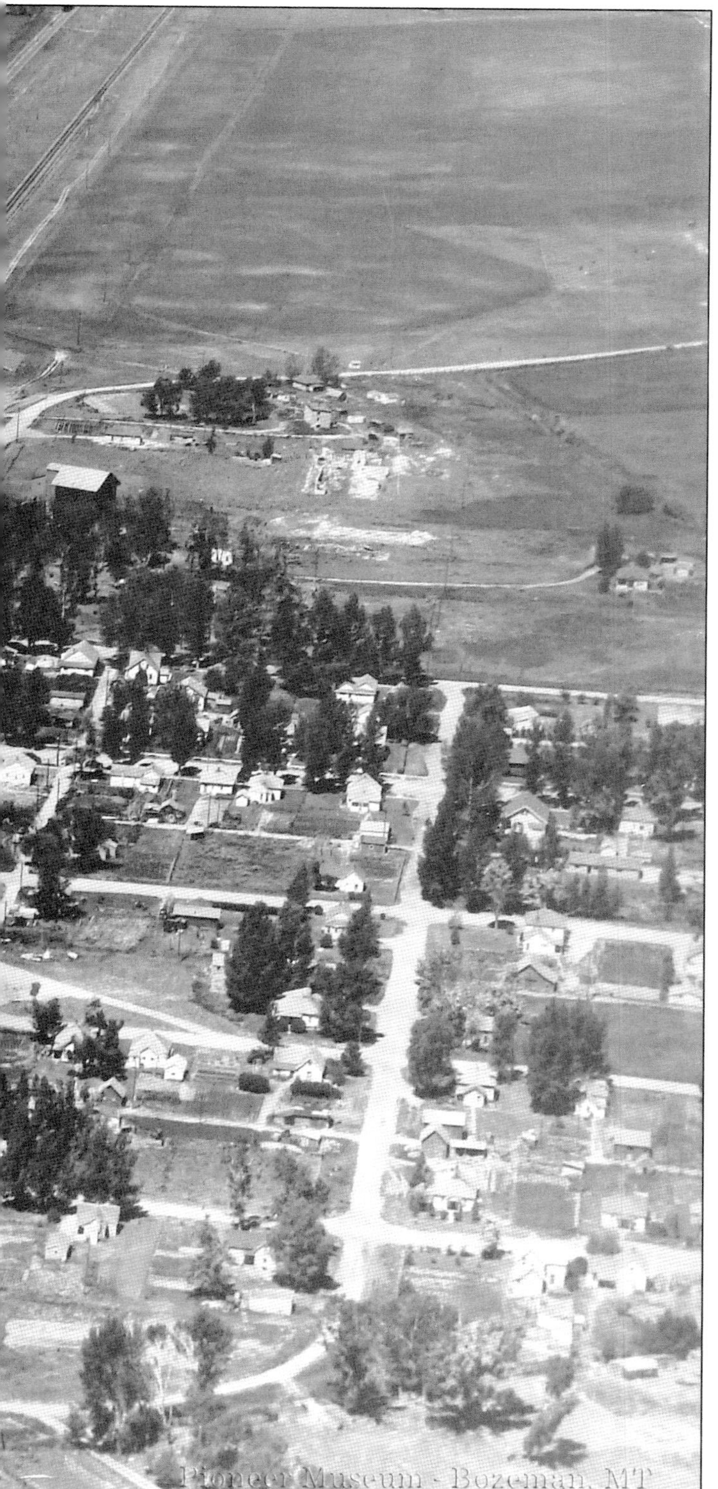

In this pre-1940 aerial view of the town of Manhattan, the business district (to the left of the railroad tracks) and many residences are visible. Both businesses and residences are set apart from the railroad, which retained considerable right-of-way. The trees pictured were mostly planted by residents, partly as a shelter from blowing winter snows and partly as a reminder of the greenery that many residents—most of whom, in the early days, hailed from the Eastern United States, Midwest United States, or Denmark—remembered with fondness from their earlier homes.

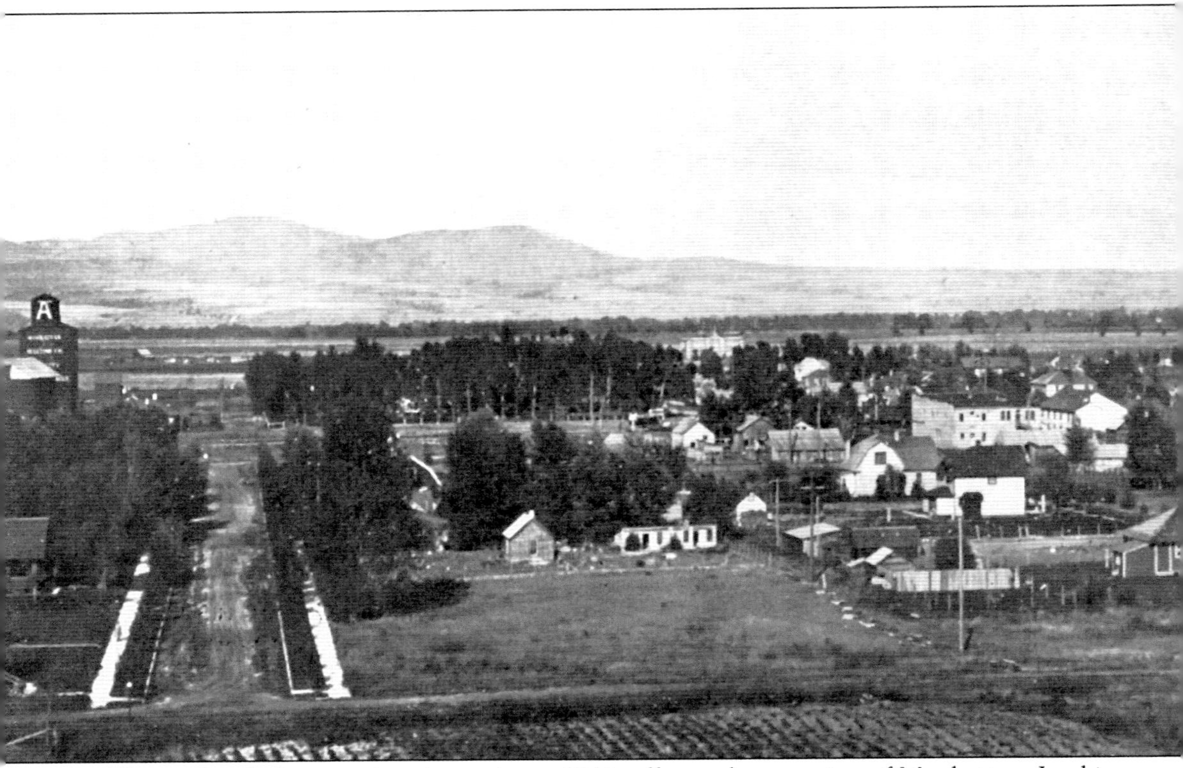

This undated photograph, taken prior to 1940, offers a close-up view of Manhattan. Looking northward from the vantage of the railroad tracks (not visible), the Manhattan Malting Company buildings are visible to the far left, while the westernmost ridges of the Bridger Mountains tower in the far background. The streets are unpaved, and a church is visible in the lower right corner. A variety of residences, from simple to more elaborate, are nestled in the trees. The business district, not pictured, is on the near side of the railroad tracks. While some buildings would be torn down and others built in the coming decades, the basic layout of the town remained the same for years to come.

Four

Churchill and Amsterdam

The Holland Settlement

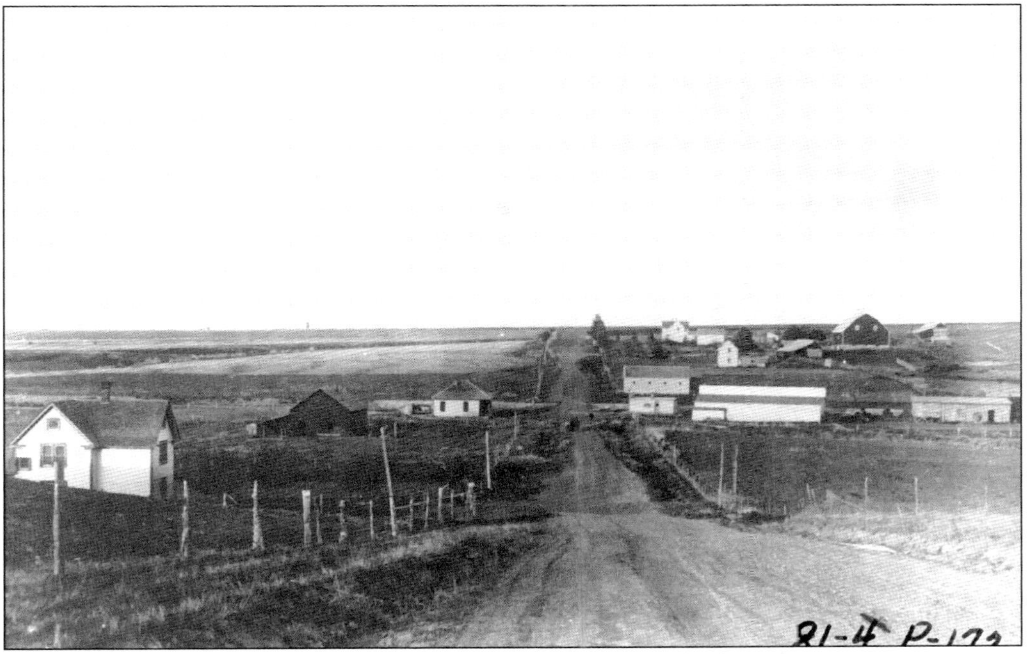

By the early 20th century, several Dutch families had settled south of Manhattan in a community called the Holland Settlement. Soon, the Holland Settlement area would take formal shape as the communities of Church Hill (eventually spelled Churchill) and Amsterdam, the latter formed in 1911 in order to accommodate the continued influx of Dutch immigrants. This 1912 view of Amsterdam faces west.

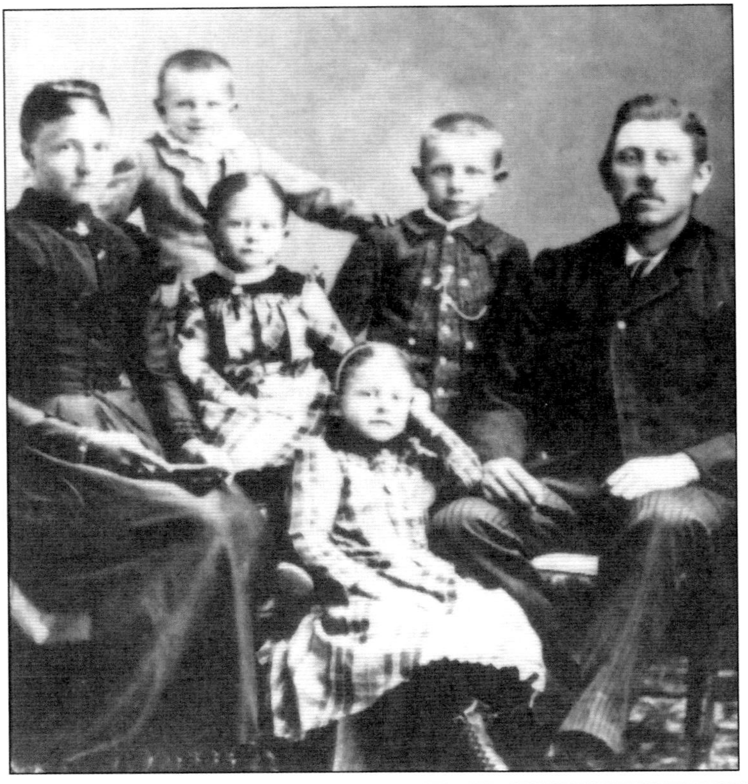

Among the earliest Dutch immigrants to the Holland Settlement area were Peter Alberda and his family, pictured here in this 1893 portrait. From left to right are mother Heina, children Henry, Elizabeth, Nellie, and William, and father Peter. Like many early settlers in the area, the Alberdas were from the Groningen province in the northern Netherlands. Others were originally from Friesland, another province in the northern Netherlands. The Holland Settlement would remain homogeneous for decades.

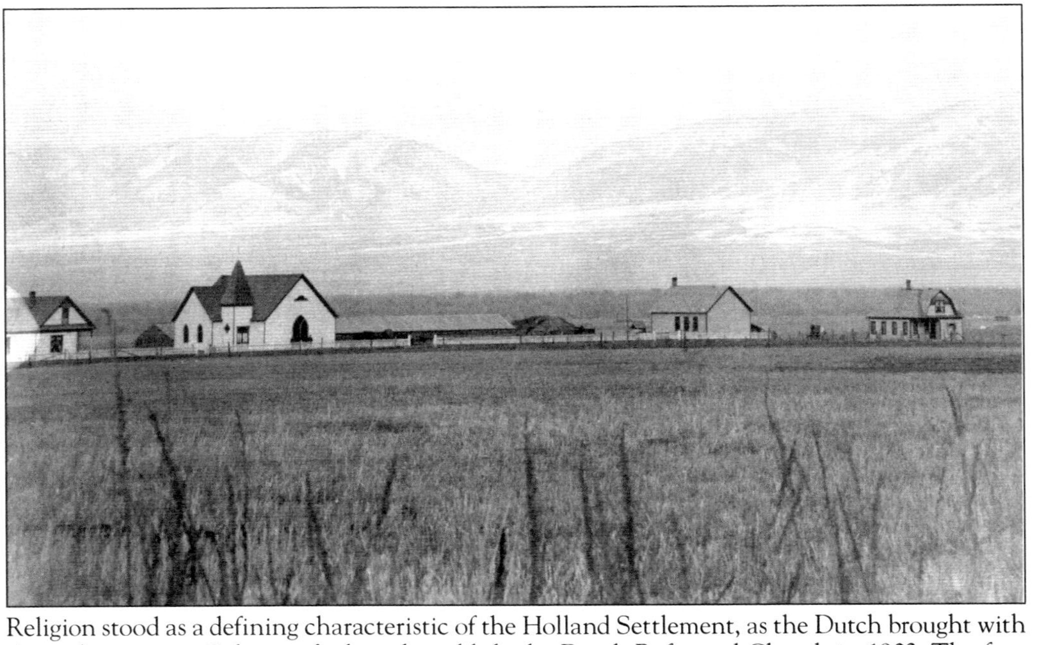

Religion stood as a defining characteristic of the Holland Settlement, as the Dutch brought with them their native Calvinist faith and established a Dutch Reformed Church in 1903. The four buildings pictured in the field in this 1904 photograph are, from left to right, a manse, church, school, and teacherage (teacher's house). An agricultural shed is behind the buildings.

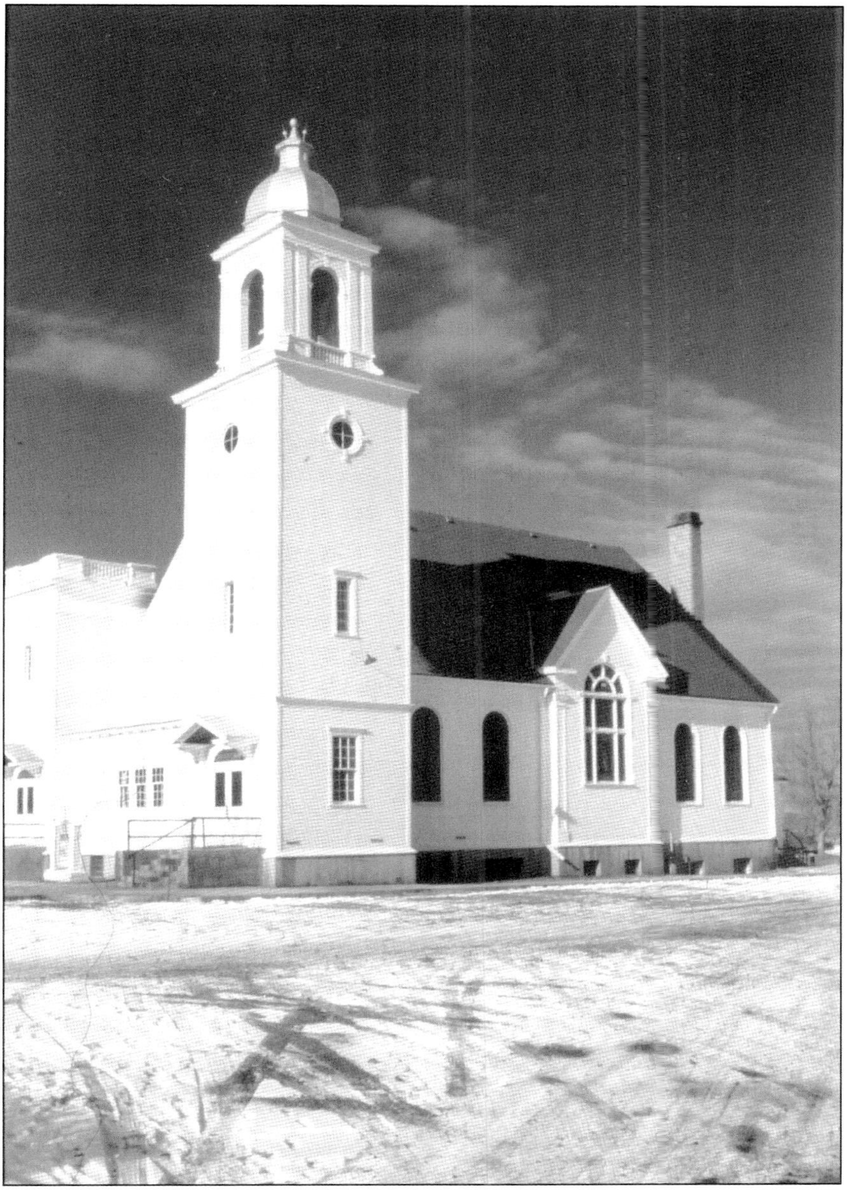

Presbyterians in the Gallatin Valley originally helped resettle Dutch immigrants in Manhattan and the Holland Settlement. Early church services in the settlement were held in Peter P. Van Dyken's homestead house under the direction of Rev. Andreas J. Wormser, a Presbyterian minister. However, Dutch Calvinism differed somewhat from the Calvinism of Presbyterians, leading to the establishment of the Dutch Reformed Church in the settlement, affiliated with the Christian Reformed Church in North America, itself founded in 1857 by early Dutch immigrants to America. The Holland Settlement's 1903 Dutch Reformed Church originally consisted of 19 families and five bachelors. Peter Van Dyken served as both a church elder and justice of the peace. Many descendants of the founding families still live in the area, and the surnames remain common: Van Dyken, Kimm, Kamp, Broekema, Alberda, Braaksma, and Weidenaar. The community grew quickly, and in 1911, a new church building (pictured) was constructed upon a nearby hill.

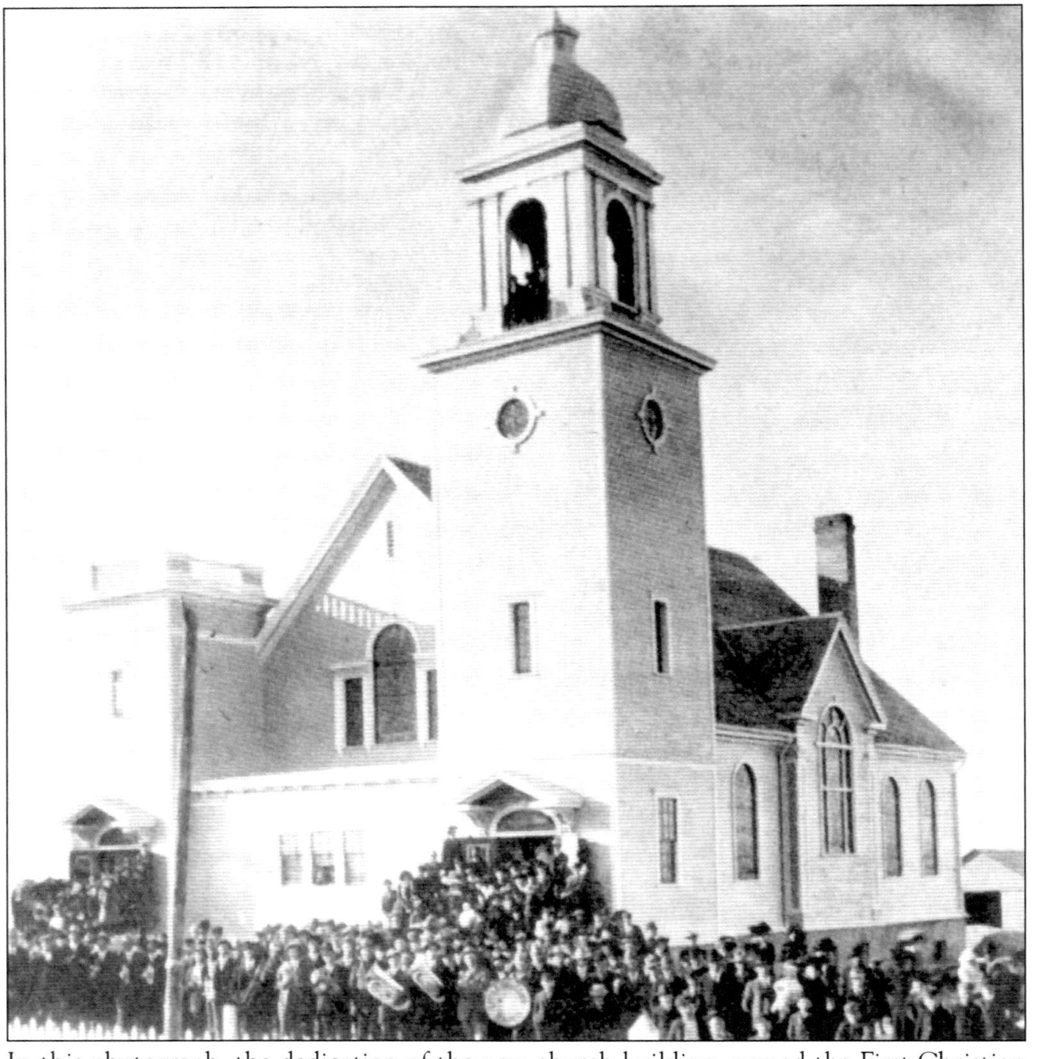

In this photograph, the dedication of the new church building, named the First Christian Reformed Church, takes place on March 17, 1911. The size of both the building and the crowd at the dedication service is indicative of the increase in families to the area. In early decades, many within the Holland Settlement attended services at the original Reformed Church building. This second, larger church building also served as a community center. The settlement soon took upon itself a new name, Church Hill (later Churchill), in recognition of the central role the church on the hill played in the life of the community. Many families in the adjoining community of Amsterdam also worshipped at Church Hill's Christian Reformed Church.

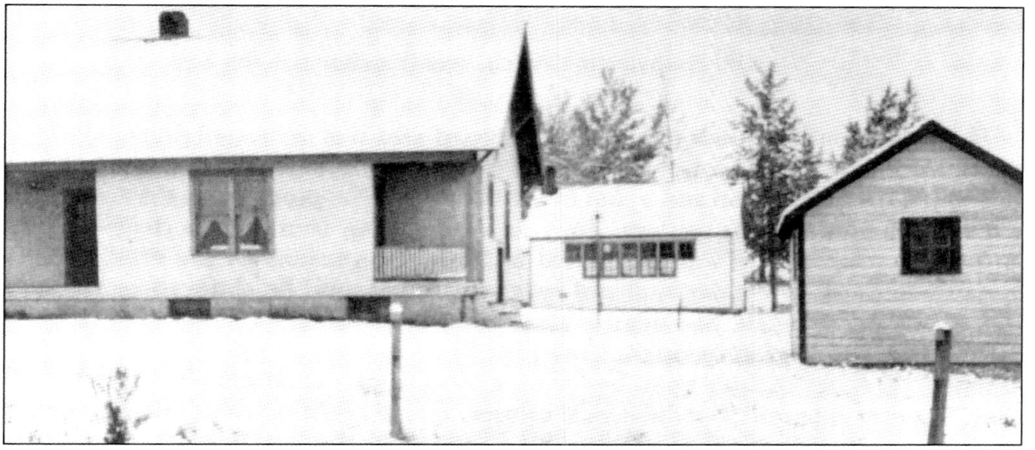

Education was also important to the early Hollanders of Churchill and Amsterdam. Classes began in 1894. Pictured here is the Hills School and teacherage. Built on land donated by Henry and Jennie VanDyken Broekema, the (initially) public school was located near the Hills Cemetery. During its half century of existence, the school was, at times, a Christian school and, at other times, a public school.

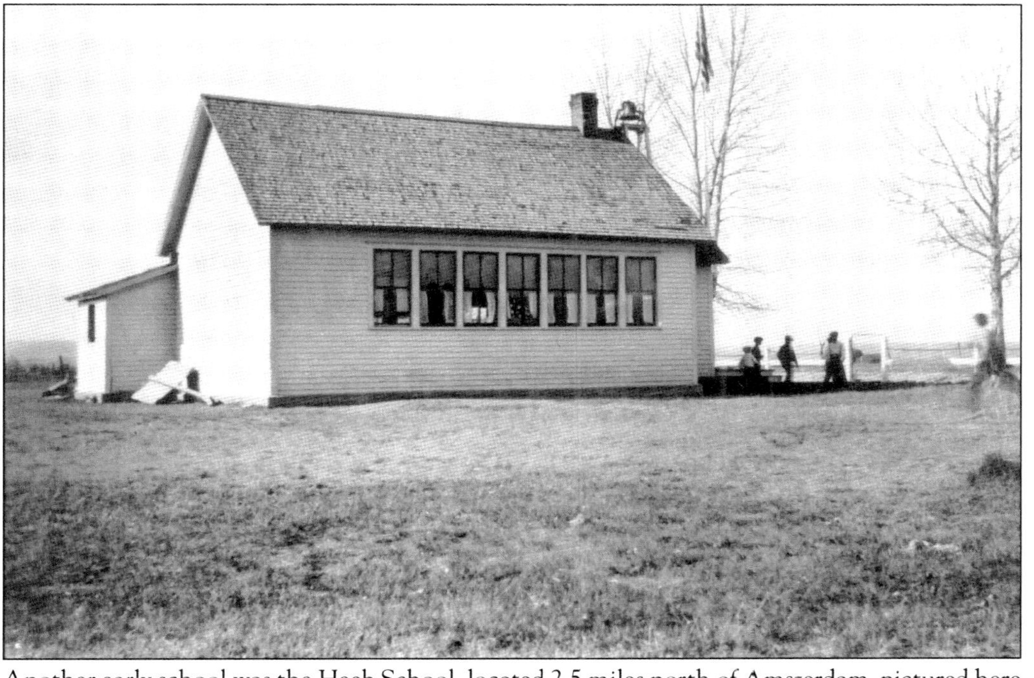

Another early school was the Heeb School, located 2.5 miles north of Amsterdam, pictured here with students standing outside. The land and some building materials for the school were donated by Henry Heeb, who also founded the Gallatin Valley Female Seminary that was later absorbed by the Presbyterian Church.

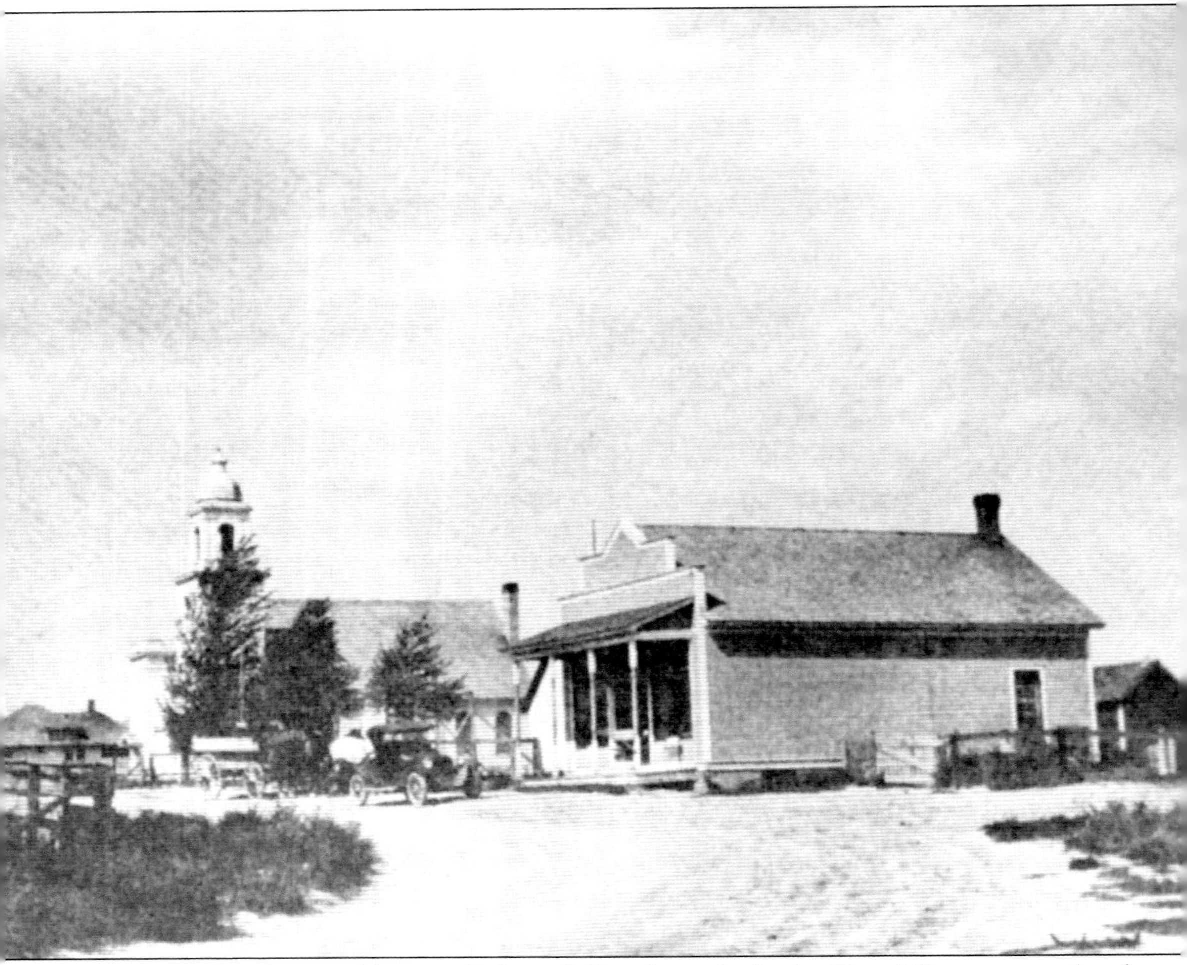

Shortly after the new Christian Reformed Church was built, the Churchill store, owned and operated by Aggie Ganzevoort, opened in 1912 on a lot adjacent to and east of the church. Visible to the left of the store in this photograph is the church. The Churchill store was located on the main road that ran through the community, with the road bending to the south at the juncture with the store. Offering general merchandise to area residents, the store remained open into the 1930s, at which time the Great Depression contributed to its closing. In this undated photograph, both an automobile and a horse and buggy are parked in front of the store. During the early decades of the century, Amsterdam and Churchill grew to a population of several hundred persons. The two communities, however, never became incorporated.

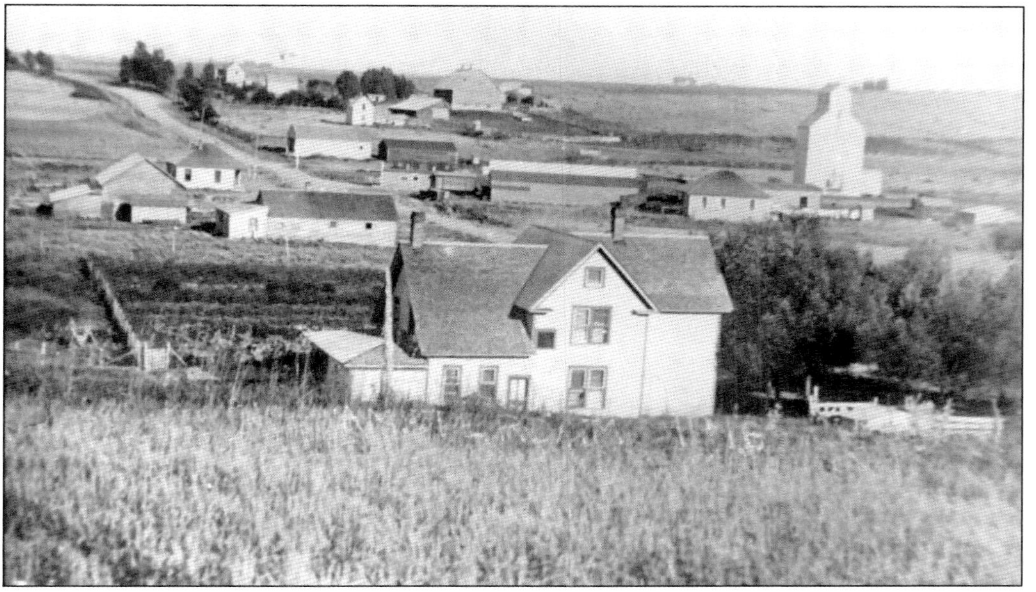

The community of Amsterdam is pictured above in 1915. The rural nature of the town is evident. Farmhouses, barns, outbuildings, a grain elevator, and several groves of trees are visible, surrounded by open space. Amsterdam and Churchill (the latter not pictured) were situated in close proximity of one another.

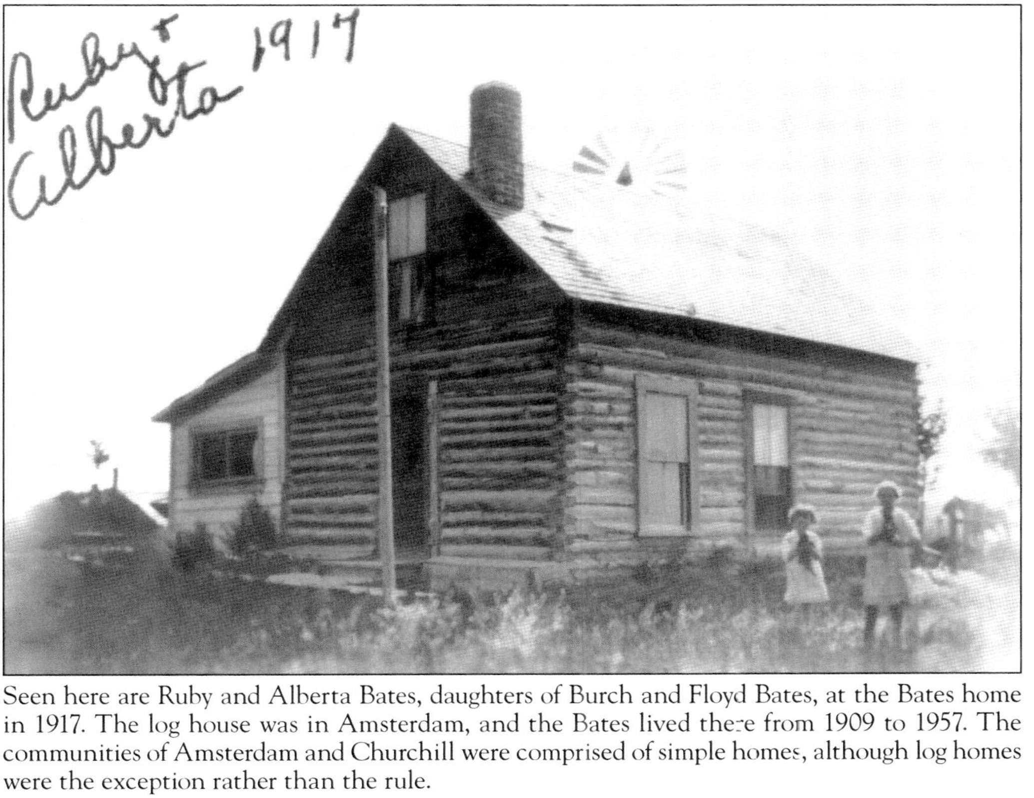

Seen here are Ruby and Alberta Bates, daughters of Burch and Floyd Bates, at the Bates home in 1917. The log house was in Amsterdam, and the Bates lived there from 1909 to 1957. The communities of Amsterdam and Churchill were comprised of simple homes, although log homes were the exception rather than the rule.

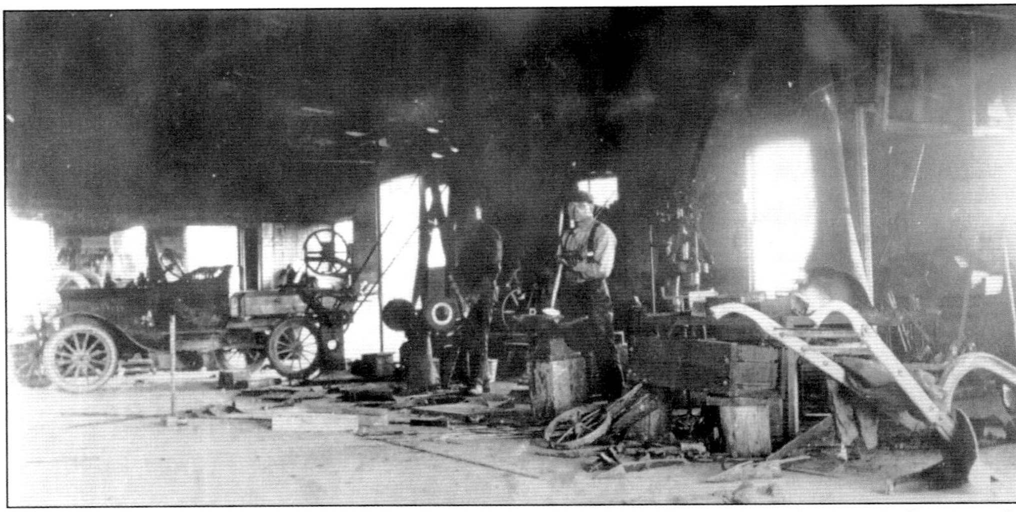

John T. Kamp is pictured inside his blacksmith shop in Amsterdam in this 1915 photograph. Kamp is standing beside the anvil, while another man is running the grinder to his left. While blacksmithing in the Gallatin Valley traditionally involved the crafting of agricultural implements and horseshoes, the early years of the automobile afforded opportunities to repair metal and steel automobile parts.

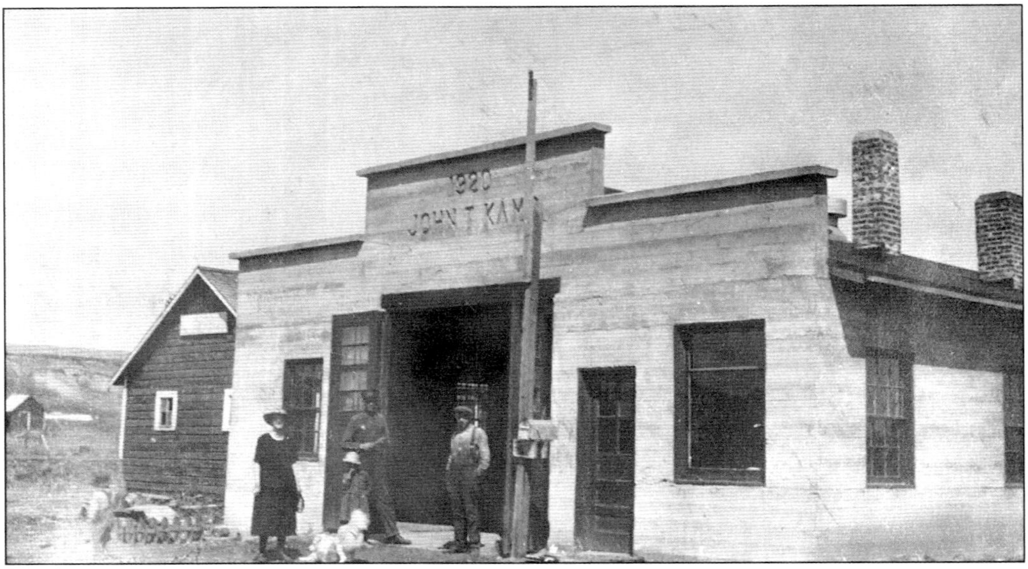

In this 1920s photograph, John and Betsy Kamp stand outside Kamp's newly constructed Blacksmith Shop with their two children and the family dog. Because of the continued prominence of agriculture in Amsterdam and Churchill, blacksmithing remained a viable business well into the 20th century.

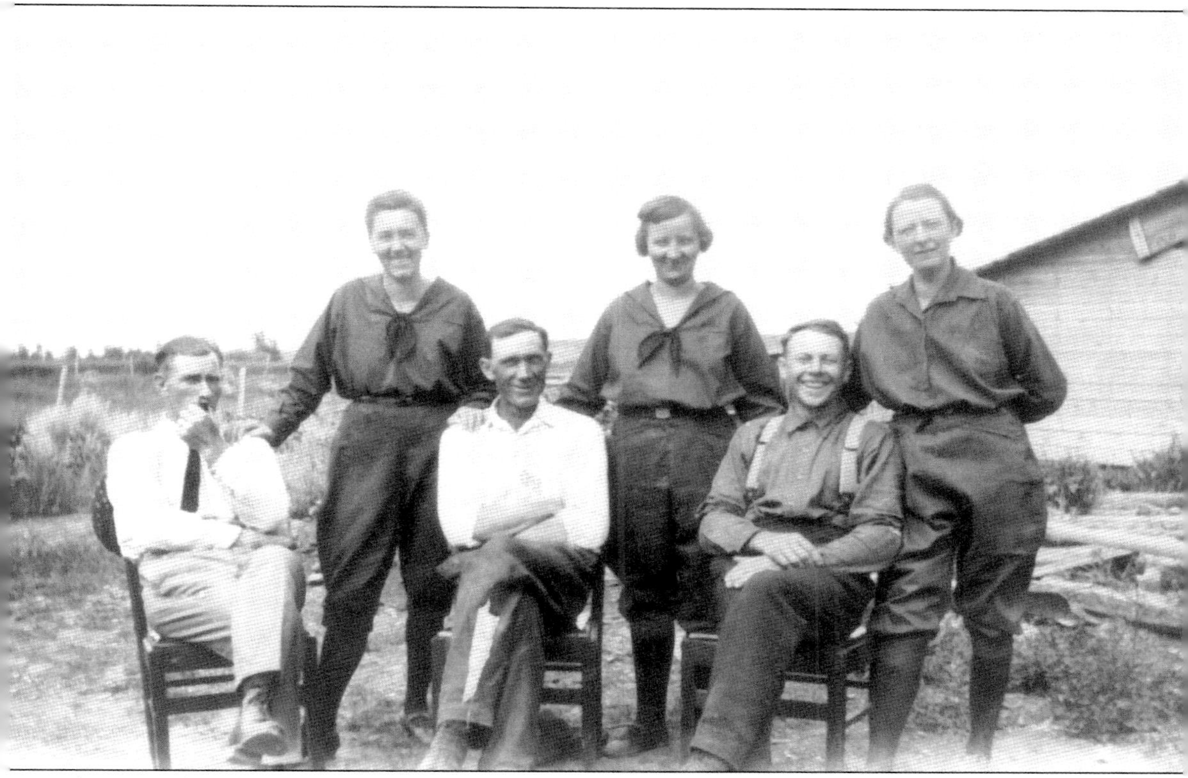

Three couples relax behind Kamp's Blacksmith Shop in this undated photograph. From left to right are Ike and Tena Osterhert, Nick and Marie Nap, and John and Betsy Kamp. Marie and Betsy were sisters. Whether laboring in the shop or in the fields, life in 1920s Amsterdam and Churchill consisted of hard work, yet community residents valued family ties and a common faith. In addition, the quiet, open spaces and surrounding mountain views provided a sense of peace and well being unobtainable in big city life in America. Many descendants of the Kamp families still live in the Amsterdam and Churchill area.

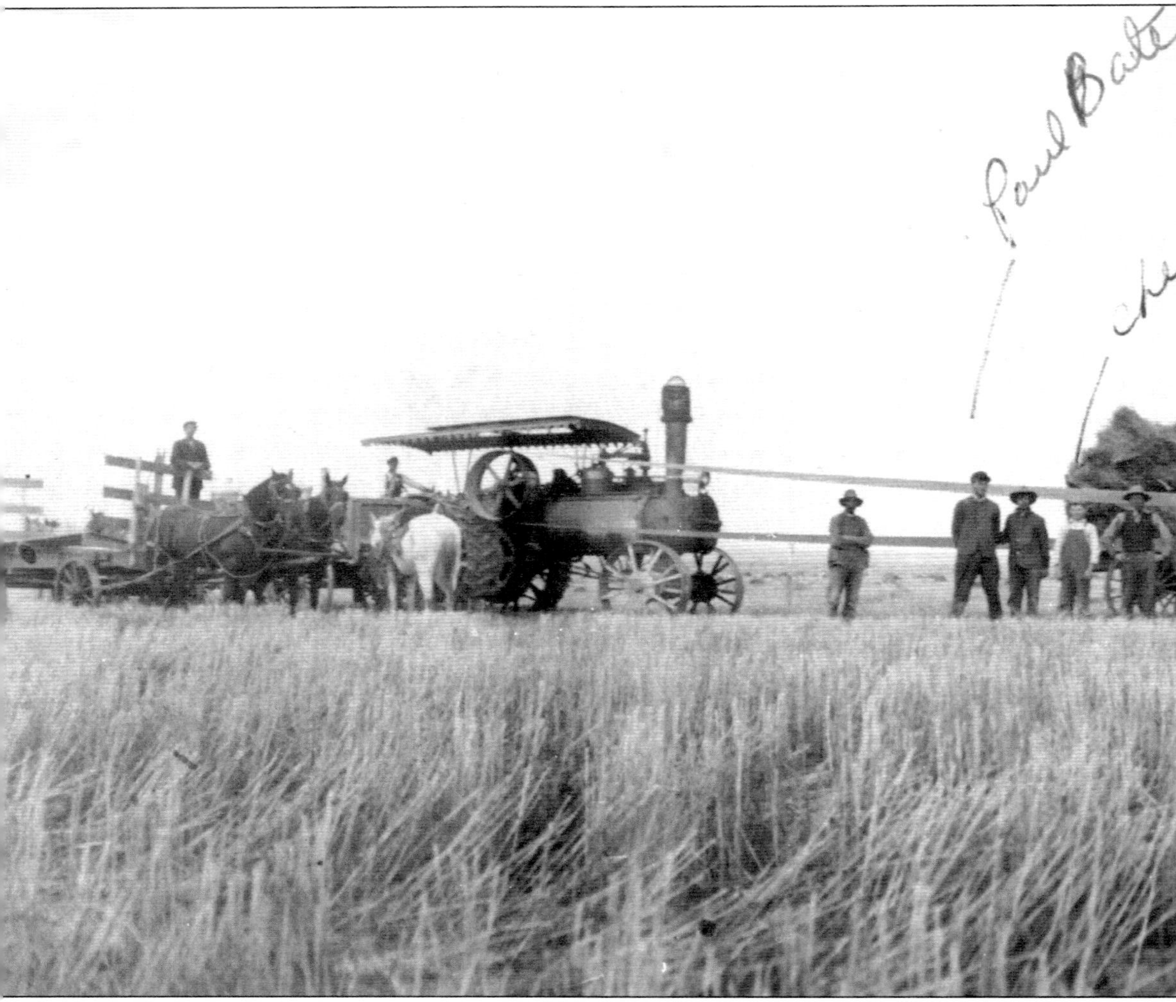

The farmland surrounding Amsterdam and Churchill was a prime area for growing barley, wheat, and other crops. Harvesting and threshing were community events, as depicted in this 1915 photograph. A combination of horsepower and machine power were required for the task in this era. At least 14 men are pictured here, including Sam Rykels, Nick Nap, Paul Bates, and

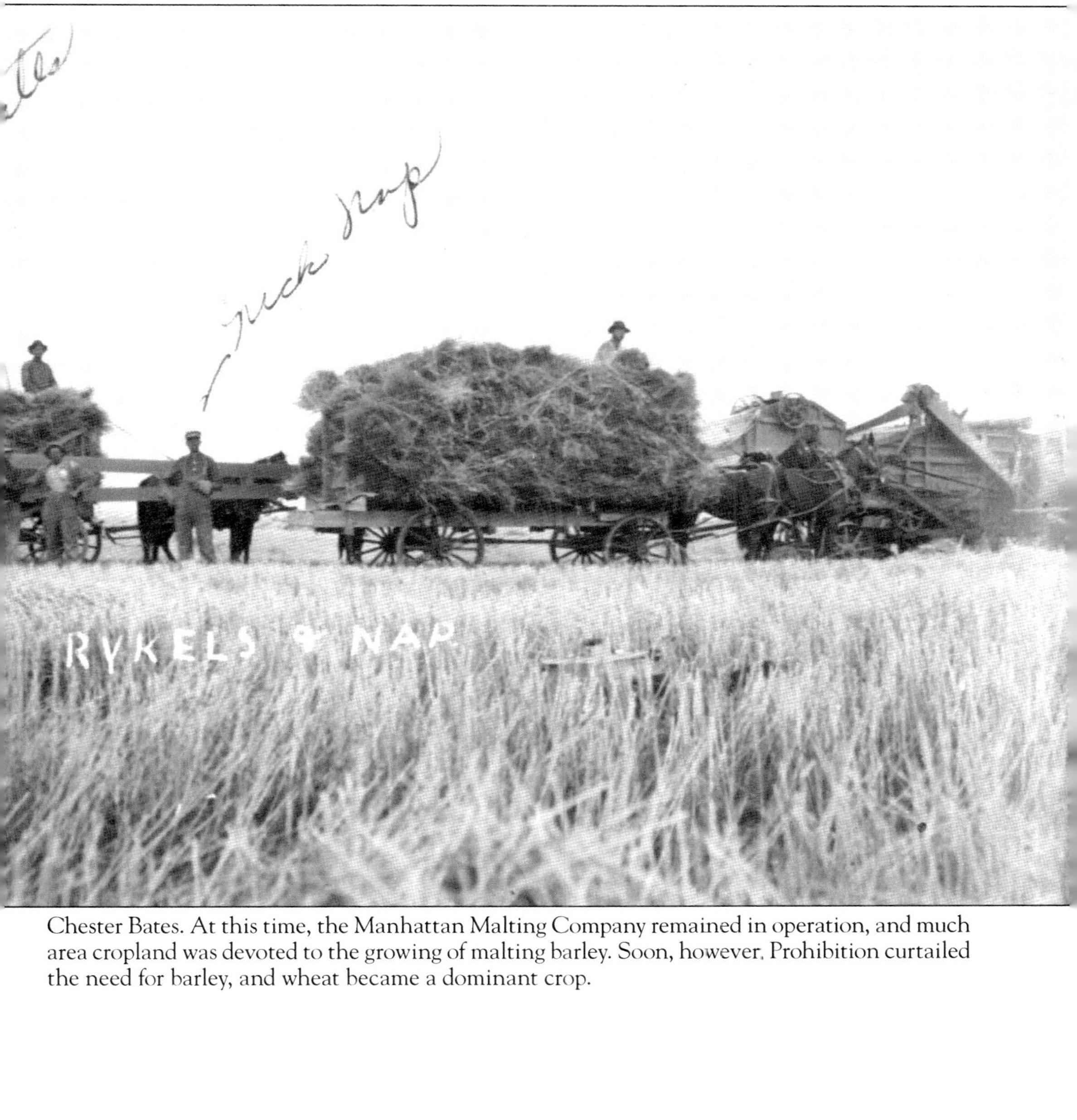

Chester Bates. At this time, the Manhattan Malting Company remained in operation, and much area cropland was devoted to the growing of malting barley. Soon, however, Prohibition curtailed the need for barley, and wheat became a dominant crop.

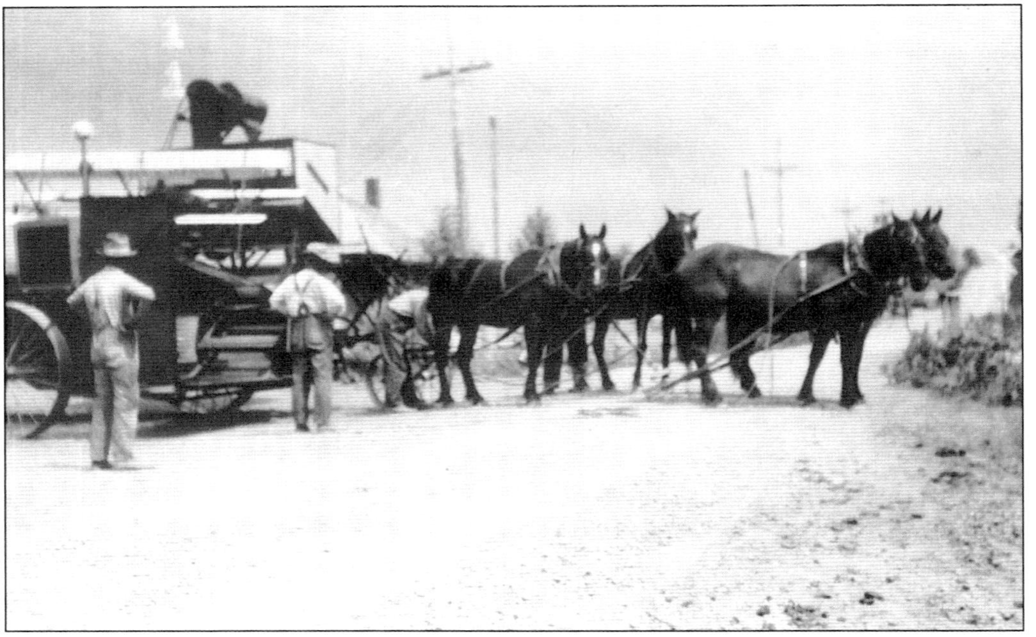

In the 1920s, Amsterdam and Churchill absorbed numerous new Dutch families and individuals arriving from the Netherlands, Canada, and other Dutch settlements in America. Many of the newcomers initially worked for established farmers such as Henry Kimm. Pictured here is a new combine, purchased in 1925 by Burch R. Bates.

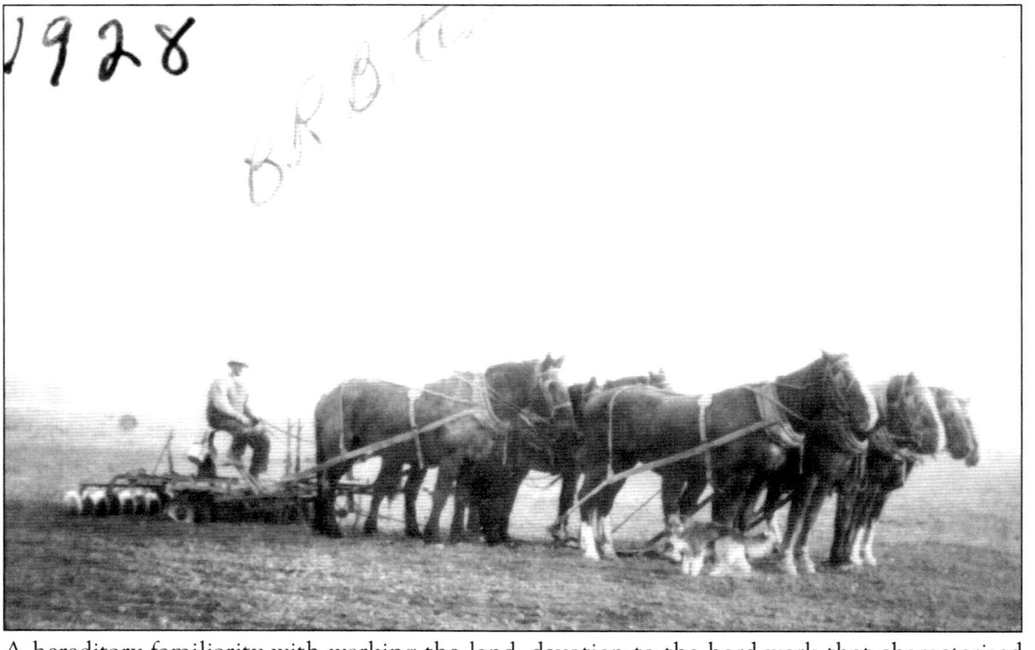

A hereditary familiarity with working the land, devotion to the hard work that characterized farming, and a common faith bound together the early pioneers and the newcomers that arrived in the third decade of the 20th century. Many of the newer arrivals settled in the area permanently. In this 1928 photograph, Burch R. Bates is disking west of Amsterdam.

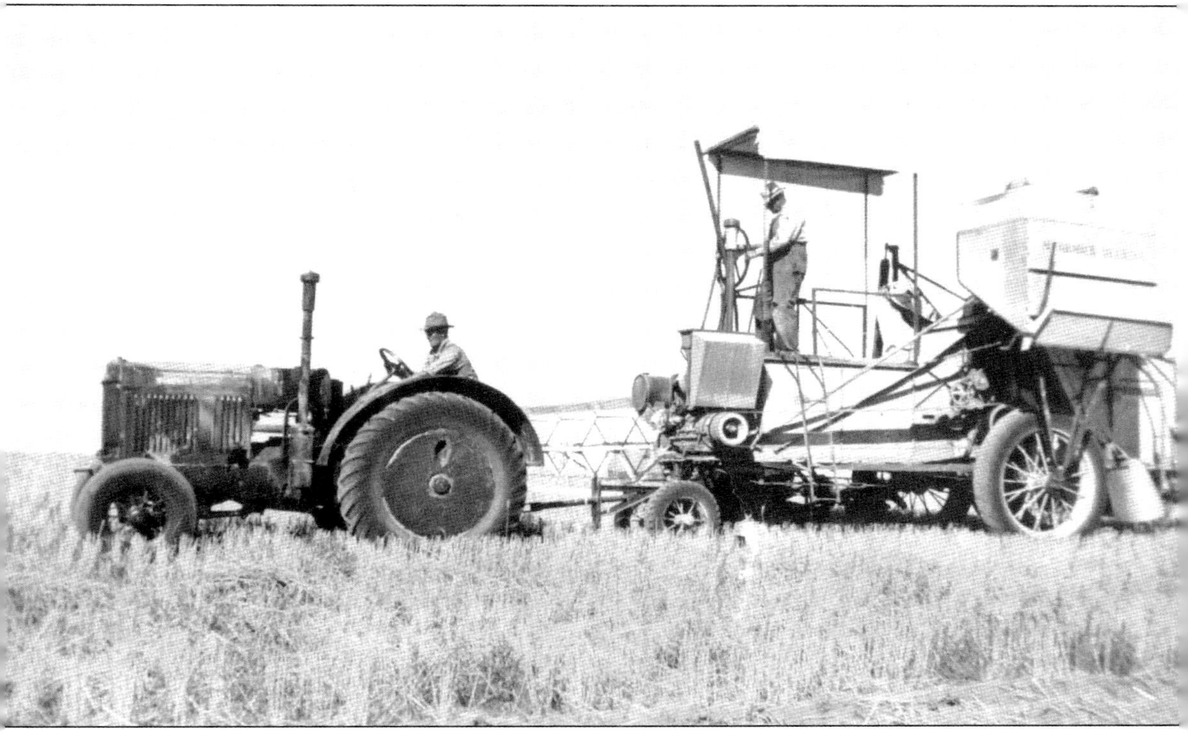

The continued progression of the Bates' family farm equipment is visible in this 1937 photograph of a new tractor-pulled combine. Paul Bates drives the tractor while Burch R. Bates operates the machinery. With each new generation of farm equipment, farmers in Amsterdam and Churchill were able to more efficiently and productively work the fields that radiated out from the communities in all directions. By now, the land supported a variety of crops. While wheat remained a constant, seed potatoes had also become a major cash crop. Many seed potatoes grown near Amsterdam and Churchill were shipped to Idaho where they were planted and grew to maturity as famed Idaho potatoes. In addition to farming, dairy cattle were common.

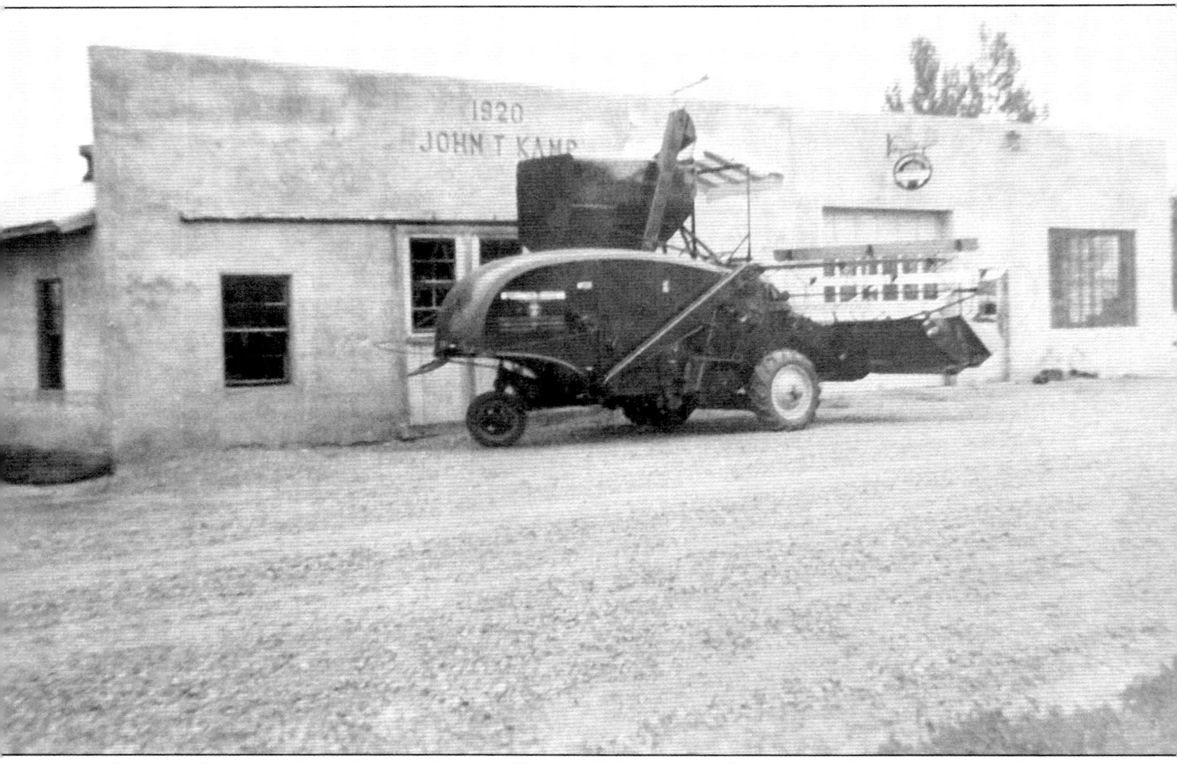

The land surrounding Amsterdam and Churchill, some of it irrigated by water from the nearby West Gallatin River, retained its fertility year after year, the whims of weather notwithstanding. By the mid-century, crop rotation, fertilizer, new developments in weed and pest control, and increasingly sophisticated farming methods in general led to greater yields and better products. Farm machinery played no small role in crop improvements. Within the span of two decades, equipment pulled by teams of horses, and later pulled by tractors, was replaced by self-propelled equipment. Pictured in this 1944 photograph is a combine parked in front of John T. Kamp's blacksmith shop. The old and the new are contrasted, as the combine is the first self-propelled model owned by Avery and Burch Bates.

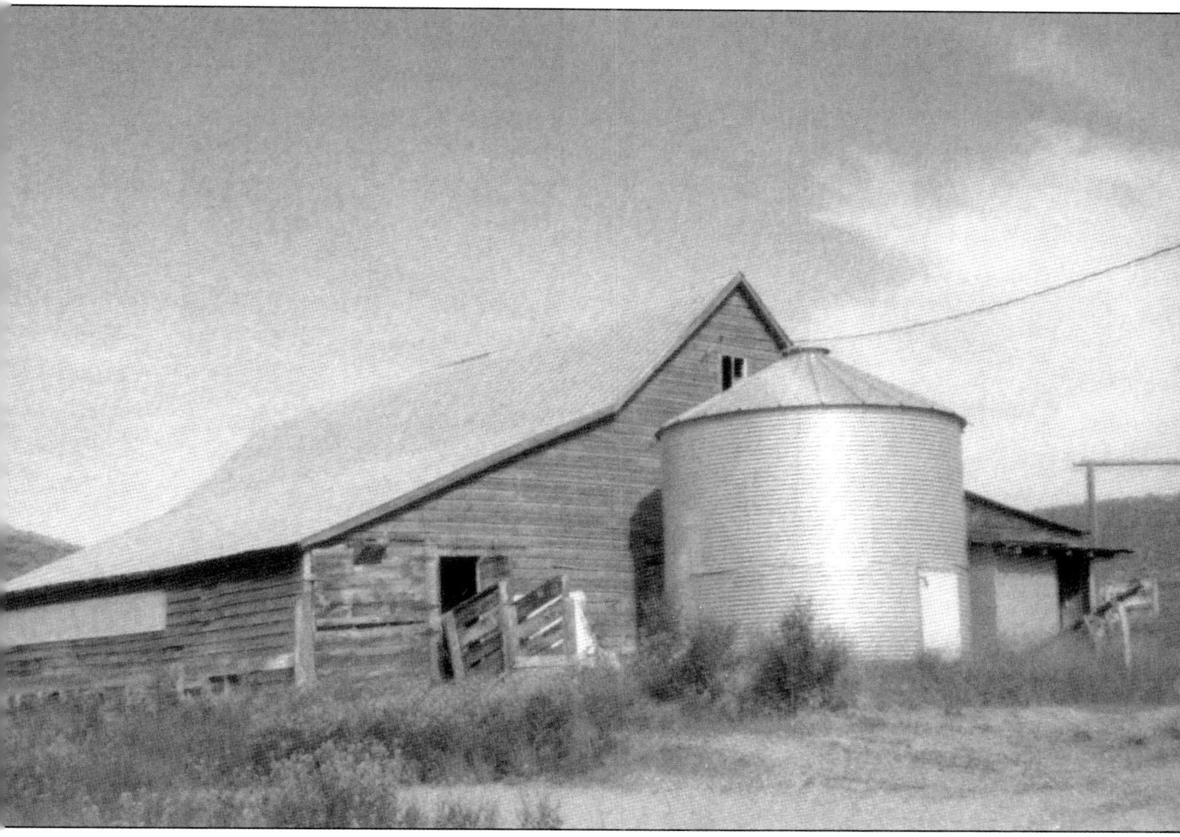

In this undated photograph, the William Broekema homestead is pictured. While the first homestead in the Holland Settlement, this image represents the property decades after it was settled. Immigrants from Groningen province in the northern Netherlands, the Broekemas were community and church leaders in the Holland Settlement, with William serving as one of the original elders in the Dutch Reformed congregation. In a pattern oft-repeated among other families, relatives followed William from the Netherlands to the Holland Settlement. Hendrick "Henry" Broekema, also from the Groningen province, came to live with his uncle William and married Jennie Van Dyken in 1915. Resourceful, the couple raised dairy cows, chickens, and hogs. They also grew grain and alfalfa. Their chickens numbered in the hundreds, and they shipped eggs by train for sale in Butte. Jennie's hot applesauce cakes were well known in the community.

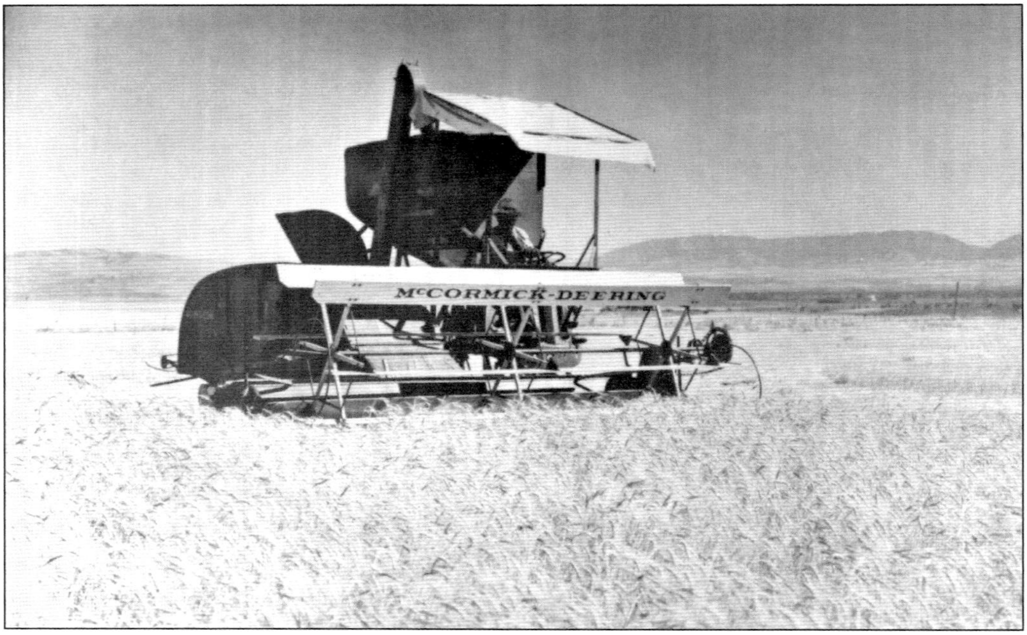

In wheat fields like those near Churchill and Amsterdam, a chapter in the history of corporate farm machinery was coming to a close. The self-propelled McCormick-Deering name pictured on this combine in this 1940s photograph was a trademark of International Harvester Corporation. Following some 50 years of "harvester wars," an antitrust lawsuit, and the Great Depression, the John Deere Corporation was finally on the verge of unseating IHC. By the end of the 1940s, the "McCormick-Deering" name disappeared.

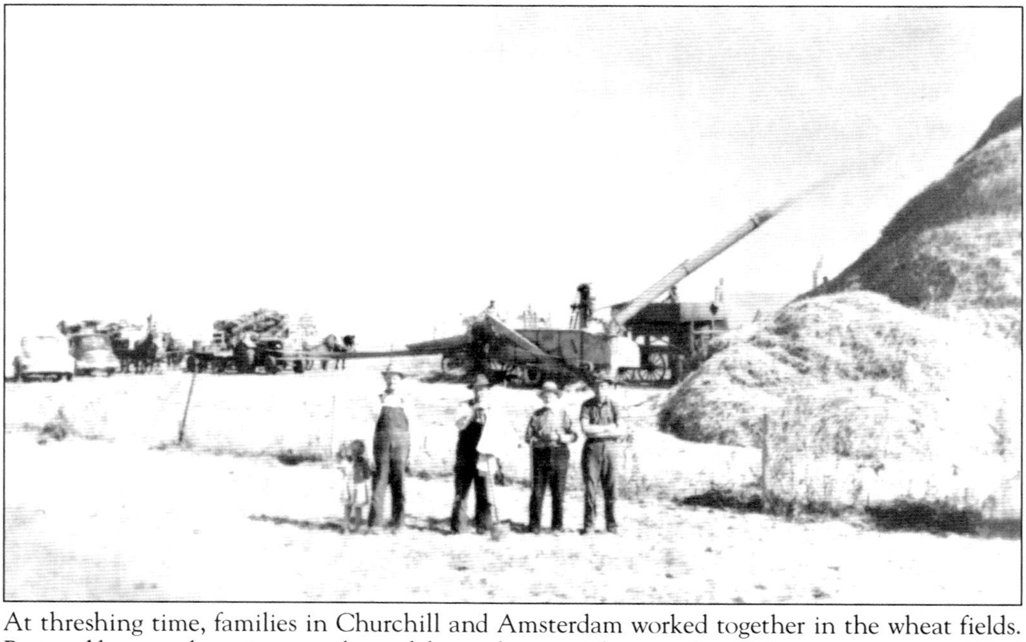

At threshing time, families in Churchill and Amsterdam worked together in the wheat fields. Pictured here are longtime members of the settlement. They are, from left to right, a young Ethel Kimm, Nick Kimm, Klaus Dykema, Dirk Dykema, and Bert H. Van Dyken.

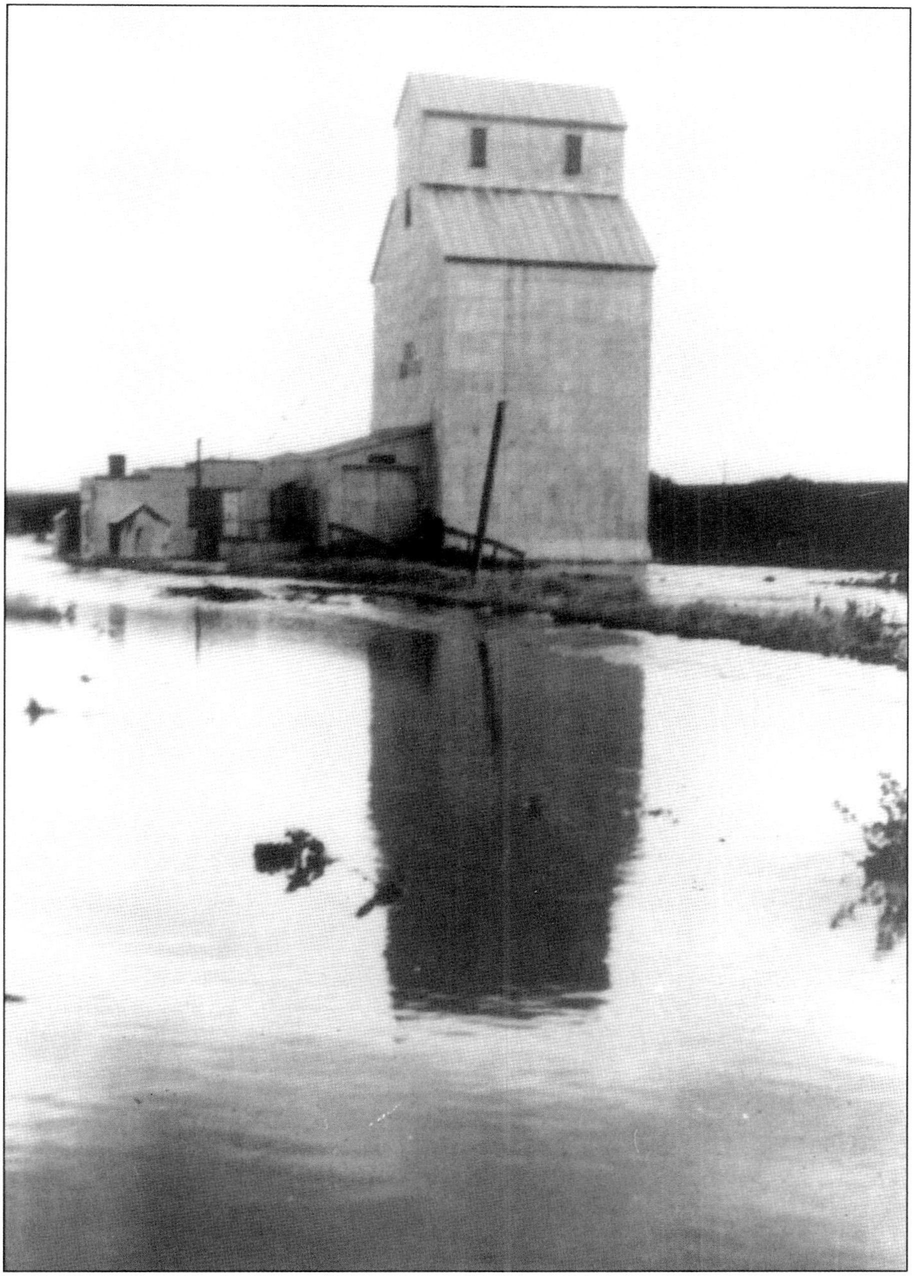

Warm spring weather in the wake of deep mountain snowpacks often brought unwanted and sometimes dangerous flooding in the Gallatin Valley. Sudden summer cloudbursts could also result in flash flooding. In this undated photograph with the Amsterdam grain elevator standing in the background, a July rainstorm dumped enough water in the area to create several inches of standing water in places. Dryland farming, by now common in the Churchill and Amsterdam area, depended upon the timing and amount of moisture in order to produce a good crop. Too much moisture could delay planting or harvesting, while too little could result in a stunted wheat crop with low yields.

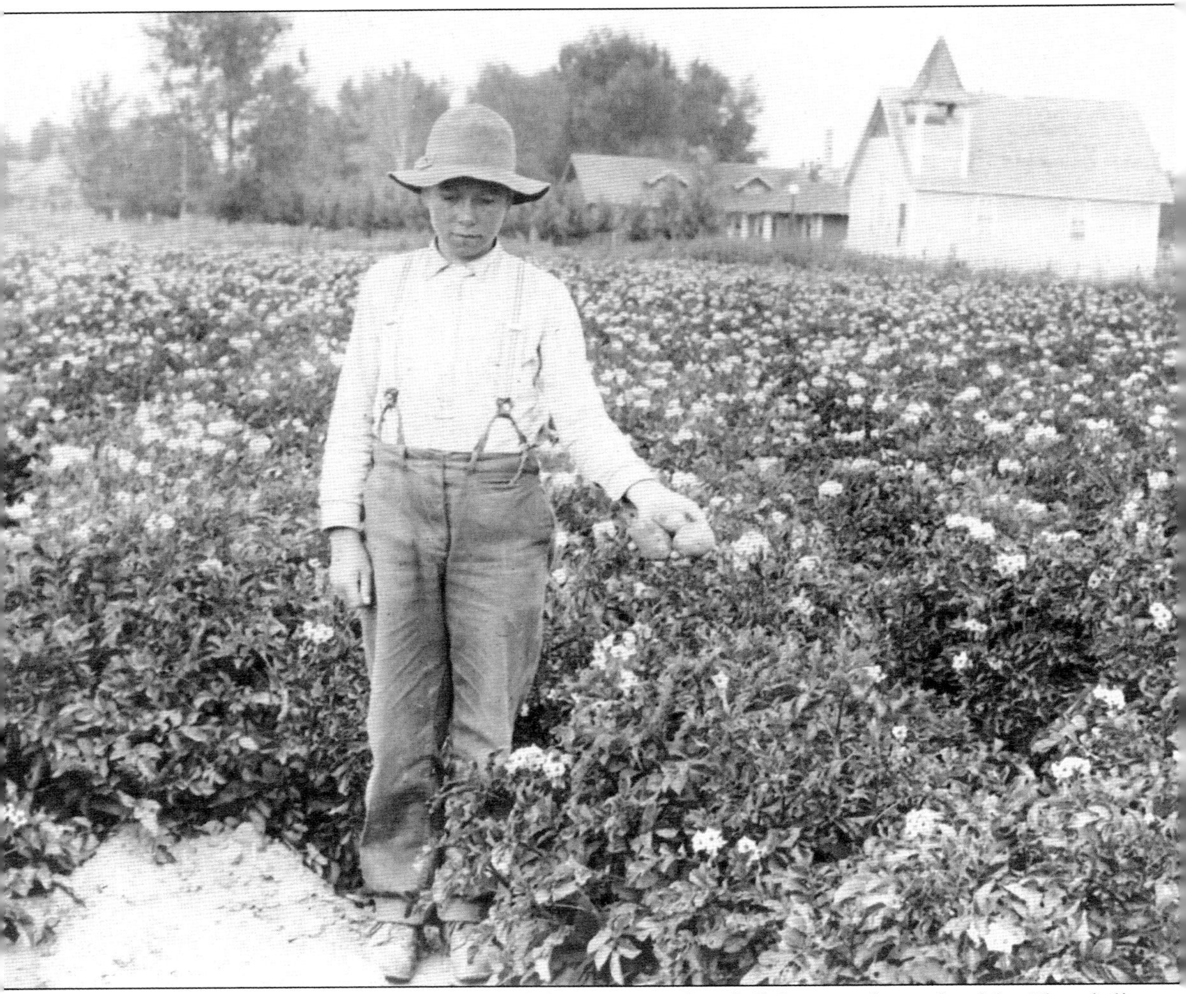

The Manhattan Christian School, founded in 1907 in Churchill, became the pride of the Churchill and Amsterdam communities. Christian private schools were established in the communities' early days, testimony to the deep Dutch Reformed faith of immigrant settlers. Expressions of faith also played a role in the area's public schools, such as the one visible in the background of this photograph, and in some cases, schoolhouses vacillated over time as public and private institutions. The Manhattan Christian School centralized early Christian private school efforts, allowing families to train their children in reading and arithmetic, as well as theology. When not in school, children typically helped their parents in the fields. In this 1917 photograph, young George Van Diest stands in a potato field. By the 1920s, potatoes were a major crop in the Churchill and Amsterdam area.

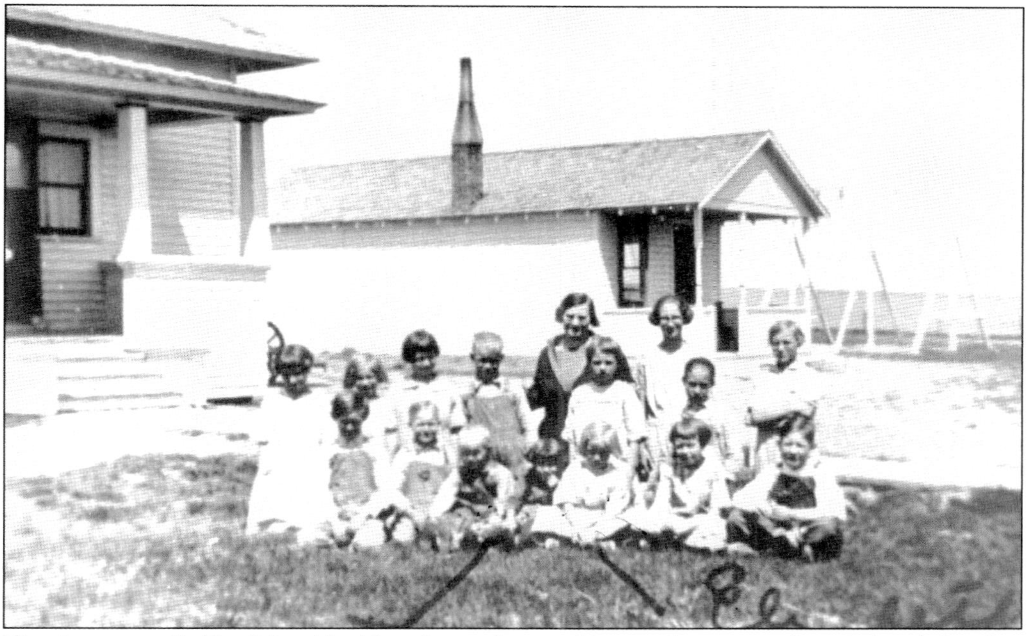

The Armstrong Public School building, located west of Amsterdam, opened in 1916 and closed in 1945, after which a new building was constructed and the name was changed to the Amsterdam Public School. In this 1927 photograph, the fourth-grade class is pictured. In the first row, Tom Kamp is third from left, and Elizabeth Kamp is fifth from left.

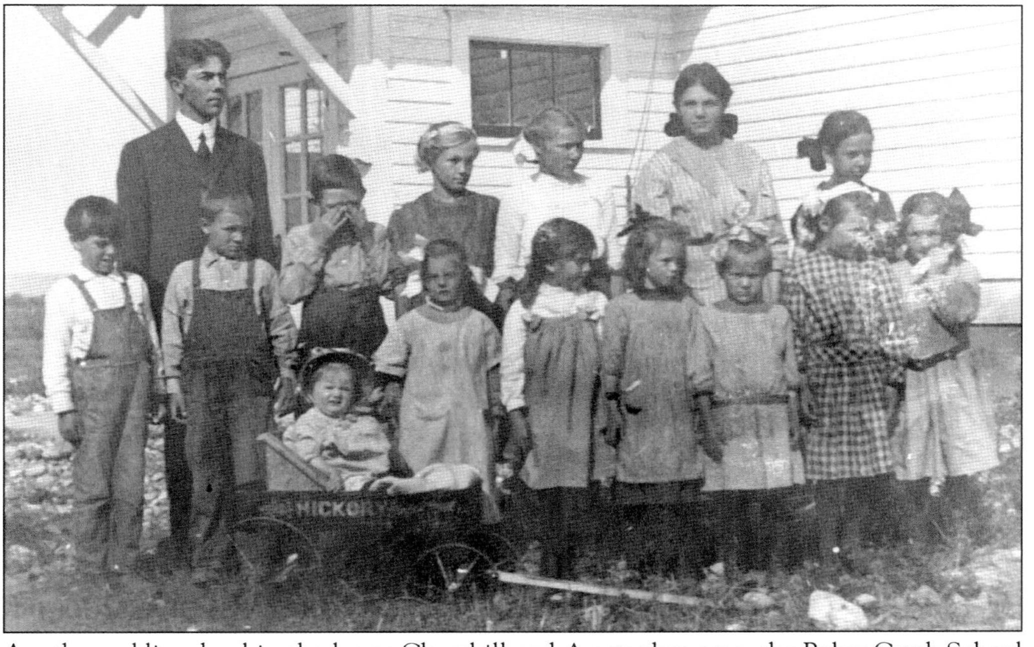

Another public school in the larger Churchill and Amsterdam area, the Baker Creek School building was open from 1912 to 1940. Pictured in this undated photograph is teacher Oliver Crawford with students in front of the school building. Note how formally dressed Crawford is, as well as the range of ages represented among the students.

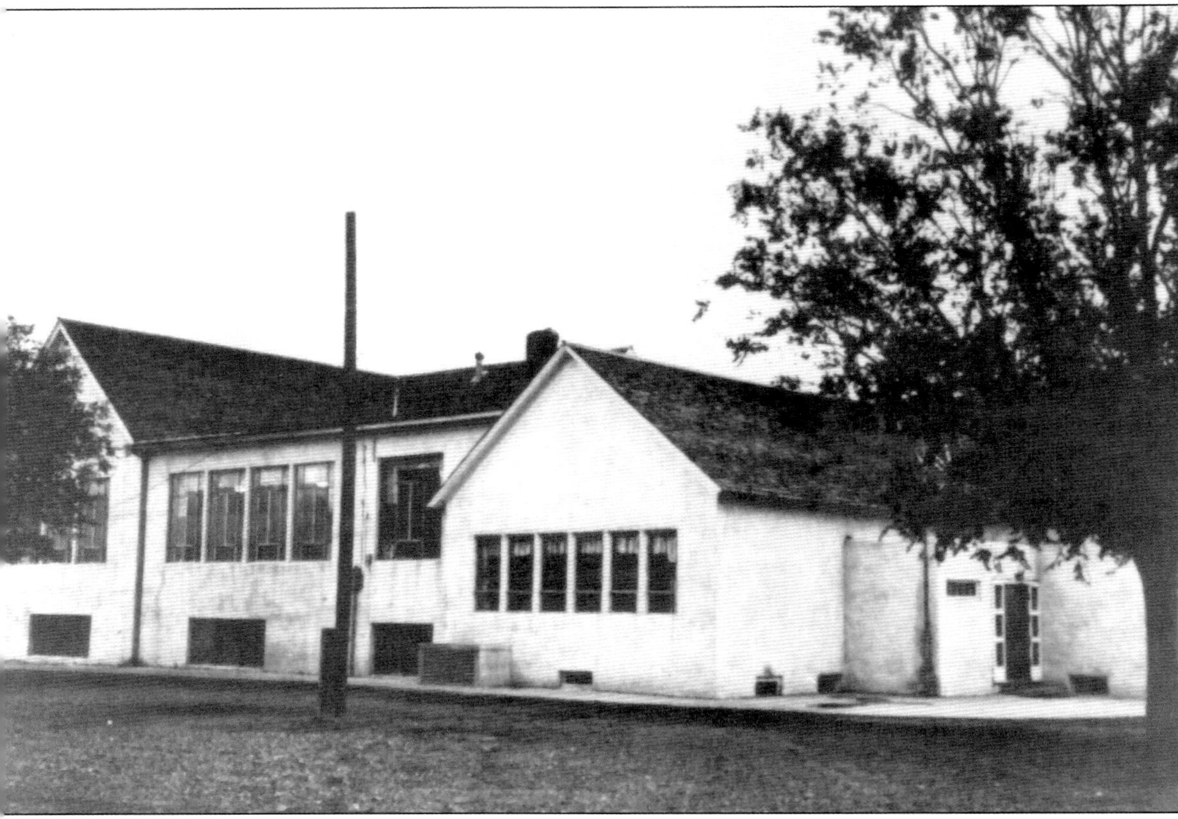

Manhattan Christian School, located next door to the Christian Reformed Church in Churchill, was recognized as one of the leading private schools in the state of Montana by the mid-century. Expanding to three buildings in the 1920s, the school struggled during the Great Depression and experienced difficulty paying teachers. However, the school survived, resuming growth by the late 1930s and initiating bus routes in the 1940s. In the late 1940s and 1950s, the school expanded, adding a high school. The high school building pictured here burned in 1957, and the school expanded considerably when rebuilding afterward. A two-part video of the history of Manhattan Christian School is available on the school's Facebook page.

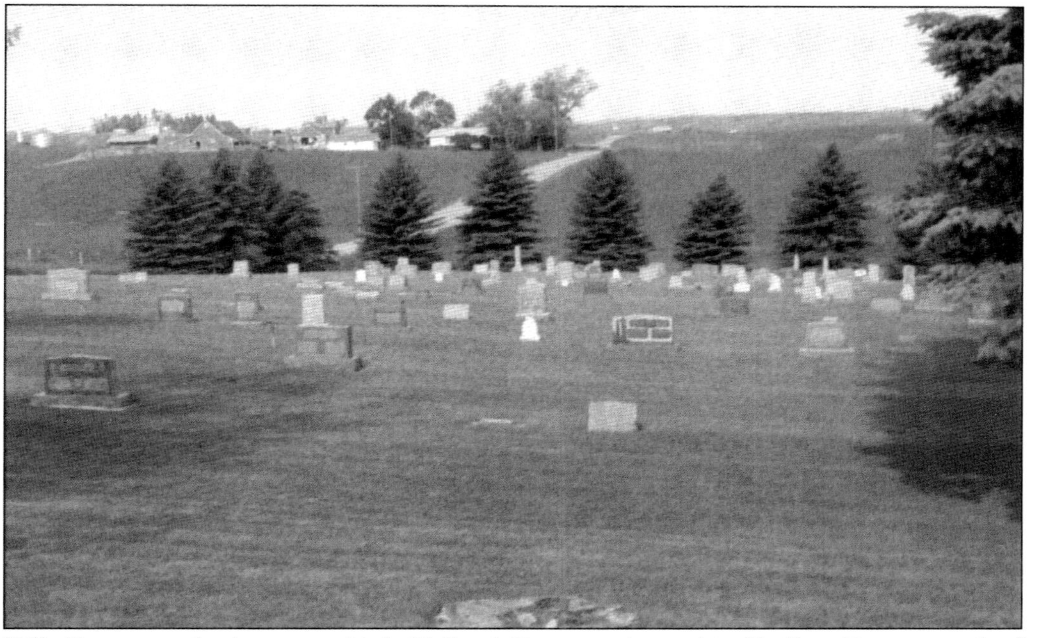

Hills Cemetery, also known as Little Holland Cemetery, located in Godfrey Canyon south of Amsterdam and Churchill, is pictured above. One of 27 named cemeteries in Gallatin County, members from a number of the area's early settler families are buried in the cemetery.

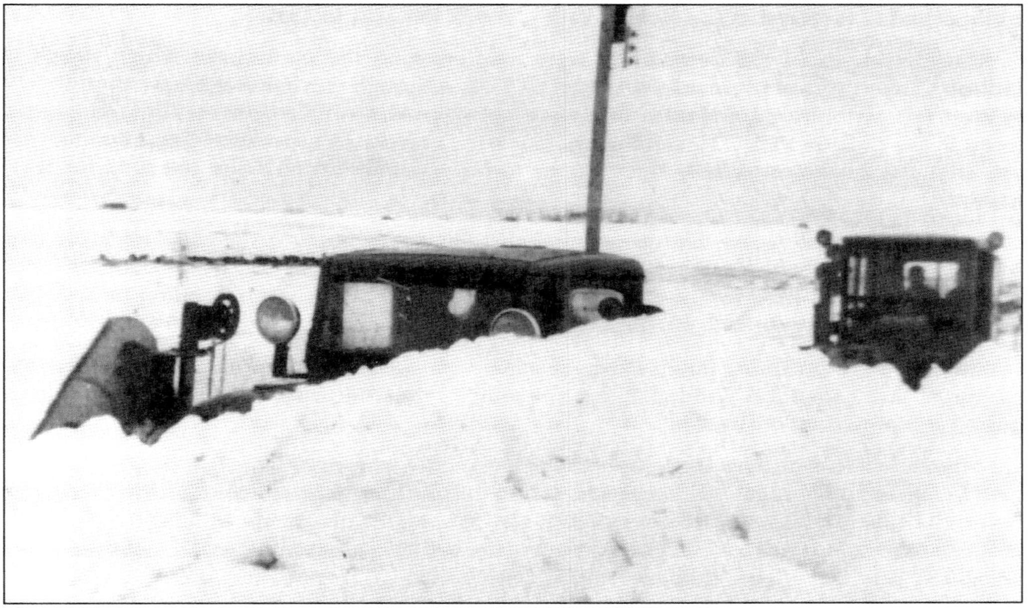

Pictured here are snowdrifts from a winter storm in 1948–1949. Late 1948 turned unusually cold. Then the blizzard of 1949 began on January 2. Frigid temperatures and severe snowstorms lasted for the next six weeks. The prolonged storms were notable enough that the February 7, 1949, edition of *Time* magazine reported that South Dakota, Wyoming, and Nebraska recorded 18 snowstorms in a period of 27 days. Montana did not experience the worst of the storms, yet the snowfall for the season was unusually deep.

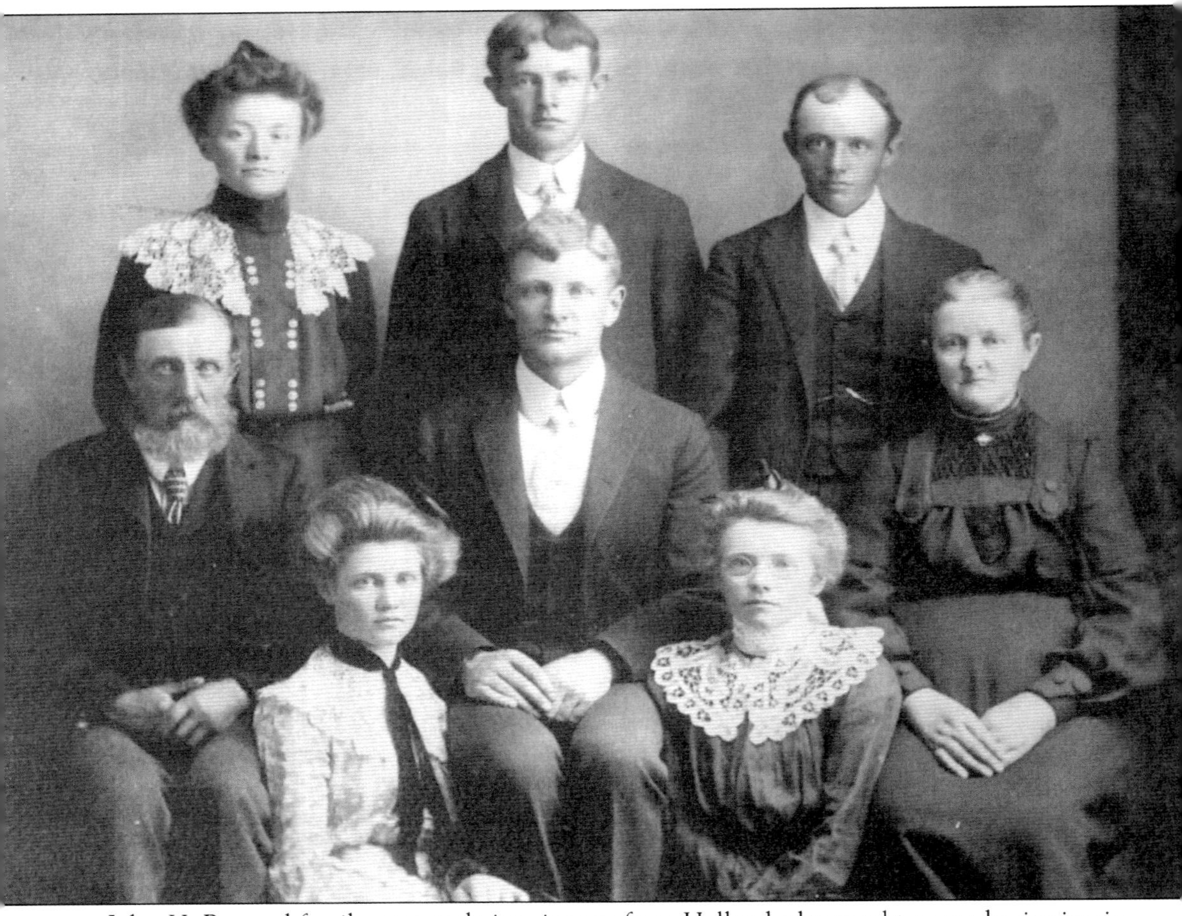

John H. Bos and family were early immigrants from Holland who sought a new beginning in Montana's Holland Settlement. Pictured here, from left to right, are (first row) Martha and Alice; (second row) John H., unidentified, and Jennie Van Dyken; (third row) Hannah, Clauson, and Henry. The Bos family name still lives on in the Churchill and Amsterdam area.

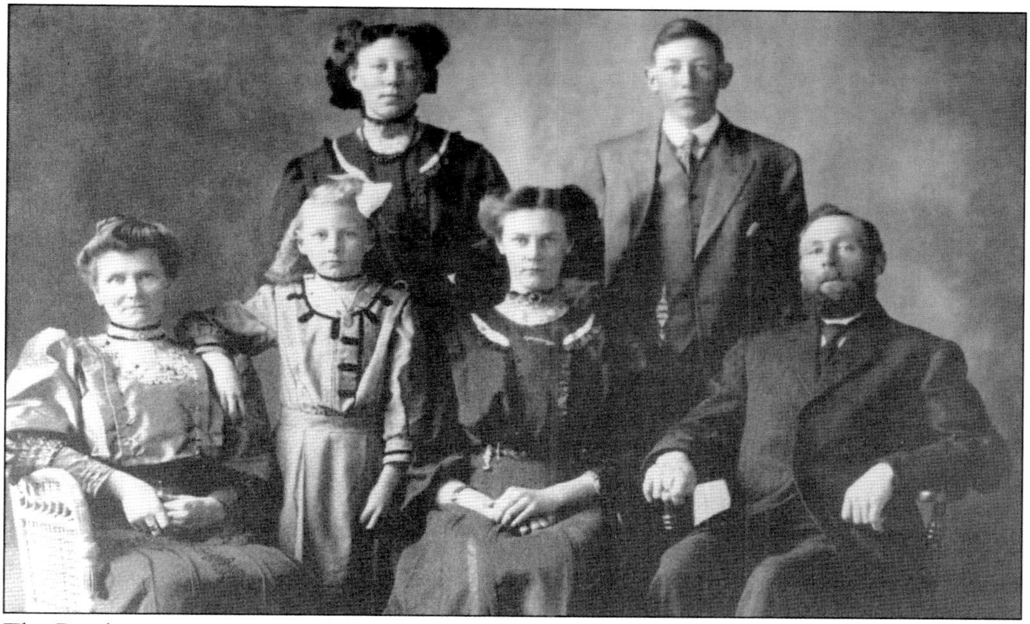

The Broekemas were among the earliest Dutch settlers in the Churchill and Amsterdam area. Pictured here, from left to right, are Mrs. Broekema, Phyllis, Lavina, Anna, Bill, and William Broekema. In the ensuing decades to the present, descendants and relatives of William have remained active in community and church life.

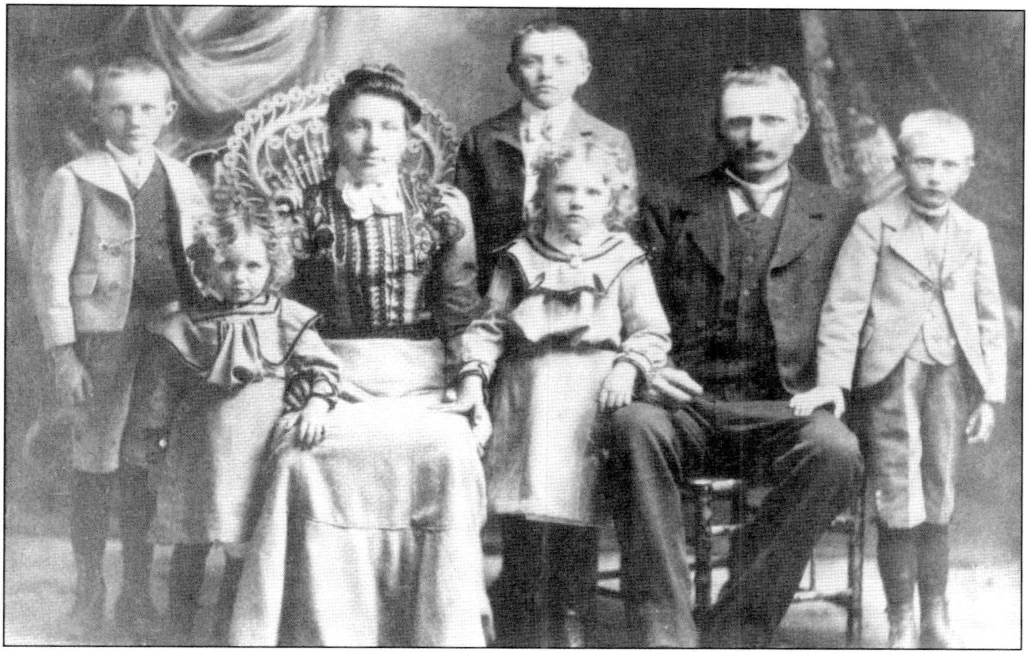

In this c. 1900 photograph is the Kimm family, early settlers in the Churchill and Amsterdam area. They are, from left to right, Nick, Trinia, Willemina Kimm, Ranger, Weke, Jacob R. Kimm, and Henry. The Kimm name remains common in the area, both in households and places. Several large seed potato operations are currently owned by Kimm family members.

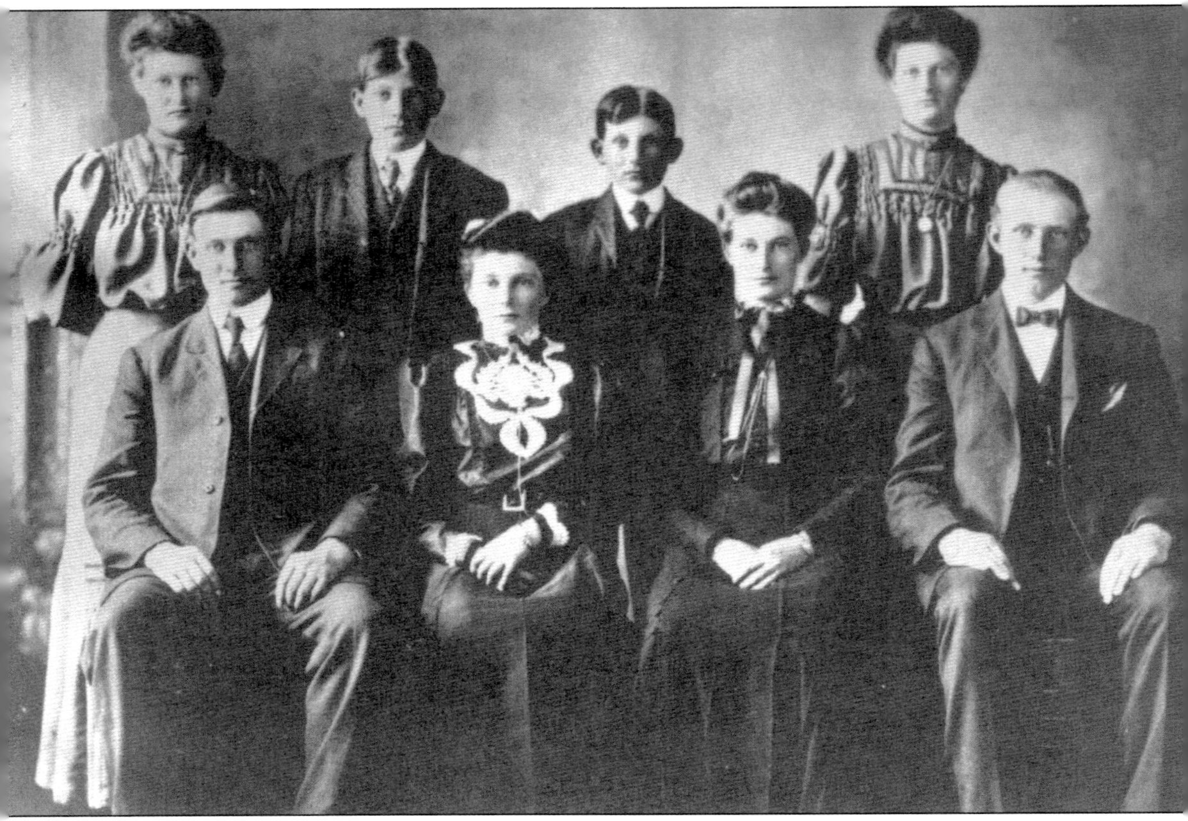

The Van Dykens were also among the earliest settlers in the Holland Settlement. Pictured here, from left to right, are the Van Dyken children: Lena, Pete, Paul, Effie, Henry, Jennie, Kate, and Ralph. The family prospered over the years, and the family name is still found throughout the Gallatin Valley today.

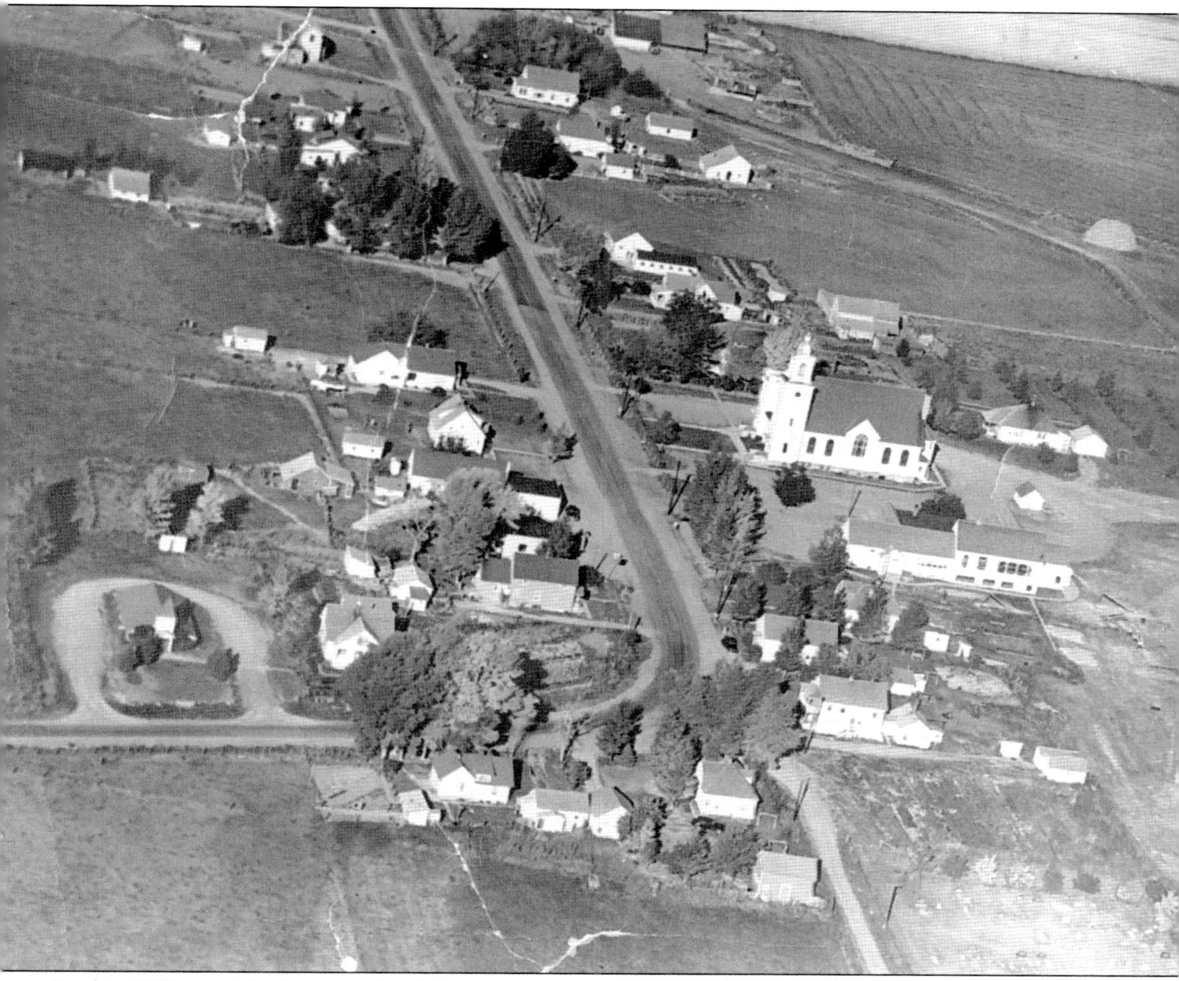

In this 1950s aerial photograph of the community of Churchill, several landmarks are visible. Churchill Road, unpaved yet much improved from earlier decades, enters from the top (west) and bends around to the left (south). The large building in the right center is the Christian Reformed Church, established in 1903. Immediately below the church is Manhattan Christian School, prior to the fire that destroyed much of the school in 1957. Near the bend in the road and just to the right with a car parked in front is the old general store. In the bottom right-hand corner is the community cemetery.

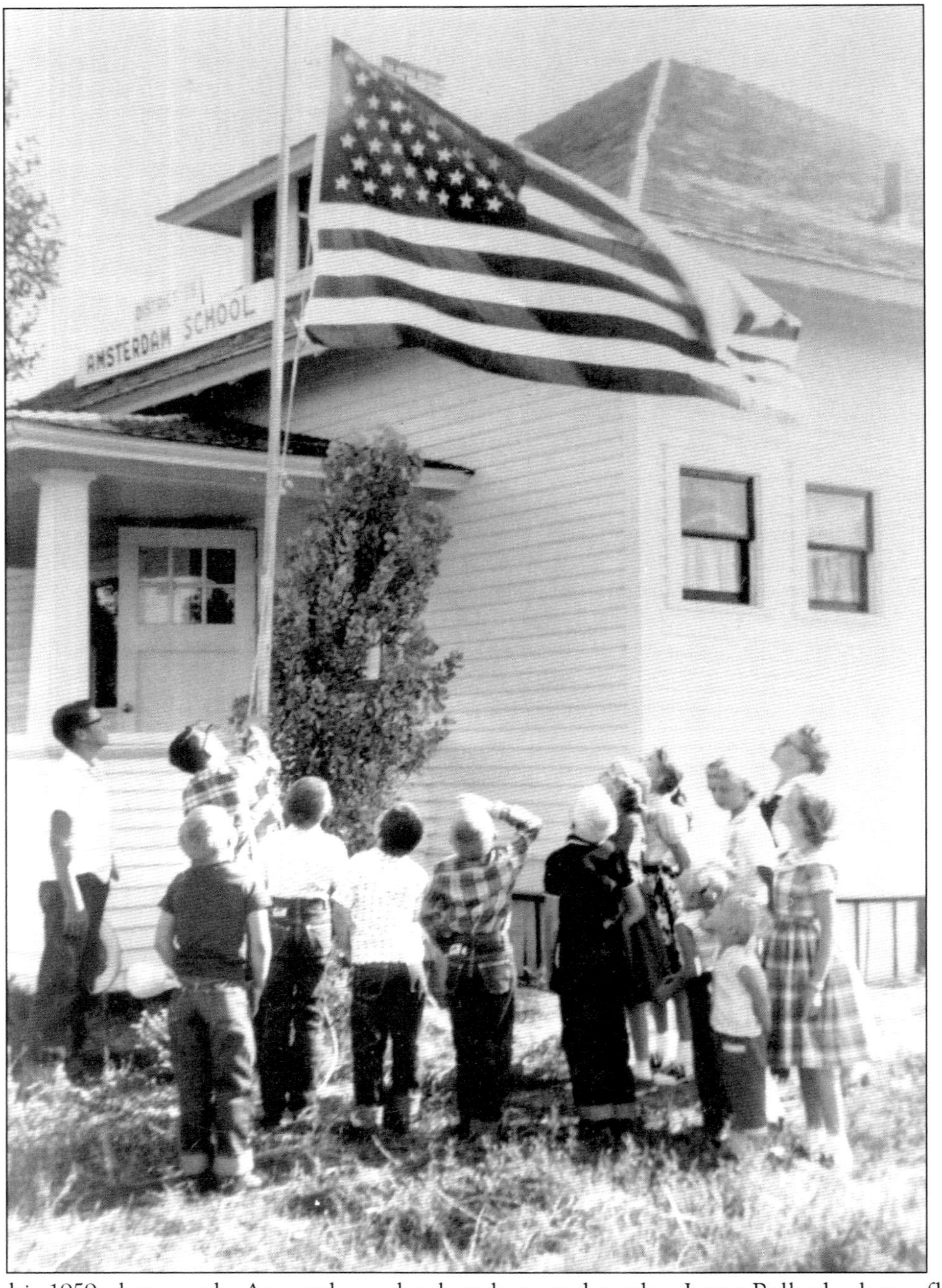

In this 1959 photograph, Amsterdam school students and teacher Jenny Ballard salute a flag that was a gift to the school from Montana US Congressional Representative (and later senator) Lee Metcalf. Metcalf served as Montana's assistant attorney general prior to World War II and participated in the Normandy invasion and the Battle of the Bulge during the war. At the time of his death in 1978, he was one of the most veteran members of the US Senate, and in 1983, Congress created the Lee Metcalf Wilderness area in southwestern Montana in honor of the senator. Patriotism and faith characterized the Dutch communities of Churchill and Amsterdam.

BIBLIOGRAPHY

Belgrade Chamber of Commerce. *Belgrade, Montana: The First 100 Years, 1886–1986*. Dallas, TX: Taylor Publishing, 1986.
Churchill-Amsterdam Historical Society. *A Goodly Heritage*. 1977.
Iverson, Ronald J. *The Princess of the Prairie: A History of Belgrade, Montana*. Privately published, 1965.
Kroes, Rob. *The Persistence of Ethnicity: Dutch Calvinist Pioneers in Amsterdam, Montana*. Urbana: University of Illinois, 1992.
Niven, Francis L. *Manhattan Omnibus, Stories of Historical Interest of Manhattan and Its Surrounding Communities*. Privately published, 1989.
Smith, Phyllis. *Bozeman and the Gallatin Valley: A History*. Helena, MT: Two Dot, 1997.